Language for Daily Use

Explorer
Edition

BROWN
Explorer Edition

Authors

Mildred A. Dawson

M. Ardell Elwell

Eric W. Johnson

Marian Zollinger

RAYMOND PICOZZI, Literature Consultant
CAROL PELAEZ, Project Editor

New York   Chicago   San Francisco   Atlanta   Dallas   *and*   London

Language for Daily Use

HARCOURT BRACE JOVANOVICH

ACKNOWLEDGMENTS

For permission to reprint copyrighted material, grateful acknowledgment is made to the following sources:

Abelard-Schuman, Ltd.: From *The Secret in the Wall* by Jean Bothwell, Abelard-Schuman, Ltd., 1971.

The Associated Publishers, Inc.: "Sky Pictures" by Effie Lee Newsome from *Gladiola Garden*.

Atheneum Publishers, Inc.: From "Let's Marry Said The Cherry" and "Upton Weller" from *Let's Marry Said The Cherry* by N. M. Bodecker (A Margaret K. McElderry Book). Copyright © 1974 by N. M. Bodecker.

The Christian Science Monitor: "Unfolding Bud" by Naoshi Koriyama from *The Christian Science Monitor,* 7/13/57. © 1957 The Christian Science Publishing Society. All rights reserved.

Hilda Conkling: "Dandelion" from *Poems by a Little Girl* by Hilda Conkling. Copyright 1921, 1947 by Hilda Conkling.

The Dial Press: From *Canal Boat to Freedom* by Thomas Fall. Copyright © 1966 by Thomas Fall.

Doubleday & Co., Inc.: "I Wish That My Room Had a Floor" by Gelett Burgess, from the book *Lots of Limericks.* Copyright © 1961 by Louis Untermeyer, copyright © 1961 by Richard Taylor. From *Paul Bunyan and His Great Blue Ox* by Wallace Wadsworth. Copyright 1926 by George H. Doran Company.

E. P. Dutton & Co., Inc.: "The Pirate Cook" from *Around and About* by Marchette Chute. Copyright © 1957 by Marchette Chute. From the book *Lad: A Dog* by Albert Payson Terhune. Copyright, 1919, 1926, 1959 by E. P. Dutton & Co.; renewal, copyright, 1947 by E. P. Dutton & Co., Inc.

Farrar, Straus & Giroux, Inc.: "springtime" from *Spin a Soft Black Song* by Nikki Giovanni. Copyright © 1971 by Nikki Giovanni.

Nikki Giovanni: "the reason i like chocolate" by Nikki Giovanni. © 1974 by Nikki Giovanni.

Harcourt Brace Jovanovich, Inc.: "Trees" from *The Little Hill* by Harry Behn. Copyright, 1949, by Harry Behn. "Bubbles" from *Wind Song* by Carl Sandburg. Copyright © 1960, by Carl Sandburg.

Harper & Row, Publishers, Inc.: From *Charlotte's Web* by E. B. White. Copyright © 1952 by E. B. White. From *The Wheel on the School* by Meindert DeJong. Copyright, 1954, by Meindert DeJong. From *Tinkerbelle* by Robert Manry.

Harper & Row, Publishers, Inc.: Illustration by Garth Williams from *Little House In The Big Woods* by Laura Ingalls Wilder. Pictures copyright © 1953 by Garth Williams.

Hartford National Bank and Trust Company: From a letter by Henry van Dyke from *A Book of Letters,* compiled by S. S. Center and L. M. Saul, Meredith Press.

Harvey House, Publishers, New York, New York: "Solidarity" by Amado Nervo from the book, *Spanish-American Poetry* edited by Seymour Resnick, published by Harvey House.

Holt, Rinehart and Winston, Publishers: "The Runaway" from *The Poetry of Robert Frost* edited by Edward Connery Lathem. Copyright 1923, © 1969 by Holt, Rinehart and Winston, Inc. Copyright 1951 by Robert Frost. "The sea was calm" by Carlton Minor from *The Voice of the Children* by June Jordan and Terri Bush. Copyright © 1968, 1969, 1970 by The Voice of the Children, Inc. From *The Saturdays* by Elizabeth Enright. Copyright 1941 by Elizabeth Enright Gillham. Copyright © 1969 by Robert M. Gillham.

Henry Lincoln Johnson, Jr.: "Trifle" by Georgia Douglas Johnson from *American Negro Poetry,* edited by Arna Bontemps.

Little, Brown and Company in association with the Atlantic Monthly Press, and *Harold Ober Associates, Inc.:* From *The Incredible Journey* by Sheila Burnford. Copyright © 1961 by Sheila Burnford.

Macmillan Publishing Co., Inc.: "The Coin" from *Collected Poems* by Sara Teasdale. Copyright 1920 by Macmillan Publishing Co., Inc., renewed 1948 by Mamie T. Wheless. "What Is Once Loved" from *Alice All By Herself* by Elizabeth Coatsworth. Copyright 1937 by Macmillan Publishing Co., Inc., renewed 1965 by Elizabeth Coatsworth Beston.

Naomi Long Madgett: "Woman with Flower" from *Star by Star* by Naomi Long Madgett (Detroit: Harlo, 1965).

The New York Times Company: "Hold Fast Your Dreams" by Louise Driscoll. © 1916 by The New York Times Company.

Smithsonian Institution Press: "To the Cedar Tree" from "Ethnology of the Kwakiutl" by Franz Boas, 35th Annual Report, Bureau of American Ethnology, 1921.

The Viking Press: From *The Cheerful Heart* by Elizabeth Janet Gray. Copyright © 1959 by Elizabeth Janet Gray.

Western Publishing Company, Inc.: "A Modern Ballad: The Ups and Downs of the Elevator Car" by Caroline D. Emerson from *Story Parade.* Copyright 1936, copyright renewed by Story Parade, Inc.

PHOTO CREDITS

Photographs are all HARBRACE by Oscar Buitrago and Erik Arnesen except those listed below. KEY: t, (top); c, (center); b, (bottom); r, (right); l, (left). COVER: Joern Gerdts/Photo Researchers. Page 2, NASA; 11, Jeffrey Foxx/Woodfin Camp & Associates; 20, NASA; 33, Ed Barnas/Design Photographers International; 41, Michal Heron; 42, John Sanford/Monkmeyer; 43, Herbert Lanks/Monkmeyer; 78, C.H. Brinton; 82, Edmund Appel; 85, Stephen Green-Armytage/Photo Researchers; 92, Freda Leinwand/Monkmeyer; 100, (l) Allen Green/Photo Researchers, (r) Fred J. Maroon/Photo Researchers; 101, (t) Focus On Sports, Inc.; 123, Smithsonian Institute; 139, Leonard Kamsler; 145, Walter D. Osborne/Photo Researchers; 165, Photo Trends; 178, Peter D. Capen/Terra Mar Productions; 180, R.D. Estes/Photo Researchers; 185, Chris Bry/Design Photographers International; 187, Herbert Lanks/Monkmeyer; 191, Mimi Forsyth/Monkmeyer; 212, Albert Moldvay/Photo Researchers; 222, Fritz Henle/Photo Researchers; 238, (l) Evelyne Appel, (r) Leonard Le Rue III/Monkmeyer; 250, Jack Fields/Photo Researchers; 288, Joern Gerdts/Photo Researchers; 301, Bettmann Archive; 313, Peter Arnold.

ART CREDITS

Don Bolognese: 15, 16, 120, 171, 173, 278, 283, 308; Judith Brown: 38, 190, 255–256; Renee Daily: 260; Diane Dawson: 5–6, 76–77, 302–303; Michael Deas: 22, 135, 195, 240, 280; Al Fiorentino: 4, 36–37, 112, 144, 183, 233, 261, 290; Arthur Friedman: 27, 89, 102, 103, 164, 193; Michael Garland: 248; Bill Greer: 65, 162, 204, 266, 296, 298, 299; Fred Harsh: 39, 56, 58, 59, 140, 141, 182, 207, 217; Oscar Liebman: 10, 35, 149, 169, 225, 300; Rosalind Loeb: 7; Richard Loehle: 116, 161, 226, 236, 264–265, 309; John McIntosh: 63, 70, 94, 96, 127, 234, 276, 284; Sal Murdocca: 88, 143, 214, 286; Amy Meyers: 71, 208, 230; Mike Quon: 138, 146–147, 179, 186, 258; Miriam Schottland: 24, 67, 83, 209, 262; Bob Shein: 20, 159, 168, 277, 304; Pat Stewart: 13, 28, 57, 80, 229, 252, 285, 307; Bruce Waldman: 30, 69, 86, 192, 305.

Contents

In this chapter you will discuss ways to become a good listener. You will also work with some words that people often use incorrectly. Here is your chance to find out what you already know about these subjects.

Tryout I.   Listening Skills

Copy the three phrases below that best complete the sentence beginning "A good listener. . . ."

1. writes down every word a speaker says.
2. tries to pick out a speaker's main points.
3. counts how many times a speaker says "and um."
4. pays close attention.
5. makes mental pictures of what the speaker says.

Tryout II.   *let* and *leave*

Write each sentence below. Choose the correct word in parentheses.

1. "(Leave, Let) me see the treasure map," said Bearded Bart to the pirate captain.
2. The captain roared, "(Leave, Let) it alone!"
3. "Will we (leave, let) at midnight?" asked Bart.
4. "Aye," said the captain, "and I will (left, let) you row the boat to the island."

Tryout III.   Unnecessary Words

Write each sentence below. Choose the correct word or words in parentheses.

1. Do you know where the zoo (is, is at)?
2. I want to get (off, off of) the bus there.
3. I know where it (is, is at).
4. Get (off, off of) the bus at the next stop.

Tryout
Time

Listening and Speaking

Millions of people all over the world sat spellbound before their radio and television sets, listening to the two American astronauts orbiting the earth.

The astronauts also listened intently as their directors spoke to them from ground stations around the world.

CAPSULE COMMUNICATOR, HAWAII: All systems on the ground look good. . . .

FLIGHT DIRECTOR, HOUSTON: You're having him get out?

CC: Roger, Flight, we're GO.

FLIGHT DIRECTOR: Tell him we're ready to have him get out when he is.

CC TO GEMINI: We just had word from Houston. We're ready to have you get out whenever you're ready. Give us a mark when you egress the spacecraft. . . .

The vitally important exchange of directions and comments continued throughout the flight.

As the spacewalk came to an end, this conversation took place:

FIRST ASTRONAUT (inside spacecraft) TO THE CAPSULE COMMUNICATOR: This is Jim. Got any message for us?

CAPSULE COMMUNICATOR: Gemini 4. Get back in.

SECOND ASTRONAUT (outside spacecraft): O.K., I'm on top of it right now.

FIRST ASTRONAUT: O.K., come on in. . . .

SECOND ASTRONAUT: All right . . . I'll open the door and come through there.

Did you ever stop to realize that you and an astronaut need to have one skill in common? You both need to be good listeners. How well do you suppose astronauts could perform their missions if they did not listen carefully to the directions they received from the ground? How successful would they be if they could not make use of the information sent to them? Probably they would do no better at their work without good listening skills than you would do in the classroom without them. The ability to listen well is essential to astronauts above the earth. It is essential to you, too.

To Discuss

1. Does your mind wander sometimes when you are listening? When? Why?
2. Is it easier for you to listen when you are alone or when you are in a group? Why?
3. Is it easier for you to listen when you know you will be questioned on what you hear? Why?
4. Do you think there is any difference between hearing and listening? If so, what is the difference? Name some things you *hear*. Name some things to which you *listen*.

Listening for the Plot

Just about everyone likes to listen to stories. *How* good are you at it? Are you able to recall the characters and events after you have been told a story so that you can retell it accurately?

To find out just how good a listener you are, close your book and listen to the story your teacher will read to you. Close your eyes, too, if you wish.

Why the Sea Is Salty

A Scandinavian Folktale

Once upon a time there was a miller who had a magic mill. This mill could grind out whatever he wanted: tablecloths, milk, or gold—anything! He had only to say "Grind gold, and do it both quickly and well," for the mill to start producing gold. Stopping the mill, however, was another matter.

As you may imagine, the mill was often in use. Soon the miller had a fine farmhouse and plenty to eat and money enough to last for many a long year. Nevertheless, he was not satisfied. He had the mill make so much gold that, just to keep it from going to waste, he covered his farmhouse with golden shingles.

The farmhouse became famous throughout the country. It glittered in the moonlight and sparkled in the sun. Ships far out at sea used it as a lighthouse.

One day a sea captain came to visit the miller. The captain had seen the golden farmhouse and heard of the magic mill. He asked the miller, "Can your mill make salt?"

"Oh, yes," said the miller proudly. "Salt, and anything else you can name."

The captain wanted the mill more than anything, for he was tired of making dangerous voyages to buy salt. He thought, "If I owned the mill, I could have it grind out all the salt I need."

"I'd like to buy your mill," said the captain.

"No, no," replied the miller. "I couldn't think of parting with it. How would I live without it?"

"You'd manage very well," said the captain. "You have this fine golden farmhouse, and you're the richest man in the country. Do sell me the mill."

At last the miller agreed to sell the mill.

The miller said, "To make the mill work, you must say, 'Grind salt, and do it both quickly and well.'" With those instructions, the captain grabbed the mill and hurried away to his ship.

The captain placed the mill on the deck of his ship and sailed out to sea. Then he spoke to the mill: "Grind salt, and do it both quickly and well." The mill began to grind salt, and it ground salt till the ship looked as if it had been sailing through a snowstorm. The captain wanted to stop the mill, but he had forgotten to ask how to do it. No matter what he said and no matter what he did, the mill kept grinding salt. It ground salt until the ship sank. The mill sank with the ship to the bottom of the sea, and still it kept on grinding. Even today, it is grinding; that is why the sea is salty.

To Discuss

1. Which plot details were easy to remember? Which were easy to forget? Why do you suppose this was so?
2. Can you think of anything you might have done to help you remember what happened better?

● Practice

As a class, choose a television program, built around a story, that most of you can watch this evening. Watch this program, and when it is over, retell it by writing in two or three paragraphs. Bring your retold version into class to compare it with other pupils' versions.

Listening to Directions

One situation that calls for you to be a good listener comes up whenever you are given directions. The main trick in listening to directions is to pay close attention.

When directions are long, it is useful to make notes. For school assignments, the notes should contain page numbers, topics, and other details.

When directions are short or when it is inconvenient to make notes, use different techniques. One way to remember directions is to think of a few key words. For example, suppose your mother says, "On your way home from school, buy six oranges. Then, please stop at Mrs. Kulak's to pick up a package she has for me." To keep the two things in mind, remember these key words in this order: *oranges* and *Mrs. Kulak.*

Another way to remember directions is to picture each step in your mind as it is given to you. For example, if someone tells you to "Turn right at the large white farmhouse," try to remember what it looks like and take a mental snapshot of it.

To Discuss

1. When do you need notes to recall directions?
2. What other ways can you use to recall directions?

● Practice

As your teacher reads some directions, you can check your ability to listen and to follow them. You may want to have paper and pencil at hand.

Listening for Information

Radio and television stations frequently broadcast excellent informational programs, featuring speakers who are authorities on their subjects. Learning to listen and to remember what you hear on such programs will add to your knowledge. You may become a better student and a more interesting person, too.

How to Listen and Remember Information

Sit where you can hear and see.
Find out what the speaker's purpose is.
Decide what parts of the speech meet your needs or interests.
Make mental pictures of points to remember.
Review the points, in order, to fix them in your mind.

To Discuss

1. Do you know what the word *concentrate* means? How can concentrating help you to listen well?
2. Why is it useful to be able to pick out the main points that a speaker makes? How does knowing the main points help you to organize the information in your mind?

● Practice

On the next page, there are pictures that a speaker on television used when telling about ways in which human beings have kept records in writing. Look at the illustrations while your teacher reads, from page 10, the story the speaker told. Afterward, close your book and discuss what you heard.

ILLUSTRATION 1: Here is my cat.
Her name is Patches.

Voici ma chatte. (Vwä-see mä shät.)
Elle s'appelle Patches.
(El sä-pel Pät-ches.)

ILLUSTRATION 2: 太空人回来了

Astronaut has returned.

ILLUSTRATION 3: HEREISMYCAT
APSIEMANREH
TCHES

ILLUSTRATION 4: Recitation

ILLUSTRATION 5: Water   Heaven   Rain

ILLUSTRATION 6: Early Greek:

Late Greek:

Latin:

Some Facts About Writing Systems

In Illustration 1 you see a language system in which an alphabet is used to form words. The letters match the sounds of the words.

Not all people write their language with an alphabet, though. As Illustration 2 shows, the Chinese use drawn figures, or characters, to stand for their words.

Most languages that do use an alphabet follow the same order we use in writing—from left to right. The earliest Greek records, however, show writing from left to right on one line, right to left on the next, and so on, without separations of words or any punctuation. This method of writing was called *boustrophedon,* meaning "as the ox plows." If we used it, our sentences would look like those in Illustration 3.

Before our alphabet was developed, at least two other civilizations had written languages. The Egyptians carved their sacred records in stone, using symbols called *hieroglyphics,* shown in Illustration 4. The Mesopotamians used tablets of wet clay for their writing. Using a pointed stick, they made wedge-shaped marks called *cuneiform,* as shown in Illustration 5, in the clay.

Our alphabet was developed at least 3,000 years ago, probably by the Phoenicians, who then passed it on to the Greeks. The Greeks found that by making a few changes to fit the sounds of their words, they could use the alphabet to write their language. Later, the Romans borrowed the letters from the Greeks, and made changes to fit their language, Latin. See Illustration 6.

Now, we use this Roman, or Latin, alphabet to show the sounds that make up our words.

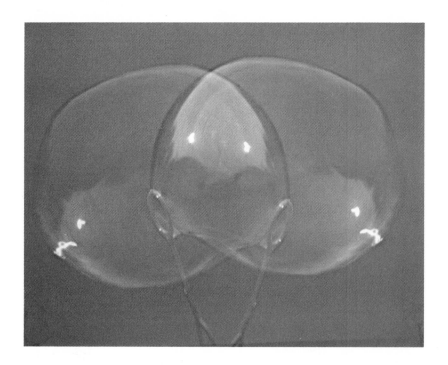

Bubbles

Two bubbles found that they had
    rainbows on their curves.
They flickered out saying:
"It was worth being a bubble
just to have held that rainbow
thirty seconds."

CARL SANDBURG

When you think of a bubble, what sorts of things do you think about? Do you think of a spherical body of gas contained in a thin liquid envelope? Probably not. Carl Sandburg uses bubbles as an image in a poetic statement. He is not asking you to think of the scientific definition of a bubble, but rather to remember other qualities a bubble may have. What are some of these? What do you think of when you think of a rainbow? If you were a bubble, would you say the same thing that these two bubbles said? Why? Try to think of other images you could use to say the same thing that Sandburg is saying here.

How Our Language Grows

Your Own Language

Does everyone in your class speak the same way? If you think they do, you might be surprised. Although we all seem to understand each other, we often use different pronunciations for the same word and even different words for the same thing.

If this idea seems strange to you, the idea that you speak in a dialect is also probably something new. We tend to associate the word *dialect* with persons whose speech is different from our own. The truth is, we all have a dialect. The part of the country where we live, our parents' speech and where they come from, the influence of others around us, are all responsible for creating our dialects.

Here are some examples. In some parts of the country, if you wanted a large, overstuffed sandwich on a roll, you would ask for a submarine; in other places you would have to ask for a hoagie; and somewhere else the same thing might be called a hero. If you asked for a milkshake to go with your sandwich, in some places you would get a thick drink with ice cream in it, while in other areas you would get a drink that is more like milk. Perhaps you would prefer an orange soft drink, orange tonic, orange soda, or orange pop. They are all names for the same thing.

Of course, we do not always use different words to talk about the same thing. If we did, we would never understand people from other parts of our own country.

Sometimes, however, even when we use the same words, we say them in different ways. For instance, do you say "pa*r*k the ca*r*" or "pa*h*k the ca*h*?" Does *greasy* rhyme with *easy* or *fleecy* in your dialect? We may all speak the same language, but we each also speak a dialect.

1. Say the groups of words below aloud. Do you pronounce each word in the group alike? If not, which ones are different? Which ones do you say differently from your classmates?

   Don/dawn   pin/pen   out/boot/route
   leg/egg   cot/caught   where/were
                week/wick/creak

2. What word or words do you use for each object or action described below? Do your friends use the same words?

   1. the flat, round food made out of batter and served with syrup and butter for breakfast
   2. missing school without permission
   3. the hardware that water comes out of above the sink
   4. the worm used for fishing
   5. the brown paper container you use to carry groceries
   6. a super-highway with limited access
   7. the utensil used for preparing fried foods on the stove

Using Your Voice Effectively

If you want people to listen to you, you should speak clearly and loudly enough to be heard easily. Clear speech depends on *volume, rate,* and *articulation.*

To Discuss

1. What happens when you turn the *volume* up on the radio or the television set? What is another word for *volume*?
2. What is a *rate of speed*? What is a *rate of speaking*? Is your own rate of speaking too fast? Too slow? Ask a friend.
3. *Articulation* has to do with the distinctness or clearness of sounds. Give examples of poor articulation.

● Practice

1. The sounds spelled by the italicized letters in the words below are sometimes completely left out when you speak—perhaps because of rapid speech or carelessness. Read each word aloud correctly.

fis*ts*	lib*r*ary	fif*th*	wid*th*	wha*t*
kep*t*	*e*leven	in*t*erest	fin*d*	wi*th*

2. What sounds should you say for the italicized letters in the names below? Read the names aloud correctly.

*R*obert	Em*i*ly	Ch*r*is	Dor*o*thy
Wi*ll*iam	Mil*d*red	Louise	Jac*qu*eline

3. Read aloud the words below. Say the italicized parts of the words carefully and distinctly.

len*g*th	po*e*try	pic*t*ure	wan*t to*
work*ing*	heigh*t*	pro*b*ably	leave *them*
*al*ready	re*g*ular	*going to*	di*d you*

Using Words Correctly: *let* and *leave*

Two verbs which are often used incorrectly are *let* and *leave*. The verb *let* means "to allow." The verb *leave* means "to go away from" or "to go away." *Left* is the past form of *leave*. It is incorrect to use *leave* when you mean "allow."

Listen for these verbs as you read aloud the following sentences:

Let

1. Please *let* me go to Carol's house.
2. I want to *let* her use my backpack.
3. Bill has *let* her borrow his canteen.

Leave

1. We want to *leave* the party early.
2. Ginger *left* the house before ten.
3. Has she *left* because she was bored?

● Practice

1. Read each sentence below aloud. Choose the correct word in parentheses.

    1. At midnight, the two pirates (left, let) the ship.
    2. "Shhh!" said the captain. "Don't (leave, let) anyone hear us."
    3. They rowed to the island where the treasure had been (left, let).
    4. "We can (leave, let) the boat on the beach," said Bart.
    5. Bart (left, let) the captain lead the way.
    6. The captain (leave, let) Bart carry the shovel.

2. Write two sentences, using *let* and *has let* correctly.
3. Write three sentences, using *leave*, *left*, and *has left* correctly.

Unnecessary Words

Use words that help you say what you mean. Avoid unnecessary words.

Read the questions below:

1. Where was he?
2. Do you know where she is staying?

Notice that the meaning of each question is perfectly clear. It is unnecessary to end either question with the word *at*.

Now think of the meaning of *off* in each sentence below.

1. The jockey swung *off* her horse.
2. Sol stepped *off* the curb.

Notice that the meaning of each sentence is clear. It is unnecessary to add *of* to *off*.

● Practice

Read each sentence aloud. Choose the correct word or words in parentheses.

1. Where were most pirate ships (anchored, anchored at)?
2. Many ships dropped anchor just (off, off of) the coast of Florida.
3. Do you think this is where some pirate treasure is (buried, buried at)?
4. I wish I knew the right place to (dig, dig at)!

Checkup I.   Listening Skills

Copy the sentences below that describe a student with good listening habits.

1. Josie paid close attention to what was said.
2. Meg didn't understand Lila's directions, but she was too embarrassed to ask a question.
3. Sarah remembered the brief directions by thinking of key words.
4. Leigh just asked a question that Sue asked five minutes ago.

Checkup II.   *let* and *leave*

Write each sentence below. Choose the correct word in parentheses.

1. The captain (left, let) Bart dig up a heavy chest.
2. He (leave, let) Bart carry it to the boat.
3. Bart jumped into the rowboat with the chest and (left, let) the captain standing on the shore.
4. "Don't (leave, let) me here!" wailed the captain.
5. "I will (leave, let) you swim to the ship," said Bart as he rowed away.

Checkup III.   Good Usage

Write each sentence below. Choose the correct word or words in parentheses.

1. I know where Edie (is hiding, is hiding at).
2. She ran (off, off of) the road.
3. She hid in the shed where the tools are (kept, kept at).

Checkup

In this chapter you will be studying sentences. Here is your chance to find out how much you already know.

Tryout I. Sentences

Some of the word groups below are sentences; the others are fragments. Copy the ones that are sentences and punctuate them correctly.

1. Can you point to the North Star
2. Handle of the Big Dipper
3. Castor and Pollux
4. Jupiter has twelve moons
5. Watch that shooting star

Tryout II. Subject and Predicate

Copy each sentence below. Draw a vertical line between the complete subject and the complete predicate.

1. The mountain lion is a big cat.
2. The animal has a long slim body and a long tail.
3. Three other names for the mountain lion are cougar, panther, and puma.
4. This fierce animal stalks through the underbrush.
5. The big cat leaps with crushing force upon its prey.

Tryout III. Finding Simple Subjects and Verbs

Copy each sentence below. Underline the simple subject with one line and the verb with two lines.

1. Margo visited Assateague Island.
2. She saw many wild ponies.
3. A mare nibbled marsh grass.
4. Up and down the field ran two foals.
5. They played a running game.
6. In the distance stood a stallion.

2

Tryout
Time

Tryout IV.   Writing Sentences Correctly

Rewrite these groups of words so that they form complete sentences.

1. Did you go to the concert on Friday it was fantastic.
2. The first group sang. My favorite song.
3. The lead singer wore a purple velvet suit. With silver buttons down the front.
4. Next, Melody Maylor sang she writes all of her own songs.
5. She can really play the electric piano, too, have you ever heard her?
6. Finally, the Banana Splits came onto the stage, they invited people from the audience to join them.
7. After the concert. We went to the stage door and waited for the singers.
8. Our long wait was finally rewarded we got some autographs.

Tryout V.   Writing Paragraphs

Read the following paragraph and decide how its structure can be improved. Then copy the paragraph, making the improvements.

At noon, we arrived at the famous Hawk's Nest in West Virginia. We stood high up and looked down on New River Gorge. it was a sheer drop of almost 150 meters down to the river. Once I saw the Grand Canyon of the Colorado. at the end of the Gorge, New River joins the Gauley River

2

Writing Good Sentences

What are the four kinds of sentences? Find a sentence below that illustrates each kind:

1. Venus is a planet.
2. Can people live on Venus?
3. Look for information about planets.
4. How hot it is on Venus!

Here are some facts about the four kinds of sentences:

A **statement** is a sentence that tells something. It ends with a period. It is also called a **declarative sentence.**

A **question** is a sentence that asks something. It ends with a question mark. It is also called an **interrogative sentence.**

A **command** or **request** is a sentence that gives an order. It ends with a period. A command or request is also called an **imperative sentence.**

An **exclamation** or **exclamatory sentence** expresses surprise or strong feeling. (The exclamation may be in the form of a statement, a question, or a command, but it ends with an exclamation point instead of a period or question mark.)

Statement: Cape Kennedy is in Florida.
Question: Where is Cape Kennedy?
Command or *Request:* Look it up on a map.
Exclamation: You can't find it!
Don't you see it even now!
Look here!

● Practice

1. Read the following groups of words and tell which ones are not sentences. Those that are sentences will do one of these things: make a statement, ask a question, or give a command.

   1. Where is the camping site
   2. Because we have to put up the tent
   3. Where is my sleeping bag
   4. Forgot my flashlight
   5. A mosquito just bit me
   6. Tell us a story at campfire

2. Copy the groups of words above that are sentences. Punctuate them correctly.

3. Write a statement, a question, and a command or request. Be sure you begin and end each sentence correctly.

4. Study the following exclamations. Be ready to tell whether each exclamation is expressed in the form of a statement, a question, or a command. Then read the sentences aloud, letting your voice show that they are exclamations.

   1. Go away!
   2. What are we going to do!
   3. I won't do it!
   4. What a show that was!

Check Test 1: Correct Words

Read each sentence aloud. Choose the correct word.

1. Aren't there (any, no) pickles in the refrigerator?
2. There is (no, any) mustard in this jar!
3. May I have (a, an) tomato and (a, an) onion?
4. Isn't there (any, no) salt or pepper?
5. How can I eat (a, an) hamburger without (any, no) ketchup?

If you need more help, turn to page 335 in the Review Handbook.

The Two Parts of a Sentence

A sentence has two parts: (1) a **subject** that names what the sentence is about; and (2) a **predicate** that tells about the subject.

Study the sentences below. Which words in each sentence name what the sentence is about? Which words tell something about the subject?

1. The kindergarten children visited our room.
2. Each member of the class told a story.

In sentence 1, *The kindergarten children* is the subject; *visited our room* is the predicate. In sentence 2, *Each member* is the subject; *told a story* is the predicate.

Now study the subjects and predicates in these sentences.

SUBJECT	PREDICATE
1. Our club	publishes a weekly newsletter.
2. Six club members	supply most of the news items.
3. Some of us	proofread the copy.

▶ The **subject** of a sentence is the part that names what the sentence is about.
▶ The **predicate** of a sentence is the part that tells something about the subject.

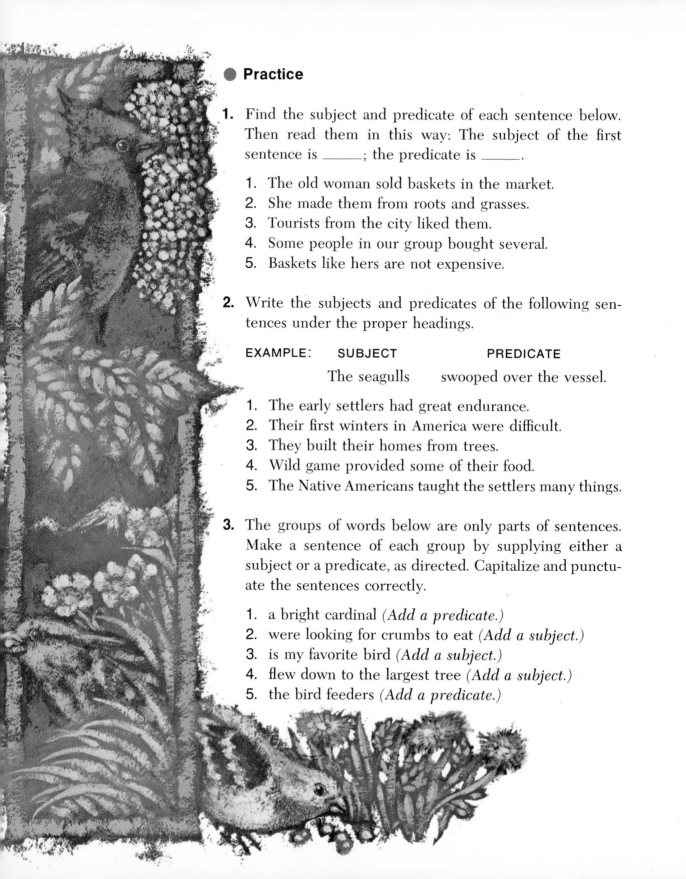

● **Practice**

1. Find the subject and predicate of each sentence below. Then read them in this way: The subject of the first sentence is _____; the predicate is _____.

   1. The old woman sold baskets in the market.
   2. She made them from roots and grasses.
   3. Tourists from the city liked them.
   4. Some people in our group bought several.
   5. Baskets like hers are not expensive.

2. Write the subjects and predicates of the following sentences under the proper headings.

   EXAMPLE: SUBJECT   PREDICATE
              The seagulls   swooped over the vessel.

   1. The early settlers had great endurance.
   2. Their first winters in America were difficult.
   3. They built their homes from trees.
   4. Wild game provided some of their food.
   5. The Native Americans taught the settlers many things.

3. The groups of words below are only parts of sentences. Make a sentence of each group by supplying either a subject or a predicate, as directed. Capitalize and punctuate the sentences correctly.

   1. a bright cardinal (*Add a predicate.*)
   2. were looking for crumbs to eat (*Add a subject.*)
   3. is my favorite bird (*Add a subject.*)
   4. flew down to the largest tree (*Add a subject.*)
   5. the bird feeders (*Add a predicate.*)

The Simple Subject

The subjects you have been studying are called **complete subjects.** Study the sentences below. All the words at the left of the vertical lines belong to the complete subjects.

1. My best friend | bought a chemistry set.
2. Many types of experiments | interest me.
3. I | want a chemistry set of my own.

In each complete subject above, there is a key word which is the main part of the subject. It is called the **simple subject.**

In the sentences above, the simple subjects are *friend, types,* and *I.*

The other words in a subject change or limit the meaning of the simple subject. For example, the words *My best* in sentence 1 limit the meaning of the word *friend* to a particular friend. The words *Many* and *of experiments* limit the meaning of *types* in sentence 2 to particular types. Words or groups of words that limit or change the meaning of a word are called **modifiers.**

The word *I* in sentence 3 above is both the complete subject and the simple subject because it is the only word in the subject.

▶ The **subject** of a sentence is the part that names what the sentence is about.
▶ The **simple subject** is the main part of the subject.
▶ The **complete subject** is the simple subject plus any modifiers.

25

1. Copy the complete subject of each of the sentences below. Then draw a line under the simple subject.

1. The Mohicans depended upon trees.
2. Wood fires kept them warm.
3. Their spears were made of wood.
4. The fruits of the trees furnished them food.
5. The bark of the birch furnished fibers.

2. In the sentences below, look first for the complete subject. Then find the simple subject and write it in a column headed "Simple Subject." Place the other words of the subject under the heading "Modifiers."

EXAMPLE: That robin on the grass fell from its nest.

SIMPLE SUBJECT	MODIFIERS
robin	That, on the grass

1. The local newspaper comes out at noon.
2. Important news of the day is on the front page.
3. News of less importance is covered later.
4. My favorite part of the paper is the comics.
5. My parents always look at the ads.

What Predicates Tell About the Subject

So far you have learned that the predicate of a sentence is the part that tells something about the subject. Now study the predicates in the following sentences. See what they tell about the subjects.

1. In this sentence, the predicate tells what the subject is doing.

   My friends | were carrying an old wagon wheel home.

2. In this sentence, the predicate tells what the subject was.

   Pam | was my partner.

3. In this sentence, the predicate describes the subject.

   Old wheels | are well made.

4. In this sentence, the predicate tells what happened to the subject.

   The pail | was knocked over by the cow.

● **Practice**

1. Write two sentences in which the predicate tells what the subject is, was, or will be doing. Sentence 1 above will help you.
2. Write two sentences in which the predicate tells what the subject is, was, or will be. See sentence 2.
3. Write two sentences in which the predicate describes the subject. See sentence 3.
4. Write two sentences in which the predicate tells what is, was, or will be happening to the subject. See sentence 4.

The Verb in the Predicate

The predicates you have been studying are called **complete predicates.** Look again at the example sentences on page 25. All the words at the right of the vertical lines belong to the complete predicate.

The key word (or words) in the predicate of a sentence is the **verb.** Another word for the verb in the predicate is the **simple predicate.** In this book the term *verb* is used rather than "simple predicate."

The verbs in the sentences on page 25 are *bought, interest,* and *want.* The other words in the complete predicate complete the verbs. Sometimes words in a complete predicate modify the verb.

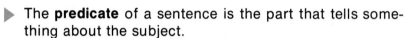 The **predicate** of a sentence is the part that tells something about the subject.

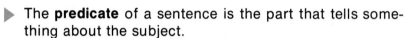 The **verb** is the main part of the predicate of a sentence.

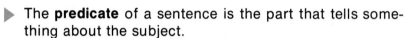 The **complete predicate** is the verb and any words that modify or complete the verb.

● **Practice**

1. Copy each sentence below. Draw a vertical line between the complete subject and the complete predicate. Be prepared to read your answers aloud in class.

   1. The castle stands in that dark forest.
   2. A high wall surrounds the castle.
   3. A wide moat discourages unwelcome visitors.
   4. A famous family still lives there.
   5. Many tourists stay in the village nearby.

2. Now look for the verb in each sentence. Draw two lines under each verb. Then find the simple subject in each sentence. Draw one line under each simple subject. Be prepared to read your answers aloud in class.

How Our Language Grows

More Than One English

Is English always English? If you heard someone from England say that he or she was going to leave the *flat* to *queue up* to *hire* a car for a *fortnight's holiday,* would you know that someone was leaving an apartment to stand in line to rent a car for a two-week vacation?

Not only do we spell and pronounce words differently from the way the English do, but many of our words and phrases are quite different from theirs. If you asked for a *sweet biscuit* in England, you would get a cookie. If you asked for a *biscuit,* you'd receive a cracker. To call your lawyer long distance, you would *ring up* your *solicitor* on a *trunk call.* You might have to change a *tyre* (tire) near a *fly-over* (overpass), hang your clothes in the *cupboard* (closet), or store the *tinned* (canned) food in the *larder* (pantry). You might put the *rubbish* (trash) in the *dustbin* (garbage can), *wash up* (do the dishes), and then take your *carrier* (shopping) bag to the *sweet shop* (candy store) in the *centre* of town.

1. Look up the following words in a dictionary. What do they mean in England?

   | form | waistcoat | lorry | post |
   | lift | pram | chemist | draughts |

2. Match the following lists of American and English words.

AMERICAN	ENGLISH
1. raincoat	a. pushcar
2. movie	b. hair grip
3. stroller	c. mackintosh
4. bobby pin	d. boot
5. trunk (of car)	e. cinema

✓ Check Test 2: Homonyms

The words *rain* and *reign* sound alike, but they differ in spelling and meaning. Such words are called **homonyms.**

The two sets of homonyms most frequently confused are *to, two,* and *too* and *there, their,* and *they're.* Complete the following exercises to review your knowledge of how to use them.

1. Write each sentence below. Use *to, two,* or *too* in place of each blank.

1. A thirsty crow came _____ a water jar.
2. The water was _____ low for the crow _____ reach.
3. An idea occurred _____ the crow.
4. It dropped pebble after pebble _____ the bottom of the jar.
5. Slowly, the water rose closer _____ the top.
6. The crow dropped _____ more pebbles in and at last could begin _____ drink.

2. Write each sentence below. Use *they're, there,* or *their* in place of each blank.

1. The spaceships are on _____ way.
2. They have landed over _____!
3. The Martians are getting out of _____ spaceship now.
4. _____ coming down the street!
5. I hope _____ friendly.

If you need more help, turn to page 344 in the Review Handbook.

Sentence Patterns: Word Order

Look at the sample of Japanese writing below.

太郎さんは私の本を読みました。

Written in our alphabet, the sentence looks like this.

Taro-san watakushi no hon o yomimashita.

(Mr. Taro) (my) (book) (is reading)

Examine the translation underneath the Japanese sentence. Is the order of the words different from that in an English sentence? How would we express this thought?

In English, we arrange words in a specific order, depending upon our meaning. To express the thought, "Pam chased the rabbit," we would not say:

Rabbit the Pam chased.

Nor would the thought be expressed in this way:

The rabbit chased Pam.

The first group of words makes no sense at all. The second group of words is a good English sentence, but it does not express the meaning intended. The order of words in an English sentence is very important to sense and to meaning.

Unscramble the following word groups to make each one a sentence that is correct and sensible.

1. loves to skate Linda my sister
2. years she has five been skating for
3. an ice team is she on hockey
4. morning she practices every at six o'clock
5. year last won medal a she in figure competition skating

The Order of Subject and Predicate

In most sentences, the subject comes before the predicate. Because *subject followed by predicate* is the usual order, it is called the **natural order.**

Sometimes, to provide variety in sentences or to emphasize something, the natural order is reversed. Then the subject follows the predicate. Such sentences as these are said to be in **inverted order.** Look at these example sentences.

NATURAL ORDER: A flickering light flashed across the bay.
A frog leaped across the path.
The scout crept into the woods.

INVERTED ORDER: Across the bay flashed a flickering light.
Across the path leaped a frog.
Into the woods crept the scout.

The Simple Subject and Verb

When you are looking for the simple subject and the verb in a sentence, always look first for the verb. It is easier to find the verb than to find the subject. Then form a question by asking *Who?* or *What?* before saying the verb. Your answer will be the subject. This plan works well with any sentence, whether its subject and predicate are in natural or inverted order. Follow this plan to find the simple subject and verb in this sentence.

Over the hill came the rider.

ASK: What is the verb?
ANSWER: *came*
ASK: *Who* or *what* came?
ANSWER: *rider* (simple subject)
simple subject — *rider;* verb — *came*

● **Practice**

1. Find the simple subject and the verb in each sentence below. Tell which two sentences follow natural order.

1. On the starting blocks stood the swimmers.
2. Off went the starting gun.
3. Into the water dove the six swimmers.
4. At the far end of the pool waited the judge.
5. Suddenly two swimmers pulled ahead.
6. Up came a hand at the end of the pool.
7. Through the air rang the cheers of the crowd.
8. A new champion grinned at the cheering fans.

2. Rewrite the following statements, changing the order of subject and predicate.

1. The battalion rode into the forest of Sherwood.
2. The bugles sounded far off across the hills.
3. Peace came after a fierce battle.
4. King Richard galloped into the banquet hall.

The Order of Words in Questions

In some questions, the simple subject and verb are in natural order—simple subject first, verb next.

> Who knocked on the door?
> Who hit the home run?
> What is the matter?

What are the simple subjects and verbs in the questions above?

Now look at the arrangement of the simple subject and verb in these questions.

1. Where are you going?
2. Did the salesperson leave?
3. Where is my sister?

What is the verb in sentence 1? What is the simple subject in sentence 1? To find the answers, did you follow the two steps which you studied on page 32? Examine the steps again with sentence 1.

ASK: What is the verb?
ANSWER: *are going*
ASK: *Who* or *what* are going?
ANSWER: *you*
      simple subject—*you;* verb—*are going*

Notice that the verb contains two words. The simple subject in a question often comes between two parts of a verb. Now follow the same steps with sentences 2 and 3.

To find the subjects and verbs of some questions, you may need to rearrange the questions first. Put the subject and verb in natural order, starting the question as you would a statement. For example:

1. You are going where?
2. The salesperson did leave?
3. My sister is where?

Copy the questions below on your paper. Draw two lines under the verb in each sentence. Draw one line under the simple subject. If it will help you, rewrite some of the questions. The numeral in parentheses after each sentence tells whether the verb is one word or two words.

1. When is Phil's birthday? (1)
2. Are we giving a party for him? (2)
3. Would he like a surprise party? (2)
4. Will you bake a cake? (2)
5. Who will address the invitations? (2)
6. How much ice cream shall I buy? (2)
7. Where is Phil's sister? (1)
8. Can she bring Phil to my apartment on Saturday? (2)
9. Were you thinking about making a gift for Phil? (2)
10. What shall I make for him? (2)

COMPOSITION: SENTENCE DEVELOPMENT

A. Study the picture below. Write five sentences in which you describe the harbor and the people in the picture.
B. Write five more sentences in which you tell what is happening in the picture. Tell what you see, hear, and smell.

The Subject in Commands and Requests

A sentence that gives a command or makes a request often begins with the verb. Sometimes the word *please* comes first.

> (you) Find your way through the maze.
> (you) Turn left at the corner, sir.
> (you) Please wait a minute, Jack.

Usually in sentences of command or request, the subject is not stated. It is understood to be *you*. This is also true when the sentence includes a person's name before the request.

> Carlos, (you) wait for me.
> Mother, (you) please wake me early.
> Joan, (you) read your part slowly.

Sometimes *you*, the subject of a command or request, *is* expressed, as in this example.

> *You* go ahead.

▶ The subject of a command or request is understood to be **you.**

Look again at all the example sentences on this page. Notice that five of them contain commas. The name of the person to whom you are talking is always set off by a comma. If the name appears in the middle of a sentence, two commas are needed, as in the examples below.

> Call me, Vito, as soon as possible.
> Please, Ruth, try to be on time.

● Practice

Write each sentence below. Use commas to set off the name of the person addressed. Insert the understood subject in parentheses.

1. Billy take a turn at bat.
2. Throw that player out umpire!
3. Please Laura hit a homer.
4. Fight on team!
5. Run for it Henry.

What Is Once Loved

What is once loved
You will find
Is always yours
From that day.
Take it home
In your mind
And nothing ever
Can take it away.

ELIZABETH COATSWORTH

What does Coatsworth mean when she tells you to take something home in your mind? Think of some people or things that you have loved. How do you feel when you think about them, even when they are not with you?

Reading Aloud

Read the following lines silently and note the rhythmical phrasing of the sentences. Prepare to read the passage aloud in such a way that others will enjoy listening to you.

The huckleberry thickets had grown all summer in dense green carpets beneath the oaks. Now they were like rust-tinged clouds floating on the ground around distant bends. Acorns peppered the earth everywhere and chipmunks gathered them with urgent purpose. The spots began to disappear from fawns, and the blunt ends of the velvet-covered racks of bucks began to sharpen and take their final shapes.

—From *Canalboat to Freedom*
THOMAS FALL

To Discuss

1. Whenever you plan to read a selection aloud, why should you first read it silently? State the reason in a sentence that begins this way:

   Prepare for oral reading by reading the selection silently to make sure. . .

2. Look back to page 14 and read the section "To Discuss." Make a statement about oral reading for each of the following qualities: volume, rate of speaking, articulation.

● Practice

Make up sentences in which you use the words listed below. Read your sentences aloud to the class. Be sure to pronounce the letters in heavy black type.

recognize   government   **s**inger   once

Writing Sentences Correctly

You know that a sentence is a group of words that has three characteristics: (1) it has a subject and a verb; (2) it makes sense by itself; and (3) it begins with a capital letter and ends with a punctuation mark. Sometimes, people put groups of words together as if they were sentences when they are not. Sometimes people break off a part of a sentence. Sometimes they run more than one sentence together.

Avoiding Sentence Fragments

When you write a sentence, keep all of its parts together. Do not punctuate a part of a sentence as if it were complete. A sentence part punctuated as a complete sentence is called a **sentence fragment.** Which group of words below is a sentence fragment?

You will have to lock the door. When you leave.

When you leave is a sentence fragment, incomplete by itself. It is incorrectly punctuated as a sentence. You can avoid the sentence fragment by keeping the parts together in this way.

You will have to lock the door when you leave.

Which group of words below is a sentence fragment? Rewrite the word groups to avoid the fragment.

Finding the key under the mat. Jennie let herself inside.

REMINDER: Avoid writing sentence fragments as if they were sentences. Keep the parts of a sentence together.

1. After each numeral below, there is one complete sentence and one sentence fragment. Tell which word group, *a* or *b*, is a sentence fragment. Then read the two word groups aloud as one sentence. Write the sentences correctly on the board.

   1. (a) We saw a bank of clouds.   (b) Drifting slowly by.
   2. (a) See that wonderful view.   (b) Of Crater Lake.
   3. (a) In the last leg of the climb.   (b) Don noticed the broken arrow.

2. Some of the word groups below are sentences, and some are sentence fragments. Decide which ones are fragments. Then copy the fragments on your paper, adding words of your own to make them complete.

   1. Some superstitions.
   2. You should never walk under a ladder.
   3. Opening an umbrella in the house.
   4. Means seven years of bad luck.
   5. You can knock on wood for good luck.
   6. A chicken's wishbone.
   7. Another good luck charm is a rabbit's foot.
   8. Throw salt over your left shoulder.
   9. Groundhog Day is February 2.
   10. Sees its shadow.
   11. There are stories behind such superstitions.
   12. With increased scientific understanding.

Avoiding Run-ons

Another common error in writing is to run sentences together, forgetting to use capital letters and end punctuation marks. Read the passage at the top of the next page. Then answer the questions below it.

My father taught Carmen and me to ice-skate we now belong to the school skating team, our team will compete with yours next Saturday.

Where are capital letters and periods needed in the passage above? How many sentences are there? Write them correctly on the board.

REMINDER: Separate two or more sentences from each other with capital letters and punctuation marks. Reading your sentences aloud will serve to check them.

● **Practice**

Write the following paragraph, using capital letters and end punctuation correctly.

Pedro followed the canyon wall, he watched the sheep from a distance, his dog, old Fidelio, was on the job one ewe wandered away from the flock, what good sense the dog used, he just quietly nosed her back into the herd.

Going Ahead

Use in sentences the subjects and predicates listed below. Add words and word groups to each part of the sentence to increase interest for the reader. Avoid fragments and run-ons.

EXAMPLE: The boy plodded on.

Hungry and tired, the boy plodded on, anxious to get his sheep home before nightfall.

SUBJECT	PREDICATE
1. The dog	tended the sheep.
2. The moon	shone.
3. The wind	was cold.

Writing Paragraphs

As you know, a paragraph is a group of sentences about a single idea or topic. To make the main idea of a paragraph clear, a writer may use one sentence to state or hint at the topic. Often, the first sentence is the **topic sentence.** You may find it helpful in writing good paragraphs to make your first sentence the topic sentence. Then write other sentences to develop the main idea.

In studying a paragraph to see whether it can be improved, ask yourself these questions:

1. Does the first sentence hint at the topic?
2. Does every sentence keep to the topic?
3. Does every sentence develop the topic?

Read the two paragraphs that follow. See if you can think of a way to improve each one.

Cumulus clouds are white and fluffy and have rounded domes. Some of them are a thousand meters high. To really appreciate their size and shape, you should see them from an airplane, as I did last summer. I was flying to Montana to see my grandfather, and I stayed on his farm all summer. From above, these clouds looked liked great rolling seas of white fog. We circled those that towered over our airplane. When we flew around a cumulus cloud, I could see that it looked like many clouds stacked together. I suppose that accounts for the name *cumulus,* which means "accumulation" in Latin.

Cirrus clouds look delicate and filmy. When you look at them, they seem filmy and you can see the sky through them. They are thin, feathery clouds. Clouds that are white and very thin are called cirrus clouds.

To Discuss

1. Refer to the three questions on page 42 as you check the content of each of the paragraphs you just read. Which of the two paragraphs seems better to you? Explain why.
2. How can the first paragraph be improved? What test of a good paragraph does it fail to meet?
3. What is wrong with the second paragraph? Suggest ways to improve it.

How to Write a Paragraph

Have your topic clearly in mind.
Write a first sentence that will suggest the topic.
See that every sentence keeps to the topic.
See that every sentence develops the topic.
Indent the first word of the paragraph.
Begin and end each sentence correctly.

COMPOSITION: WRITING A PARAGRAPH

A. Write a paragraph about cirrus clouds, using some of the details below.

> Cirrus clouds are thin and delicate.
> The word *cirrus* means "curl" in Latin.
> Formed at an altitude of nearly 6,000 meters, they are the highest clouds.
> They consist of crystals of ice.
> They look like white feathers.

B. Write a paragraph on one of the topics below or on a topic of your own choice. Follow the guides above.

> a book you have read
> a famous inventor or scientist
> a place you have visited
> a famous event

A Book to Read

TITLE: **Mrs. Frisby and the Rats of NIMH**
AUTHOR: Robert C. O'Brien
ARTIST: Zena Bernstein
PUBLISHER: Atheneum

Mrs. Frisby, widow of the late Jonathan Frisby, was raising her family alone, but she had a terrible problem. The Frisby family (who are field mice) made their winter home in a cinder block in Farmer Fitzgibbon's field. When the ground thawed each spring, the animals that lived in the field moved to their summer homes to escape being injured or even killed by the big metal blades of Farmer Fitzgibbon's plow. But Mrs. Frisby's son, Timothy, was quite ill. He had to have bed rest in order to get well. How could Mrs. Frisby move him to safety?

In solving this problem, Mrs. Frisby makes the acquaintance of a colony of most extraordinary rats: rats that had electric lights, an elevator, and an extensive library in their burrow. These rats had known her husband, Jonathan. But how? What could explain these mysterious, intellectual rats?

Mrs. Frisby and the Rats of NIMH won the Newbery Medal the year it was published. This award is given each year to "the author of the most distinguished contribution to American literature for children."

Checkup I.　Sentences

1. Read the word groups below. Decide which ones are complete sentences. Write the sentences and punctuate them.

1. Casey Jones was an engineer
2. His train was the *Cannonball*
3. Have you heard the ballad of Casey Jones
4. Always brought his train in on time
5. A monument to Casey Jones
6. What a fearless hero

2. Write three sentences: a statement, a question, and an exclamation.

3. Write three commands or requests. In two of them, use the name of a person to whom you are talking.

Checkup II.　Subject and Predicate

Copy each sentence below. Draw a vertical line between the complete subject and the complete predicate.

1. The bobcat is smaller than the cougar.
2. It is named for its short tail.
3. The bobcat is about the size of a small dog.
4. This little wildcat frightens many people.

Checkup III.　Finding Simple Subjects and Verbs

Copy each sentence below and at the top of page 46. Underline the simple subject once and the verb twice.

1. Once a family owned a small goat.
2. The small goat grew into a big nuisance.
3. That pest ate anything.
4. One day the goat ate the father's favorite red shirt right off the clothesline.
5. Was the father ever mad!

Checkup

6. He tied that poor goat to the railroad track just before train time.
7. But the goat coughed up the red shirt.
8. The engineer quickly stopped the train.
9. Do you know the folk song about this smart goat?

Checkup IV. Writing Sentences Correctly

Rewrite these groups of words so they form correct sentences.

1. James Watt experimented. With steam engines in the eighteenth century.
2. In 1825 George Stephenson drove the first passenger train a horse could outrun it.
3. Trains were called Iron Horses they replaced real horses for transportation.

Checkup V. Writing Paragraphs

Read the paragraph below. Decide how its structure can be improved. Then copy the paragraph, making the improvements.

Their hind feet are webbed. They have flattened tails. Beavers are well-suited to life in the water. When beavers dive under the water, they can close their nostrils tightly. An otter has webbed hind feet, too.

In this chapter you will add to your word-building techniques and your study skills. Here is your chance to find out how much you already know.

Tryout I. Prefixes and Suffixes

1. Make two words from each of the words below by adding a prefix or a suffix. Use different prefixes and suffixes.

play   out   regular
build   coat   appoint
charge   hand   cast

2. Write each word below correctly, adding a suffix that begins with a vowel.

hope   love   peace   care

3. Write each of the above words correctly, adding a suffix that begins with a consonant.

Tryout II. Finding Entries in a Dictionary

The guide words on a certain dictionary page are **honest-hooky.** Write the words below that you would find on that page.

honey   hone   hoodwink
hoodlum   hoot   honorary
homing   honorable   homeward

Tryout III. Finding Word Meanings

Read the sentences below. Try to discover the meaning of each italicized word from its context in the sentence. Write the meaning for each.

1. He had the *crafty* look of a fox.
2. The *ferocious* dog growled and bared its teeth.
3. Are the refreshments *adequate* for twenty guests?
4. You may be sure about it, but I am *dubious.*

Tryout Time

Good Study Habits

Organizing for Study

Good study habits are important to doing good work in school, and organization is important to good study habits. How well do you organize your study? What would a "study profile" of you show? Think about sitting down to do your homework. Then answer these questions about yourself.

1. *Assignment:* Do you understand exactly what you are to do?
2. *Supplies:* Do you have at hand all books and supplies that you need?
3. *Working conditions:* Do you work in the best lighted, quietest place you can find?
4. *Timing:* Do you estimate how long the assignment will take you? Do you give yourself enough time? Do you start your homework at a regular time every day?
5. *Concentration:* Do you avoid interruptions after you start work? Do you keep your mind focused on your work?

To Discuss

1. Talk over the check questions above. Why are they important in organizing study?
2. Are you pleased or displeased with your "study profile"? What good study habits do you have? What study habits do you need to develop?

Keeping Good Records

A personal notebook or notepad can be valuable in helping you to organize your work. In it you can take good, clear notes on assignments you must do. You can also keep lists of books that you want to read or have read, as well as lists of words that you have learned.

Taking Notes on Assignments

You may want to devote one section of your notebook to assignments. Read the following summary of an assignment. Remember that these notes tell what to do, where to go for information, how to get the information, and when the assignment is to be finished.

> Mon., Nov. 12. English
> Report on history of Thanksgiving Day. Find references in library. Look up history in card catalogue. Use encyclopedia. Look through poetry books in room for Thanksgiving poem to use for report. Report due Fri., Nov. 16.

To Discuss

1. Notice that the notes above answer *W* and *H* questions: *What, Where, How,* and *When.* Tell what information is given on each of these topics:

   1. what to do
   2. where to go for information
   3. how to get the information
   4. when the assignment is due

2. Why do you think the notes are dated?

3. Why is it important to write the notes neatly and clearly?

Read the following guides for taking notes on assignments. Write the list in your notebook at the beginning of the "Assignments" section.

How to Take Notes on Assignments

Write the date of the assignment and the subject on the first line.

Record the details of assignments accurately.

Use *W* and *H* questions to see that the information is complete.

Write the date the assignment is due.

Write neatly and legibly.

Listing Books to Read

As you hear about books that interest you, write the titles and the authors' names in your notebook. Note why you want to read each book. Tell whether it is fiction or, if it is nonfiction, whether it is a biography, science, history, or some other kind of book. Look at this example.

> ## Books to Read
> *Insects and Plants*, by Elizabeth K. Cooper. Nonfiction, science. Tells about partnerships between insects and plants. Tells how to raise silkworms.

Keeping a Reading Record

Soon after you have finished a book, make a record to help you remember it. Look at the model below.

> ## My Reading Record
> *Insects and Plants*, by Elizabeth K. Cooper. 142 pages and appendix. Science. Finished Nov. 12. Topics covered are bees and bee flowers, moths and the yucca, silkworms and the mulberry tree. Tells how to raise silkworms. Rating ***
> *The Saturdays*, by Elizabeth Enright. 175 pages. Fiction. Finished Sept. 30. Four children without a mother find out how to enjoy their Saturdays in New York. Rating ***

To Discuss

1. What facts are included in the sample entries? Give a reason for including each kind of information.
2. How do you know whether the books in the reading record are fiction or nonfiction? How did the student classify the nonfiction?
3. What rating system did the writer use? What is the first book in the reading record about? How can you tell?
4. Read the words from each entry that explain the contents of the book.
5. Which words are abbreviated? Are the abbreviations written correctly?

● Practice

Start keeping book lists and reading records in your notebook. Under "Books to Read," list a book found on your classroom book shelves or in the library that will give you more information on a topic you have been studying. Under "My Reading Record," list a good book you have recently read.

Keeping a Word List

As you read and study, you will find many words that are new to you or are used in unfamiliar ways. Such words should be kept in your notebook as a way of enlarging your vocabulary. A large vocabulary is itself one of the most useful of all study helps.

Study the model below. Notice the information included.

> Thurs., Dec. 14. Soc. studies book, pages 35-40. _function_, the particular purpose for which a thing exists. The _function_ of the Congress is to make the laws.
>
> _reign_ (pronounced rain), rule. The Revolution took place during the _reign_ of King George III.

To Discuss

1. Tell why it is helpful to know the date, subject, name of book, and pages from which the new words were selected.
2. Read from the model an example of a definition. Does the sample sentence add anything to the definition?
3. Why is it helpful to underline the words?
4. Where would you go to find meanings of words?

Going Ahead

Write a composition, serious or humorous, describing your difficulties in studying and how you have tried to overcome them.

How Our Language Grows

From Ancient Myths

What do Saturday, a panic, a volcano, an echo, and the planet Venus have in common? They all remind us of the influence of classical mythology on our language.

Hundreds of years ago the Greeks and Romans believed their gods and goddesses had a hand in everything that happened. Each god or goddess ruled over a certain area of life and had special characteristics. Many of these characteristics are still associated with the name of the god or goddess today.

1. Except for Earth, the planets in our solar system are all named for Roman gods and goddesses. List the planets. For which god or goddess was each named?

2. Many stars and constellations were named for mythological characters. Here are some. Look them up to find out for whom they were named.

   Gemini Pegasus Centaurus Hercules Perseus

   Can you find other stars or constellations named for ancient gods or goddesses? What are they?

3. Many words in our vocabulary are related to ancient mythology. Below is a list of words and the mythological character related to each. Look up each word and write its meaning. Then look up the mythological being and find out who each one was.

   titanic/Titan   iris/Iris
   cereal/Ceres   mercurial/Mercury
   bacchanalian/Bacchus   herculean/Hercules

4. Do you know where the words at the top of this page came from? If not, look up Saturn, Pan, Vulcan, Echo, and Venus.

Studying Parts of Words

You can build your vocabulary and improve your spelling by observing how some words are put together. For example, study the parts of this word:

re place ment

1. Notice that *replacement* has been formed by adding syllables to one root word. Spell the root word. Use it correctly in a sentence.
2. What syllable has been placed at the beginning of the root word? Look it up in a dictionary. How does it change the meaning of the root word? Use the new word correctly in a sentence.
3. What syllable has been added at the end of the root word? Look it up in a dictionary. How does it change the root word? Use the new word correctly in a sentence.

▶ A **prefix** is one or more syllables placed before a root word to change its meaning.
▶ A **suffix** is one or more syllables added to the ending of a word to change its meaning.

Study the words in each group below. Find the root word. What does it mean? Notice how prefixes and suffixes are used to build new words. What do the new words mean?

1	2	3	4
real	firm	claim	color
unreal	confirm	proclaim	discolor
really	firmness	reclaimed	colorless

To Discuss

Notice the spelling of *really*. The last letter of the root word and the first letter of the suffix are the same. This makes a double consonant. What other words like this do you know?

● Practice

See how many words you can build by adding prefixes and suffixes to these words. At least forty words can be made.

clean   count   cover
govern   form   press
frost   plant   appear
collect   part   satisfy

✓ Check Test 3. Correct Verb Forms

1. Write each sentence below. Choose the correct word in parentheses.

1. The dragon (blew, blown) fiery breath at Ezmerelda.
2. She (drew, drawn) her sword to slay the beast.
3. As the dragon (came, come) closer, she saw tears in its eyes.
4. The dragon's tears and the way it (blew, blown) its nose softened Ezmerelda's heart.

2. Write each sentence below. Choose the correct word in parentheses.

1. "Please (don't, doesn't) cry," said Ezmerelda.
2. "It (don't, doesn't) matter about your breath," she continued.
3. "Just (don't, doesn't) scorch any more knights," she warned.
4. "I (doesn't, don't) mean to scorch anybody," sniffed the dragon.
5. "I've tried chewing ice but that (doesn't, don't) work," the dragon wailed.
6. "(Don't, Doesn't) worry," said Ezmerelda, "we'll think of something."

If you need more help, turn to page 337 in the Review Handbook.

Adding Suffixes

Sometimes adding a suffix causes a change in the spelling of a root word. Notice how the spelling of each word below changes when a suffix beginning with a vowel is added to it.

shine	shining	slope	sloping
love	lovable	grieve	grievance

The words below are exceptions to this rule. Note that the final *e* has been kept even though the suffix begins with a vowel. Pronounce the words and notice the soft sounds of *c* and *g*.

courage   courageous   peace   peaceable

Look at the words below. What happens when a suffix beginning with a consonant is added to a word that ends in silent *e*?

spite   spiteful   sedate   sedately

Exceptions to this rule are *true* and *due*.

true   truly   due   duly

● **Practice**

Use a suffix to build a new word from each of the words below. Follow the spelling rule that applies.

believe	actual	pass	gain
conserve	hope	free	like

When a suffix that begins with a *vowel* is added to a word ending in silent *e*, the *e* is usually dropped. If a *g* or *c* comes before a final *e*, the *e* is retained when a suffix beginning with *a* or *o* is added. When a suffix that begins with a *consonant* is added to a word ending in *e*, the *e* is usually retained.

leav_ing

58

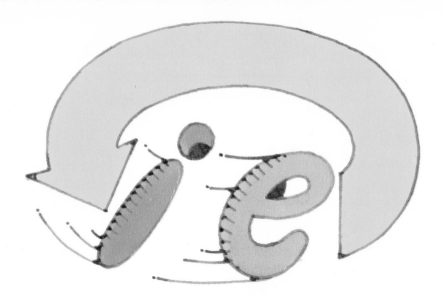

Spelling *ie* or *ei*

Study the spelling of each of the words below. In which words does the *i* come before *e*? The *e* before *i*?

chief   friend   receive   believe   eight

Notice that in only two cases does the *e* come before the *i*. In *receive*, *e* comes before the *i* after a *c*. In *neighbor*, *e* comes before the *i* when the letters have the sound of *a*. You may have heard the rule: ***i before e except after c or when sounded like a as in neighbor or weigh.***

Although you can usually follow this rule, there are some exceptions. Two examples are *foreign* and *height*.

● **Practice**

1. List all the words you can think of that are spelled according to the rule of *i* before *e*, as stated above. Make another list of exceptions to the rule. Check your dictionary for help.

2. One word in each pair below is misspelled. Choose the correct word and write a sentence, spelling the word correctly.

reign   fierce   cieling   feild
riegn   feirce   ceiling   field

> In words containing *ie*, the *i* usually comes before the *e* except after *c* or when the sound of *ie* is that of *a* as in *weigh*.

59

Using the Dictionary

The dictionary is one of the most valuable of all study tools because it can provide so much information. Study the part of a dictionary page shown below to see what kinds of information are given.

point·er [poin′tər] *n.* **1** A hand, finger, or other indicator, as on a clock or meter. **2** A slender rod used to point out things on maps, charts, etc. **3** A smooth-haired dog trained to scent and point out game. **4** *informal* A useful bit of information; hint; tip.

point·less [point′lis] *adj.* **1** Having no point; blunt. **2** Having no meaning or purpose. **3** Having no effect. **— point′·less·ly** *adv.*

Typical pointer

point of view *pl.* **points of view 1** The position from which a person looks at or considers an object, situation, etc.: an unusual *point of view*. **2** An attitude or viewpoint.

poise [poiz] *v.* **poised, pois·ing,** *n.* **1** *v.* To balance or hold in balance: The cat *poised* itself on its hind legs; The sword was *poised* in his hand. **2** *n.* Balance or equilibrium. **3** *n.* Ease of manner; self-possession.

Po·land [pō′lənd] *n.* A country in north central Europe.

po·lar [pō′lər] *adj.* **1** Of or having to do with a pole or poles. **2** Having to do with, coming from, or found near the North or South Pole. **3** Directly opposite in action or character.

polar bear A large bear with white fur, found in the arctic regions.

Po·lar·is [pō·lar′is] *n.* The North Star.

po·lar·i·ty [pō·lar′ə·tē] *n., pl.* **po·lar·i·ties** The condition of having poles with opposite properties at the ends of an axis, as in a magnet.

Polar bear, up to 8 ft. long

po·lar·ize [pō′lə·rīz] *v.* **po·lar·ized, po·lar·iz·ing** To become or make polar; give polarity to. **— po′·lar·i·za′·tion** *n.* ¶3

pole¹ [pōl] *n., v.* **poled, pol·ing 1** *n.* A long, thin, wooden or metal rod, usually rounded. **2** *n.* To push along with a pole, as a boat.

From the *HBJ School Dictionary*, © 1977 by Harcourt Brace Jovanovich, Inc. Reprinted by permission.

To Discuss

1. Where are the letter tabs? How do they help you when you are looking up a word in a dictionary?

2. Why is a knowledge of alphabetical order important in using a dictionary?

3. Where are the guide words? How do they help you?

● Practice

1. Quickly tell which letter comes before *r*; after *u*; before *h*.

2. Tell which two letters come before *m*; after *i*.

3. Tell which letters are in the first third of the alphabet; the second third; the last third.

4. Write these words in alphabetical order.

nervous   divide   length   years

heavy   several   cough   pleasure

5. Alphabetize each of these groups of words.

1. bureau, bottle, baggage, blouse, breathe
2. inquire, ivory, icicle, iron, imagine
3. sparkle, sincere, scythe, strict, scandal
4. team, tender, teacher, there, theme

6. The words in **boldface** (heavy black type) below are guide words. Tell which words that follow them would be entries on the dictionary page where these guide words appear.

1. **exceed–exclusive**   except, examine, excite, excuse
2. **juice–justice**   junior, junket, justify, juggle
3. **whip–white**   whisper, whirlpool, whittle, whole
4. **master–matter**   maple, mastery, matador, mast

Studying an Entry from a Dictionary Page

Here is a dictionary entry. Study it carefully.

ro·tate [rō′tāt] *v.* **ro·tat·ed, ro·tat·ing 1** To turn or cause to turn on or as if on an axis. **2** To alternate in a definite order: In volleyball the players *rotate*; to *rotate* crops. — **ro′ta·tor** *n.*

The earth rotates on its axis.

From the *HBJ School Dictionary,* © 1977 by Harcourt Brace Jovanovich, Inc. Reprinted by permission.

1. *Spelling:* Notice the spelling of the entry word *rotate.* What happens to the final silent *e* when *-ed, -ing,* or *-or* is added to *rotate?*

2. *Pronunciation:* The pronunciation is shown within parentheses after the spelling. Notice the aids to pronunciation.

1. *Syllables:* The word is divided into parts, called **syllables,** according to the number of vowel sounds it has. How many vowel sounds are there in *rotate?* How many syllables?

2. *Accent mark:* Find the mark after the first syllable of the entry word *rotate.* This mark shows which syllable should be given greater stress in speaking.

3. *Respelling:* The letters within the brackets tell you how the word should be pronounced. The accent mark or marks are shown, and the syllables are respelled in the way that best helps you pronounce them. For instance, the second syllable of *rotate* is respelled /tāt/. The bar over the vowel is called a **diacritical mark.** What does it tell you about how the *a* in /tāt/ is pronounced?

3. *Meaning:* How many definitions are given for *rotate?* In addition to the definition, what other aid does the dictionary give you to understand the meanings of *rotate?*

Dividing Words Correctly

As you have seen, dictionary entries show where words are broken into syllables. This is information you need in writing when you run out of space at the end of a line and find you must break a word. Since a word may be broken only between syllables, consult your dictionary to see where you should break it. Then put a hyphen at the end of one of the syllables and continue the word on the next line.

To Discuss

Look up the words below in your dictionary. Then answer the questions that follow them.

quote   prize   hyphen   estimate   muscle

1. Which words cannot be divided? Tell why.
2. Which words can be divided only in one place? Write them on the board, using a hyphen to divide them correctly.
3. Which word can be divided in more than one place? Write it on the board, correctly dividing it with hyphens.

● Practice

Divide the words below into syllables. Use hyphens correctly. Consult your dictionary.

potato	sentence	hyphenate	arrange
resistance	heavenly	student	departmental
review	undertake	injurious	practice

Using the Pronunciation Key

Different dictionaries use different systems to show the pronunciation of a word. Usually the system is explained in the front pages of the dictionary. In addition, there may also be a short key to pronunciation on the page itself. If you do not understand your dictionary's pronunciation system, refer to the *pronunciation key.*

Here is a key to the pronunciation of vowel sounds in the dictionary from which the sample page on page 60 is taken.

---

add, āce, câre, pälm; end, ēqual; it, īce; odd, ōpen, ôrder; tŏŏk, pōōl; up, bûrn; ə = a in *above*, e in *sicken*, i in *possible*, o in *melon*, u in *circus*; yōō = u in *fuse*; oil; pout; check; ring; thin; this; zh in *vision*.

From the *HBJ School Dictionary,* © 1977 by Harcourt Brace Jovanovich, Inc. Reprinted by permission.

In the pronunciation key above, note that several of the vowels have no diacritical marks at all. Such vowels are called **short vowels.** Other vowels have diacritical marks that look like bars above them. These vowels are called **long vowels.** Pronounce the letter *a* as a short vowel, and then as a long vowel. What is the difference?

● **Practice**

1. Read the list of words below. How does each vowel's short sound differ from its long sound?

hat	let	it	hot	cup
āge	bē	īce	ōpen	ūse

What other words do you know that contain the vowel sounds in the words above? Say them.

2. A special sign is used to stand for the soft vowel sound in unaccented syllables. The sign is ə. It is called a **schwa.** In the key above, find the words that tell you how to say the sound of ə.

Say these words and listen for the unaccented vowel sound of the schwa.

a way (ə wā′)   lev el (lev′ əl)   pen cil (pen′ səl)
les son (les′ ən)   lic o rice (lik′ ə ris)   fo cus (fō′kəs)

What other words do you know that contain the schwa sound? Say them.

3. Say each of the words in the pronunciation key on page 64. Listen to the different vowel sounds.

4. Pronounce every entry word on the sample dictionary page on page 60. Use the key on page 64 to help you.

Review Practice

Sentences

1. Decide which of the following groups of words are sentences, and then write each sentence correctly.

   1. what an archer you are
   2. will you be able to hit the bull's-eye
   3. the zing of the bowstring
   4. move back ten paces
   5. the way you made that arrow

2. To each group of words in section 1 that is not a sentence, add words to create a sentence. Write the sentence correctly.

3. Write three different kinds of sentences about something you saw or did today: a statement, a question, and an exclamation. Then write a command. Be prepared to read your sentences aloud with the proper expression.

Selecting the Right Definition

In your reading or listening, you may find that you need the dictionary definition of a word in order to know its correct meaning. The word you look up may have several meanings, numbered separately in the dictionary.

Do not hastily accept the first definition and stop there. Try out the definition in the sentence and paragraph where you found the word. If it fits, fine. If not, look further. Always check the meaning by the **context,** or setting, in which the word is used. Look at this example:

The hunter sent her *pointer* to look for game.

Which of the numbered definitions on page 60 fits this sentence? Why do you think so? Would any of the other definitions make sense in the sentence?

To Discuss

1. Why is it not wise to assume that the first definition of any entry word is the one you want?
2. What is meant by *context* in this sentence: Check all dictionary definitions of a word to see that it fits the context.

● Practice

Look in your dictionary for the definitions of the italicized words in the sentences below. Choose the definition that fits each sentence. Tell the meaning and substitute it for the single word.

1. We expect extremely cold winters here; they are part of the *cycle.*
2. We must send our request through proper *channels* at City Hall.
3. Only a *quirk* could have caused that old man to save every piece of string he could find.
4. These *novel* styles in sandals are comfortable.

✓ **Check Test 4.   Forms of Verbs**

Write this conversation correctly, choosing the correct form of the verbs in parentheses.

A hare once (grow) _____ very proud.

"I have never (know) _____ an animal faster than I am," he boasted.

"I will race you," said a tortoise.

"YOU?" said the hare and he (throw) _____ back his head and laughed. He (know) _____ he could win, so he (take) _____ the challenge.

The hare nearly (fly) _____ off the starting mark.

The hare thought, "I have (grow) _____ sleepy. What would happen if I (take) _____ a little nap?" So the hare (throw) _____ himself into the bushes and went to sleep.

When he woke up, he (know) _____ something was wrong. The tortoise had (take) _____ first place!

If you need more help, turn to page 341 in the Review Handbook.

Using Context Clues to Discover Word Meanings

Sometimes you do not need to look up an unfamiliar word in the dictionary. You can figure out its meaning by using the clues around it. For example:

> Dina was proud of her stamp collection because it made her feel like a real philatelist.

What do you think that the meaning of *philatelist* might be? Do the words "stamp collection" suggest a meaning?

Perhaps an unfamiliar word may remind you of a word you know. For example:

> The king did not have authoritarian power.

What word that you know is similar to *authoritarian*? If you know the word *authority*, you will probably guess the meaning of *authoritarian*.

How to Discover the Meaning of a Word

Notice how the word fits into the meaning of the sentence in which it occurs.

See if the word reminds you of one you already know.

Read the following selection. Use the guides on page 68 to help you guess the meanings of the italicized words.

In the courtyard, some of King Arthur's knights were about to leave on a *pilgrimage* that would take them on many different paths. Dressed in shining *mail*, with *visors* open, they *bade* their friends farewell. In their hands they *bore* their *lances* upright, while their shields with knightly *crests* hung at their sides. Finally, their farewells made, the knights turned their *mounts abruptly* and rode swiftly into the dawn. They had set out on the great *quest*.

Refer to the above selection to answer these questions.

1. What clues tell you that a *pilgrimage* and a *quest* are some kind of journey?
2. Does the word *shining* give you a clue to the meaning of the word *mail?*
3. Look at the word *visors.* Can you think of other words that begin with *vis*? If you know the meaning of *vision* or *visible,* can you guess the meaning of *visors*?
4. What clues can you find to help you guess the meanings of the other italicized words in the paragraph?
5. Most words have more than one meaning. The dictionary may give several meanings for a word. However, the setting, or context, in which you find a word will tell you which definition applies in that instance or situation. Which of the following meanings applies to the word *mounts* as used in the selection above?

   1. mountains
   2. gets up on
   3. horses for riding

✓ Check Test 5: Writing Abbreviations

When you take notes or make lists, you may use abbreviations. Review some of the abbreviations you learned in earlier grades by completing the following exercises.

1. Write the correct abbreviations for names of days.

2. Write the abbreviations for the names of nine months.

3. Write the abbreviations for the italicized words below:

    1. The city of Washington, *District of Columbia*
    2. Albany, *New York*
    3. Mulberry *Street*
    4. Bryant *Avenue*
    5. Harrison *Boulevard*
    6. Mill *Road*
    7. Chicago, *Illinois*
    8. *Doctor* H. M. O'Neill

If you need more help, turn to page 329 in the Review Handbook.

Going Ahead

Look at the "Pair Tree" below. Draw one like it and label the blank pears to match their homonyms. Add other pears to make a good crop. You may want to make a large copy of your tree and display it as a wall chart in your classroom.

Explanation

I hate to be a kicker
I always long for peace,
But the wheel that does the squeaking
Is the one that gets the grease.

JOSH BILLINGS

What is Josh Billings explaining here? Can you restate this idea in your own words without using the image of a squeaky wheel? Do you agree with the first two lines of the poem? What about the last two?

A Book to Read

TITLE: **Across Five Aprils**
AUTHOR: Irene Hunt
PUBLISHER: Follett

Jethro Creighton was nine years old in April of 1861 when Fort Sumter was fired upon and the Civil War began. On Saturday afternoons, his family, like many other farm families in southern Illinois, packed a picnic supper and traveled in a horse-drawn wagon to a nearby town. At their picnic, brass bands boomed and people made patriotic speeches asking for money to equip troops with uniforms and ammunition. Everyone cheered the speeches and then, with hearty appetites, settled down to their suppers. To Jethro, the coming war meant excitement, adventure, and, best of all, a change from the hard, monotonous work of farming.

But the mood of optimism and confidence vanished quickly as the war began in earnest. By April of the next year, Jethro had seen three of his brothers go off to fight; two for the North and one for the South.

Across Five Aprils tells of the Creighton family's struggles during this critical period in our country's history. Ms. Hunt's grandfather was a boy of nine when the Civil War began. The stories that he told his grandchildren — stories of uncertainty, pain, and occasional moments of joy — are the heart of this intriguing book.

Checkup I. Prefixes and Suffixes

Write each sentence below. Add a prefix or suffix to the incomplete word in order to form words you need:

1. The hare was __satisfied.
2. He knew he was speed__ and __beat__.
3. How had that tortoise moved so rapid__?
4. Maybe the tortoise would agree to __run the race.
5. "I know I could be success__ next time," thought the hare dream__.

Checkup II. Finding Entries in a Dictionary

The guide words on a certain dictionary page are **lever–lie.** Choose the words from the list below that you would find on the page.

levy	license
lest	lettuce
let	lick
liable	level
library	life
lexicon	liberty

Checkup III. Finding Word Meanings

Copy each word below on your paper. Beside each, write a word that it reminds you of and that would help you know its meaning.

secondary	differ	severity
picturesque	numerical	internship
irritant	frequency	longevity

4

Enjoying Poetry

To enjoy and appreciate a poem fully, you should hear it read aloud and also read it aloud yourself. Listen as your teacher reads the following poem.

Springtime

in the springtime the violets
grow in the sidewalk cracks
and the ants play furiously
at my gym-shoed toes
carrying off a half-eaten peanut
butter sandwich i had at lunch
and sometimes i crumble
my extra graham crackers
and on rainy days i take off
my yellow space hat and splash
all the puddles on Pendry Street and not one
cold can catch me

NIKKI GIOVANNI

How to Read a Poem Aloud

Read the poem silently for mood and meaning.
Learn the meaning and pronunciation of unfamiliar words.
Practice reading the poem aloud with expression.
Group the words to make the meaning clear.
Use your voice to bring out the rhythm of the poem.

Choral Reading

Some poems are good selections for group voices to read aloud. They may have parts in them for solos, duets, trios, quartets, or an entire group.

Listen to this poem about a pirate cook.

The Pirate Cook

Oh, once there was a pirate bold
Who thought that he could cook;
He knew just how to bake a cake—
He'd read it in a book.

He stirred it up, he stirred it down.
He stirred it carefully.
He cooked it in a cooking pot
And served it up for tea.

The crew all took a hopeful bite
And then with one accord
They lifted up the pirate cook
And threw him overboard.

The cook was not so pleased at this,
Until with joy he found
That he could sit upon his cake
And paddle it around.

He paddled it, he paddled it,
He paddled night and day,
Until a porpoise came along
And carried it away.

"That only shows," the pirate said,
"That I know how to bake;
It is not usual for fish
To care for currant cake."

"I knew that I was right," he said
And gently sank below;
And now he keeps a cooking school
To which the mermaids go.

MARCHETTE GAYLORD CHUTE

Read the poem carefully so that you understand it. Then plan a choral reading of it with a group. To help you, discuss the questions below.

1. What does each stanza have to say about the pirate?
2. Describe the cake. Read the lines from the poem that help in your description.
3. Talk over ways you could divide this poem into parts.
4. Decide how the lines should be read to bring out their meaning and feeling.
5. Practice your choral reading of the poem.
6. When you are ready, share your reading with other groups.

Word Pictures in Poems

Read the following poem and discover the word pictures the poet creates.

Sky Pictures

Sometimes a great white mountain
Or snowy polar bear
Or lazy little flocks of sheep
Move on in the blue air.

The mountains tear themselves like floss,
The bears all melt away,
The little sheep will drift apart
As though they'd finished play.

And then new sheep and mountains come,
New polar bears appear,
And roll and tumble on again
Up in the skies, blue-clear.

The polar bears would like to get
Where polar bears belong.
The mountains try so hard to stand
In one place, firm and strong.

The little sheep all want to stop
And pasture in the sky.
But never can these things be done,
Although they try and try.

EFFIE LEE NEWSOME

To Discuss

1. What are the sky pictures that the poet is talking about? What three images does she use throughout the poem?
2. Find and list the words that give motion to the sky pictures.
3. Read aloud the stanza that describes the sky pictures vanishing. Which of the descriptions is most appropriate for the animal that is disappearing?
4. Think of two or three "Sky Pictures" of your own. Write some word pictures to describe them.

Read the poem below, noticing how the poet uses word pictures to create a feeling about books.

the reason i like chocolate
is i can lick my fingers
and nobody tells me i'm not polite

i especially like scarey movies
cause i can snuggle with mommy
or my big sister and they don't laugh

i like to cry sometimes cause
everybody says "what's the matter
don't cry"

and i like books
for all those reasons
but mostly cause they just make me
happy

and i really like
to be happy

NIKKI GIOVANNI

1. What words describe how the poet feels about chocolate? Scary movies? Books?
2. Does this poem have a rhythm? Read the rhythm of your favorite lines aloud.
3. Think of word pictures you might use to tell about books. Write some of your word pictures. Put some of your word pictures in your own poem.

Patterns of Rhyme

Many poems are written with a rhyme pattern. The simplest pattern is a two-line verse that rhymes. This pattern is called a **couplet.**

Listen to a poem written in the couplet pattern.

Trees

Trees are the kindest things I know,
They do no harm, they simply grow

And spread a shade for sleepy cows,
And gather birds among their boughs.

They give us fruit in leaves above,
And wood to make our houses of,

And leaves to burn on Hallowe'en,
And in the Spring new buds of green.

They are the first when day's begun
To touch the beams of morning sun,

They are the last to hold the light
When evening changes into night,

And when a moon floats on the sky
They hum a drowsy lullaby

Of sleepy children long ago. . . .
Trees are the kindest things I know.

HARRY BEHN

1. How many couplets can you find in the poem?
2. List the pairs of rhyming words in the poem.
3. Choose your own rhymes and write one couplet or more.
4. Write a complete poem in the couplet pattern.

Read the following two poems to yourself and then write their rhyme patterns. Write "a" for the first end-of-the-line word and for every line that rhymes with it. Write "b" for the next end-of-the-line word and the other lines that rhyme with it, and so on. Compare your findings with those of a classmate.

Solidarity

Little lark, let us sing a song!
Waterfall, let us leap along!
Rivulet, let us run with mirth!
Diamond, let us be very bright!
Eagle, now let us take our flight!
Dawn of day, let us have new birth!
　　Sing a song!
　　Leap along!
　　Run with mirth!
　　Be very bright!
　　Take our flight!
　　Have new birth!

AMADO NERVO
translated by Mildred E. Johnson

The Coin

Into my heart's treasury
　I slipped a coin
That time cannot take
　Nor a thief purloin, ——
Oh, better than the minting
　Of a gold-crowned king
Is the safe-kept memory
　Of a lovely thing.

SARA TEASDALE

Poems Without Rhyme

Although many poems rhyme and have regular rhythm, not all do. Below is an example of such a poem. Read it to yourself.

Unfolding Bud

One is amazed
By a water-lily bud
Unfolding
With each passing day,
Taking on a richer color
And new dimensions.

One is not amazed,
At first glance,
By a poem,
Which is as tight-closed
As a tiny bud.

Yet one is surprised
To see the poem
Gradually unfolding,
Revealing its rich inner self,
As one reads it
Again
And over again.

NAOSHI KORIYAMA

To Discuss

1. Many unrhymed poems have words that echo the sounds of other words. In "Unfolding Bud," the long ō sound is repeated several times. Write the words that echo the long ō sound. Can you find other sounds that are echoed in this poem?

2. Repetition is often used in unrhymed poetry. Read the first line of each stanza aloud. How does this repetition, even though it is not exact, add to the poem?

Read the poem below, noticing its rhythm.

Dandelion

O little soldier with the golden helmet,
What are you guarding on my lawn?
You with your green gun
And your yellow beard,
Why do you stand so stiff?
There is only the grass to fight!

HILDA CONKLING

To Discuss

1. One thing that adds to the rhythm of this poem is the repetition of an initial consonant sound. What examples of this can you find?

2. The way this poem is punctuated also adds to its rhythmic quality. Read the poem aloud to a classmate, paying particular attention to the punctuation.

Most of us spend more time fixing the blame than fixing the problem.

ANONYMOUS

Which is easier to do: (1) blame someone or a set of circumstances for causing a problem; or (2) solve the problem? Which is more practical in the long run? Why?

How Our Language Grows

May I Borrow a Cup of Hors d'oeuvres?

For several centuries after the year 1066, England and much of what we call France were part of the same kingdom. The rulers of the kingdom spoke French, but English remained the language of the people. The rulers were, for the most part, well-educated and had large vocabularies.

We can tell something about the lives and interests of the French-speaking people living in England centuries ago by the kinds of words that made their way into our language. Many words having to do with food came from French. *Napkin, pastry, roast,* and *boil* are some examples. Many words related to fashion and social life also came from French: *apparel, costume, gown, coat, ballet, taffeta, chic, satin, melody,* and *checkers.* Since the French controlled the government, French words such as *reign, court, parliament, traitor,* and *mayor* became a part of English. Words and phrases connected with the military, art, and science often originated in French. Can you think of some of these words?

1. Below are some clues to English words related to eating that have been borrowed from French. What are the words? Can you think of others?

    1. a place where people go to eat dinner
    2. two words for the last meal of the day
    3. what you look at in sentence 1 above to decide what to order
    4. a desire for food or drink
    5. to test the flavor of something by putting it into your mouth

2. Is the French phrase *hors d'oeuvres* in your dictionary? Look it up. How should you pronounce it?

Discovering Mood in Poetry

Read the following poem silently and try to feel the mood it creates.

The sea was calm
as a breath of
cool air was
moving from
the sea

And the moon arose
revealing the long
line of the jungle
trees

As they stretch to the
mouth of the
open sea.

The moon draws up
like a drawbridge
to let the
stars see.

CARLTON MINOR

1. What words would you use to describe the mood of this poem?
2. What word or group of words in the first stanza expresses mood?
3. In the second and third stanzas what words help describe the peaceful scene?
4. In the last stanza the poet compares two things. What is being compared? What term is used for this kind of comparison—*metaphor* or *simile*?
5. Using the beginning words "The moon," write some metaphors that could fit in place of the one in the poem.

Discovering the Meaning of a Poem

The poem below tells about a young colt on a wintry evening. The colt belonged to a breed of horses common in New England—the Morgan breed. Read the poem carefully for word clues to help you discover the poem's meaning.

The Runaway

Once when the snow of the year was beginning to fall,
We stopped by a mountain pasture to say, "Whose colt?"
A little Morgan had one forefoot on the wall,
The other curled at his breast. He dipped his head
And snorted to us. And then he had to bolt.
We heard the miniature thunder where he fled
And we saw him, or thought we saw him, dim and gray,
Like a shadow against the curtain of falling flakes.
"I think the little fellow's afraid of the snow.
He isn't winter-broken. It isn't play
With the little fellow at all. He's running away.
I doubt if even his mother could tell him, 'Sakes,
It's only weather!' He'd think she didn't know!
Where is his mother? He can't be out alone."
And now he comes again with a clatter of stone
And mounts the wall again with whited eyes
And all his tail that isn't hair up straight.
He shudders his coat as if to throw off flies.
"Whoever it is that leaves him out so late,
When other creatures have gone to stall and bin,
Ought to be told to come and take him in."

ROBERT FROST

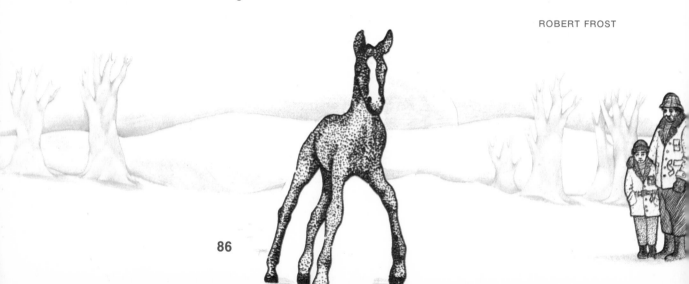

86

1. Why do you think the poet called the poem "The Runaway"?
2. What do the first two lines tell about the season and setting for this poem?
3. Who is the "We" in the second line?
4. Why did the passers-by stop?
5. Read the lines that tell how the poet first saw the little Morgan.
6. Read the line that explains why the colt snorted and then had to bolt.
7. Notice how the poet helped you hear the bolting. What is "miniature thunder"?
8. What does the poet mean when he says the colt isn't "winter-broken"?
9. How does the poet feel about the colt? Why did he think the colt was a runaway?
10. How does the poet describe what the colt looked like after he bolted?
11. Whom do you think the poet is talking about in the last three lines?

Read the following poem. What do you think the poet is saying?

Hope is a thing with feathers
That perches in the soul,
And sings the tune without the words,
And never stops at all,

And sweetest in the gale is heard;
And sore must be the storm
That could abash the little bird
That kept so many warm.

I've heard it in the chillest land,
And on the strangest sea;
Yet, never, in extremity,
It asked a crumb of me.

EMILY DICKINSON

Writing Limericks

Read these limericks, noticing the rhyme and rhythm pattern.

Old Man of Peru

There was an old man of Peru
Who dreamed he was eating his shoe.
    He woke in the night
    In a terrible fright,
And found it was perfectly true.

UNKNOWN

I wish that my room had a floor;
I don't care so much for a door;
    But this walking around
    Without touching the ground
Is getting to be quite a bore.

GELETT BURGESS

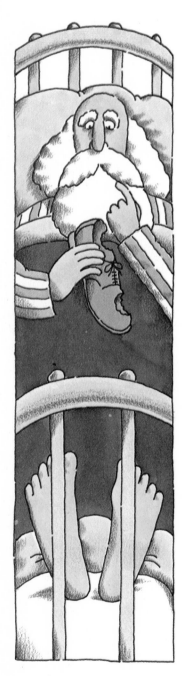

To Discuss

1. What is the pattern of rhyme in the first limerick? As your teacher reads the first limerick aloud, tap out the rhythm with one finger on your desk.
2. Is the rhyme pattern different in the second limerick? Tap out the rhythm in the second limerick by yourself.
3. Usually, the last line gives the real point of humor or the surprise ending in a limerick. Can you suggest a last line for this limerick?

> A hungry young man named de Pew
> Found a rather large mouse in his stew
>   Said the waiter, "Don't shout
>   Or wave it about . . .
> _____

What must the last line rhyme with?

4. Write your own limerick. To help you start, begin your limerick with "There was _____."

88

A Poem to Enjoy

A Modern Ballad
The Ups and Downs of the Elevator Car

The elevator car in the elevator shaft,
Complained of the buzzer, complained of the draft.
It said it felt carsick as it rose and fell,
It said it had a headache from the ringing of the bell.

"There is spring in the air," sighed the elevator car.
Said the elevator man, "You are well-off where you are."
The car paid no attention but it frowned an ugly frown

```
                              when
                  up         it
            going                 should
      started                        be
       it                                going
  And                                       down.
```

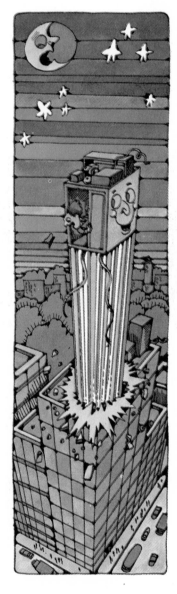

Down flashed the signal, but *up* went the car.
The elevator man cried, "You are going much too far!"
Said the elevator car, "I'm doing no such thing.
I'm through with buzzers buzzing. I'm looking for the spring!"

Then the elevator man began to shout and call
And all the people came running through the hall.
The elevator man began to call and shout.
"The car won't stop! Let me out! Let me out!"

On went the car past the penthouse door.
On went the car up one flight more.
On went the elevator till it came to the top.
On went the elevator, and it would not stop!

Right through the roof went the man and the car.
And nobody knows where the two of them are!
(Nobody knows but everyone cares,
Wearily, drearily climbing the stairs!)

Now on a summer evening when you see a shooting star
Fly through the air, perhaps it *is*—that elevator car!

CAROLINE D. EMERSON

A Book to Read

TITLE: **Let's Marry, Said the Cherry and Other Nonsense Poems**

AUTHOR/ARTIST: N. M. Bodecker

PUBLISHER: A Margaret K. McElderry Book/Atheneum

"Let's marry," said the cherry.
"Why me?" said the pea.
"Cause you're sweet," said the beet.

So begins the preparation for one of the most delicious garden weddings ever. And thus we enter the realm of glee in N. M. Bodecker's very comprehensible, nonsensical book of verse.

After reading just a few pages, you will be tapping your toe to the rhythms of strange people with odd pets, such as:

Upton Weller
(senior teller)
kept a boa
in his cellar.

You will be traveling with a chuckle to the Island of Rum (exceedingly glum) or better yet to the Island of Yorric (intensely historic). But watch out for alligators employed as elevator operators and never, never ask them to take you to the nineteenth floor. Homer Beecher (Spanish teacher) recommends this book for all lovers of nonsense.

Mr. Bodecker has illustrated his verses with whimsical characters from "armadillos" to "gorillos." Is there anyone who should be encouraged *not* to read this book?

"No way," said the hay.

In this chapter you will study nouns. Here is your chance to find out how much you know about them.

Tryout I. Common and Proper Nouns

Write these two headings on your paper: *Common* and *Proper*. Write each of the nouns below in the correct column. Use capital letters where they belong.

state	benson school	continent	city
building	mt. everest	australia	mountain
georgia	florida	wood county	street
june	sunday	swedish	river

Tryout II. Singular and Plural Nouns

Write each sentence below. Change each singular noun in parentheses to plural.

1. The (child) gave themselves two (week) to practice for the talent (show).
2. Ida and Amy played "A Serenade for (Sheep)" on the (piano).
3. Alex performed three (solo).
4. Rita juggled the (glass) and (dish).
5. Fran balanced the (box) on her front (tooth).
6. What great (performance)!
7. No one threw (tomato)!

Tryout III. How Nouns Show Possession

Change these expressions to show possession by using an apostrophe.

1. the nests of the squirrels
2. the coat of my aunt
3. the games of children
4. the den of the thieves

Tryout
Time

5

Learning About Nouns

The Noun

What is your name?
Where are you right now?
What objects do you see around you?

All of your answers to these questions have one thing in common: They all name something. One names a person—you. Another names a place—your classroom or perhaps a room in your home. The final one names things—possibly books and chairs. These names are called **nouns,** and they are one of the most frequently used parts of speech in our language.

▶ A **noun** is a word that names.

The nouns that you used to answer the questions at the top of the page named a person, a place, and things that you can see or touch. Nouns can name more, however. They can name a feeling, such as *fear,* or a time, such as *winter.* They can name a condition or state of being, such as *prosperity.* They can even name a thought or belief, such as *faith.* Can you see or touch what the nouns below name?

happiness	nation
ambition	autumn
week	secrecy
justice	hunger

1. Look around the room. What are some nouns that name things you can see or touch?
2. What are some nouns that name what you cannot see or touch?
3. Complete these sentences by adding nouns. Be prepared to tell if each noun names a person, a place, a thing that can be seen or touched, or a thing that cannot be seen or touched.

   1. We had _____ for dessert the first night of camp.
   2. Is _____ the cook again this year?
   3. One quality I look for in a counselor is _____.
   4. This summer I hope to learn about _____.
   5. A great feeling of _____ comes over me when I see the lake.

✓ Check Test 6: Forms of Verbs

The sentences below require forms of verbs you have studied in earlier grades. Write each sentence. Use the correct form of the verb in parentheses.

1. (write)   I have _____ a message to a wizard.
2. (give)   I _____ it to her raven for delivery.
3. (eat)   But the bird _____ my message!
4. (begin)   I have _____ another letter.
5. (give)   I hope my first message _____ the raven indigestion!

If you need more help, turn to page 336 in the Review Handbook.

How Our Language Grows

¿Habla español?

How's your Spanish? Because you know English, you may know more Spanish than you think you do.

We use many words in English that we think of as Spanish. Some examples are *hacienda, flamenco, fiesta, amigo,* and *sombrero.* Many other words that are part of English have also come into the language from Spanish but are not as easily identified. The following words have all come into English from European Spanish, brought to America by colonists from Spain: *burro, cargo, parasol, patio,* and *bonanza.* All of these words are spelled the same in Spanish and in English. They have almost the same meaning in both languages. Other words that have come into English from European Spanish have approximately the same meanings in both languages, but they have different spellings. Examples are: *lasso* (English), *lazo* (Spanish); *canyon* (English), *cañon* (Spanish); *ranch* (English), *rancho* (Spanish).

Latin American Spanish has contributed still other words to English. In tracing the origins of these words, we find that Spanish colonists often borrowed words from the Latin American Indian languages. Examples include: *tobacco, chocolate, tomato, potato, canoe, coyote, chili, vanilla,* and *tapioca.* In tracing the etymologies of these words, we find some interesting examples of language borrowings.

Look up the following words in a college dictionary for other examples of interesting word histories.

mascara   desperado   alligator   tornado   spaniel

What does each word mean? How has it changed? Does it originally come from European Spanish or from an Indian language?

Three Noun Signals

Look at the italicized nouns in the following sentences.

1. The *tree* is a *juniper.*
2. An *actor* appeared on the *screen.*
3. A fine *concert* will be given in the new *hall.*

Notice that each of the nouns above is introduced by *a, an,* or *the.* You may have known these three words as *articles* or *adjectives.* In this book, we shall call them **noun signals,** because they signal the approach of a noun. In fact, *a, an,* and *the* never appear in a sentence unless they are followed by a noun.

▶ *A, an,* and *the* appear before nouns; they are called **noun signals.**

Name each noun and its signal in sentence 1 above. Do the same for sentence 2. In the first two sentences the noun signals come directly before the noun. However, a noun and its signal do not always come side by side in a sentence. In sentence 3 a modifier comes between the noun signals and the nouns. Read each noun and its signal in sentence 3.

Nouns do not always need noun signals. Many times *a, an,* or *the* do not come before nouns. Study the italicized nouns in this sentence.

Mrs. Grasso always practices *honesty* in *business.*

Remember, whenever you do see *a, an,* or *the* in a sentence, you may be sure that a noun follows.

1. Tell which of the eight words listed below can be used as nouns. You can do this by testing with the noun signals in 1, 2, and 3 below. If the word fits with one or more of the signals, it can be used as a noun.

1. A _____   2. An _____   3. The _____

orange   played   forgot   speech
horses   trucks   regretted picture

2. List the nouns and the noun signals in each of the following sentences.

1. The lettuce is in the bowl.
2. We will make a good salad for the luncheon.
3. Do you have a ripe tomato in the refrigerator?
4. Please run to the store for a cucumber.
5. Get a jar of sliced pickles, too.
6. Put the sandwiches on a large plate.

A book, tight shut, is but a stack of paper!

CHINESE PROVERB

One way to paraphrase this proverb might be: A book is of no value unless it is read. Can you invent a proverb about a well-read book? About a television or a radio that is turned off?

Review Practice

Subject and Predicate

1. Copy each sentence below. Draw a line between the complete subject and the complete predicate.

   1. Ancient Egyptians kept dogs as pets.
   2. The saluki is one of the oldest breeds.
   3. Many new breeds exist today.
   4. Hounds are good hunters.
   5. German shepherds make fine watchdogs.
   6. The tiny chihuahua has a shrill bark.

2. Name the simple subject and verb in each of the above sentences.

3. Study the sentences below. In each sentence the subject and predicate are in inverted order. Name the simple subject and the verb in each sentence.

   1. On the picnic table sat a bouquet of wild daisies.
   2. Across the tablecloth hurried a hungry ant.
   3. Beneath the bench sat a timid squirrel.
   4. Around the tree buzzed a swarm of bees.
   5. Over my head flew a bluejay.
   6. Across the blue sky floated some fleecy clouds.

4. Rewrite each of the sentences in section 3, putting the subject and predicate in natural order.

COMPOSITION: DESCRIPTION

A. Select a noun that names an object in your room. Describe it using from three to five sentences, but do not give away the name. Read your description aloud and let the class guess the object.

B. Choose at least four of the following phrases and weave them into a descriptive paragraph.

a lonely child	a fierce wind
a dark night	an eerie noise
a glad surprise	a whispered warning

Sentence Patterns: Nouns and Verbs

Study the following symbols for the two parts of speech you have studied so far—*nouns* and *verbs*.

$$N = Noun$$
$$V = Action verb$$

When we combine these symbols in the same order in which nouns and verbs usually appear in sentences, we can build sentences of our own.

The sentences below follow two of the most common patterns in English sentence structure.

SENTENCE PATTERN 1: N V   Dogs bark.
Lucy won.

SENTENCE PATTERN 2: N V N   Politicians make
    speeches.
Marta picked apples.

When we add the noun signals *a, an,* and *the* to these two sentence patterns, we can build sentences similar to these.

The **N V**   The bells rang.
A N V   A firecracker exploded.
A N V the **N**   A carpenter built the house.

Now try building sentences of your own, using the sentence patterns shown by the symbols below. For each group of symbols, build two sentences that make sense. Do not use the same noun or verb twice.

1. **N V**
2. **N V** an **N**
3. **N V N**
4. The **N V**
5. **A N V N**

6. **A N V** the **N**
7. The **N V N**
8. **A N V**
9. The **N V** a **N**
10. An **N V** the **N**

Common and Proper Nouns

Look at the first picture above. What do you see? If you say "a building," your response will be correct. If you say "The Empire State Building," that will be correct, too. Similarly, you may say that the second picture shows a house or that it shows the White House.

The words *building* and *house* are nouns which name any building or any house. They are called **common nouns.** The nouns *Empire State Building* and *White House* name a particular building and a particular house. They are called **proper nouns.** Proper nouns always begin with capital letters.

Compare the common nouns and the proper nouns listed below. How are they different?

COMMON NOUNS	PROPER NOUNS
continent	Africa
country	Canada
state	Delaware
government body	Senate
document	Constitution of the United States
organization	Junior Achievement
building	Rosedale Public Library

A proper noun sometimes includes more than one word. Look at the list above. Notice that each important word in a group of words begins with a capital letter.

100

If you need review on capitalizing proper nouns, turn to pages 329–330. Study the rules and examples for capital letters.

▶ A noun that names a particular person, place, or thing is called a **proper noun.** Any other noun is called a **common noun.**

● **Practice**

1. For each common noun below, name a proper noun. Be prepared to write it correctly on the board.

author	language	city
river	book	month
state	ocean	street
continent	country	school

> Begin a proper noun with a capital letter. If a proper noun includes more than one word, begin each important word in the group with a capital letter.

2. For each proper noun below, name a common noun.

Thanksgiving	Library of Congress
Mt. Hood	Martha Washington
The United States	Audubon Society
Massachusetts	World War II

3. Write each sentence below. Begin the proper nouns with capital letters.

1. The los angeles rams is a california football team.
2. A music group called the iron sweatshirt played for the halloween assembly.
3. Pitcher satchel paige is a member of the national baseball hall of fame in cooperstown, new york.
4. On our trip to florida, we visited miami beach, disney world, and tarpon springs.

Singular and Plural Nouns

The singular form of a noun names one item or unit; the plural form names more than one. Most nouns add *s* or *es* to indicate a change to the plural form. This change in form is noticeable in both speech and writing.

Read aloud the words listed below. Listen to the plural sounds. You should hear three different sounds added to the singular form: *s*, *z*, and *ez*.

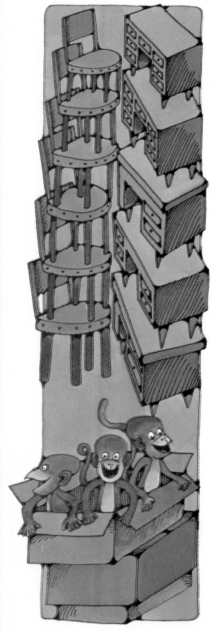

chair, chairs   wish, wishes   table, tables
lamp, lamps   lake, lakes   rose, roses
lady, ladies   crutch, crutches   clock, clocks

Now examine the written form of the plurals above. Notice that each plural ends in an *s* or *es*.

Ways of Forming Plural Nouns

Nouns form their plurals in different ways.

1. Most nouns form their plurals by adding *s* to the singular form.

     desk   desks   dance   dances

2. Nouns that end in *s*, *sh*, soft *ch*, and *x* form their plurals by adding *es*.

     match   matches   marsh   marshes
     grass   grasses   box   boxes

3. Nouns ending in *y* following a consonant change *y* to *i* and add *es*.

     party   parties   city   cities

Nouns ending in *y* following a vowel add *s*.

     monkey   monkeys   tray   trays

Irregular Plural Forms

1. Some nouns ending in *o* add *s* to form the plural.

    solo solos   Eskimo Eskimos   piano pianos

Other nouns ending in *o* add *es*.

    tomato tomatoes   potato potatoes
    hero heroes

2. Most nouns ending in *f* or *fe* change *f* to *v* and add *es*.

    leaf leaves   knife knives

A few simply add *s*.

    chief chiefs   roof roofs   safe safes

3. Some nouns follow no pattern in forming their plurals.

    ox oxen   mouse mice   child children

4. Some nouns change vowels within the word.

    woman women   tooth teeth

5. Some nouns do not change form for plurals.

    deer deer   sheep sheep

If a plural is formed by adding *s* or *es*, the dictionary shows only the singular form. If a plural is formed in any other way, its dictionary entry includes the plural spelling.

● **Practice**

Write the plural form of each noun below. If you are in doubt, consult the dictionary.

1. goose	**4.** half	**7.** gas	**10.** radio
2. house	**5.** tornado	**8.** zoo	**11.** dish
3. second	**6.** belief	**9.** self	**12.** dairy

> Form the plural of most nouns by adding *s* to the singular form.
> Form the plural of nouns ending in *s, sh,* soft *ch,* and *x* by adding *es*.
> Form the plural of nouns ending in *y* following a consonant by changing *y* to *i* and adding *es*.
> Form the plural of nouns ending in *y* following a vowel by adding *s*.

The Possessive Form of Nouns

The possessive form of a noun shows ownership. The italicized nouns in the phrases below are possessive forms. Read the phrases aloud and tell where the apostrophe is located in each possessive noun.

SINGULAR POSSESSIVE	PLURAL POSSESSIVE
the *horse's* saddle	the *horses'* saddles
the *fox's* den	the *foxes'* den

1. Most singular nouns show possession with an apostrophe and *s*.

    the *girl's* books   the *country's* flag

2. Plural nouns ending in *s* show possession with an apostrophe only.

    the *girls'* books   the *countries'* flags

3. Plural nouns not ending in *s* show possession with an apostrophe and *s*.

    the *women's* hats   the *oxen's* yoke

Form the possessive of singular nouns by adding an apostrophe and an *s*.
Form the possessive of plural nouns ending in *s* by adding an apostrophe.
Form the possessive of plural nouns not ending in *s* by adding an apostrophe and an *s*.

● **Practice**

1. Write the singular and plural possessive of each of the nouns below. Add a noun signal and a word to name what is possessed.

    EXAMPLE: ox — an ox's burden   the oxen's burden

boy	group	child	pupil	fox
monkey	lady	hero	chief	elf

2. Write the possessive forms of the nouns in parentheses.

    1. The (fog) swirling mist covered the airfield.
    2. The (runways) lights were barely visible.
    3. Tensely, the pilot studied the (plane) gauges.
    4. She strained to hear the (tower) instructions.

TITLE: **Ben and Me**
AUTHOR/ARTIST: Robert Lawson
PUBLISHER: Little, Brown

Ben Franklin has always received credit for the invention of the Franklin stove and the lightning rod. We know that he helped draft the Declaration of Independence and was a famous and well-loved man in his time. But—as you may have always suspected—behind every great person, you're sure to find a great mouse.

The "me" of *Ben and Me* is Amos, a mouse who decided to take pen in paw to set the records straight for posterity. Amos is the one who suggested how Ben build his famous stove, although Amos does give Ben credit for being a hard worker. The invention should rightly be called the Amos Stove, but the mouse had no use for fame and fortune. He and Ben debated and finally came to this agreement: Amos would aid, advise, and assist Ben with bright ideas. In return, Ben promised to provide food and a fur-hat home for Amos and his family. Amos and Ben enjoyed a wonderful partnership from that time on, except for a brief spell when Amos refused to participate in any more experiments involving electricity.

Robert Lawson, who was fortunate enough to discover Amos's manuscript, has been awarded both the Caldecott and the Newbery Medals.

Checkup

Checkup I. Common and Proper Nouns

Write each sentence below. Begin each proper noun with a capital letter.

1. Joan traveled from new york to los angeles.
2. In philadelphia she saw independence hall.
3. She crossed the mississippi river to get from illinois to missouri.
4. She stopped at rocky mountain national park in colorado.
5. At last she saw the pacific ocean.

Checkup II. Singular and Plural Nouns

Write the plurals for these nouns.

foot	daisy
leaf	roof
hero	potato
gun	church
woman	cargo

Checkup III. How Nouns Show Possession

Write each sentence below. Make the words in parentheses possessive.

1. (Children) stories have been unkind to wolves.
2. (Zoologists) studies have shown that wild wolves do not attack human beings.
3. Have you read any of (Dr. Fox) books?
4. This (author) specialty is the wolf.
5. The (wolves) worst enemies are humans.
6. Many wolves have been killed senselessly by (hunters) bullets.

In this chapter you will learn to identify and use good techniques of gathering and organizing information. Here is your chance to find out how much you already know.

Tryout I. Writing a Bibliography

List the books below in alphabetical order by the authors' last names. Write them, using the correct form for a bibliography. Use punctuation and capital letters where they are needed.

1. the king's falcon, by paula fox
2. a spy in old philadelphia, by anne emery
3. meeting in the mountains, by john b prescott
4. blue canyon horse, by ann nolan clark

Tryout II. Outlining

Copy the following part of an outline using correct punctuation and capitalization:

the moon

I facts about features we can observe
  a moonlight
    1 source of light
    2 phases of moon
  b tides
    1 relation to moon
    2 frequency
  c eclipses

Tryout III. Using *teach* and *learn*

Write each sentence below. Use the correct form of *teach* or *learn* in place of each blank.

1. Can you _____ me to play tennis?
2. Our mother has _____ us the different strokes.
3. The twins have _____ very quickly.

6

Tryout Time

Gathering and Organizing Information

Doing Research

Research is not something limited to white-coated scientists poring over test tubes. It is something you will be doing through junior high school, high school, and beyond.

Why? In order to learn, you will often be called on to do careful and patient investigation into a topic. For example, suppose that you were presented with the topic "My Community's Water Supply." How would you go about learning more about the subject?

What Questions Should You Ask?

In beginning your investigation, decide what questions you must answer. Which of the following questions would be appropriate to a study of your community's water supply?

1. What is the source of our water supply?
2. Do we have enough water? Could there be a shortage?
3. How popular is boating in our community?
4. How is the water brought to our homes?
5. What are some ways in which water is purified and which of these ways is used in our community?
6. How much water is used to fill an Olympic-sized swimming pool?
7. Who pays the cost of supplying our water?
8. Is our water tested for impurities? If so, how?
9. How many tennis courts do we have?
10. Are families billed for the water they use?

Where Can You Find the Answers?

After you have chosen your questions, think of sources where you could find the information necessary to answer them. Which of the following resources could you use to find information about your community's water supply? Remember that you will need general information about community water supplies as a background for studying your own community's water resources.

1. *Your home:* Could you find books or other materials about water resources at home? Could you observe some things about your community's water supply in your own home?
2. *Your classroom:* Could you find books, pictures, or other materials on the topic there?
3. *The library:* Are there encyclopedias, reference books, newspapers, magazines, illustrations, and pamphlets containing information on the topic? How can you find out?
4. *Government agencies, or other organizations:* In your community or state, are there organizations that have pamphlets, maps, or pictures that will help?
5. *Experts:* Are there experts on the topic who live in your community?

● Practice

Suppose that you are studying the topic "The History of the Monster in American Movies."

1. List questions that will need to be answered as you make your study. Be prepared to read them in class. Discuss the questions with your classmates and make a class list.
2. Make a list of sources that might give you the information you need. Then make a class list of sources.

Interviewing an Expert

If you are lucky, you may find that there is an expert in your community who can help you with a research project. If so, set up an interview in which you ask the person important questions.

For example, suppose that you want information on your town's police department. Call or write a letter to the police chief to arrange for an interview. Before your meeting, do some reading on police departments so that you will have some general background on the subject. Then, write down the questions that you want to ask the police officer. List them in sensible order and mark the most important ones so that you will be sure to ask them.

During the interview, listen carefully. If you do not understand an explanation, ask politely for further information.

Take brief notes during the interview. Jot down the main points and important figures or details. Use abbreviations. After the interview, review your notes and complete them so that they will be understandable to you later.

How to Prepare for and Conduct an Interview

Make arrangements for the interview by telephone or letter.

Prepare your questions carefully before the interview.

During the interview, listen carefully.

Take brief notes on the main points and any important facts and figures.

Write clearly and use abbreviations that you will understand later.

Immediately after the interview, review your notes and add to them.

● **Practice**

1. Choose a topic on which you or a classmate could speak as an "expert" after some preparation. Here are some suggested topics:

   a visit to a famous place (your choice)
   how to play a game (your choice)
   experiences as a gardener
   how to plan a camping trip
   a hobby (your choice)

2. After you have selected a topic, choose a partner. Decide which roles each of you will play in making arrangements for the interview and during the interview. Be prepared to act your roles before the class.

3. Follow the guides for interviewing above.

COMPOSITION: WRITING A NEWS STORY

A. After you have heard your classmates' interviews, select one of them as the subject of a news story. Write it as if you were a reporter for the *Morning News*. Tell who gave the interview, what the main points were, what details were surprising or new to the class, and why the information was important.

B. Write a news story in not more than three full paragraphs, telling as much as you can about some event or person in your community. The school newspaper may publish it or your room may wish to issue a class newspaper that includes some of these stories.

✔ Check Test 7: Using Words Correctly

Write each sentence below. Choose the correct word in parentheses.

1. Everyone had finally been (chose, chosen) for a team.
2. Our team (sang, sung) a song before the game.
3. The first batter (chose, chosen) a heavy bat.
4. He got a hit, but he (broke, broken) the bat.
5. The second batter (chose, chosen) another bat.
6. She (broke, broken) her bat, too!
7. As I stepped up to the plate, the bell ending recess (rang, rung).
8. I think we have (broke, broken) the record for broken bats in this game!

If you need more help, turn to pages 340–341 in the Review Handbook.

Using an Encyclopedia

Suppose that you want to do some research on ancient mummies. However, you do not know of a mummy expert in your community. How are you going to get the answers to your questions?

Actually, you do have an expert — in fact, you have thousands of them on almost every imaginable topic. Their knowledge has been brought together in an encyclopedia.

Perhaps you have encyclopedias in your home or perhaps you have seen or used them in the library. If so, you may know that there are different kinds. Some deal with only one area of knowledge, such as biography or science. Others cover all areas of human knowledge and come in sets of twenty or more volumes.

Information on some topics in an encyclopedia is not likely to change much over the years. For example, the facts about George Washington's life are fairly well researched and known. Other topics, however, undergo continuous change. For example, information about medical research that appeared in an encyclopedia ten years ago is likely to be very much out of date now. Therefore, you should be aware of just how up-to-date an encyclopedia you are using is. Look for the *copyright notice;* it gives the year the encyclopedia was published. The copyright notice is usually printed on the *copyright page,* which follows the *title page* at the front of each volume in a set.

To Discuss

1. Which topics below suggest information that is not likely to change from year to year?

Space Travel	The Wombat
Energy Sources	The First Balloon Flight

2. For which topics above would you need to refer to an encyclopedia with a recent publication date?

● **Practice**

1. List all the kinds of encyclopedias in your school or neighborhood library by checking through the card catalogue. Note whether the encyclopedias are single volumes or sets of several volumes.
2. Write the titles of the most up-to-date encyclopedias you can find on biography, music, and general knowledge.

Finding Information in an Encyclopedia

An encyclopedia has several aids to help you find the information you want. Here are five such aids:

1. The topics are arranged in *alphabetical order*. The guide letter and volume number are stamped on the spine of each book.
2. There is an *index*. Because there may be information on a topic in several articles of an encyclopedia, turn to the index to be sure of finding the information you may need. The index may often be in a separate volume labeled *Index*.
3. Each major article is divided into subtopics. *Subheadings* tell you what these subtopics are.
4. At the top of the page, there may be *guide topics*. Use them as you use guide words on a dictionary page.
5. At the end of an article, there may be *cross references* to other articles containing information on the same subject. For example, an article on the Aztecs might be followed by this cross reference:

   See also Archeology; Indian Tribes, North American; and Mexico.

To Discuss

Under what topic in an encyclopedia would you look for information on each of the subjects below? Would you need to look in more than one place? If so, why?

1. The "Green Revolution" in Raising Crops
2. Alaska Under the Russians
3. Head-hunters in the Upper Amazon
4. Strip Mining in West Virginia
5. The Use of Poison Gas in World War I

● Practice

1. What is the name of the encyclopedia you are using?
2. Find the index. Is there an index volume? Look up *Aztec* in the index. Read the references.
3. Turn to the article on your state. How is the general topic narrowed down to the most important facts? Read the subheadings.
4. Does the top of the page include two guide topics? If so, what does the first guide topic tell you? The second guide topic? Are the guides printed in heavy type?

Look at me, friend!
I come to ask for your dress . . .

I come to beg you for this,
Long-life Maker,
For I am going to make a basket for
  lily roots out of you.
I pray you, friend, not to feel angry. . . .

KWAKIUTL

The Native Americans are known for their understanding of and respect for nature. What aspect of nature is mentioned in the poem above? For what is the poet asking? If you were to ask for something from nature, what would you ask for? Why?

How Our Language Grows

Gr–r–r–r

When you make up your mind about something, do you prefer to be called *stubborn* or *determined*? How about *mule-headed*? Someone could actually use all three terms to describe the same characteristic, but the feeling created would hardly be the same.

Many words have emotional meanings. Whether we realize it or not, we often describe things in biased language. In doing so, we reveal our own feelings. We also influence the way others feel about a subject.

Do you listen to *country-western music* or shut off that *hillbilly noise*? Did your best friend just pass along some juicy *gossip* or just the latest *news*? Are some of your tastes *out-of-date*, *old-fashioned*, or simply *conservative*?

When words carry unpleasant feelings such as *stubborn, mule-headed, hillbilly,* and *gossip,* they are sometimes called **snarl** words. Words that create pleasant feelings—*slender, determined, polite*—are called **purr** words. Why do you suppose *purr* and *snarl* are used to describe such emotional language?

1. Match each purr word in the first column below with its counterpart snarl word in the second column.

promotion	gullible
generous	old
elderly	scheme
portly	propaganda
trusting	fat
plan	extravagant

2. Write each snarl word below. Then write a purr word to match each one.

   bookworm   miserly   nosey   skinny   wishy-washy

Using the Library

A school library or a local public library is a storehouse of information. In it you can find just about any reference tool you might need—dictionaries, encyclopedias, and other nonfiction books on specific topics.

How can you find the information you need among the millions of nonfiction books? Luckily, there is a well-organized system for locating the book you want.

First, you need to know that each nonfiction book is given a number, called a **call number.** Nonfiction books are arranged on the shelves in numerical order, according to their call numbers. The call number assigned to a book tells what general subject area the book covers.

The most common numbering system for nonfiction books in school and local libraries is the **Dewey Decimal System.** There are ten major subject divisions in this system of classification:

000–099	General Works
100–199	Philosophy
200–299	Religion
300–399	Social Sciences
400–499	Linguistics
500–599	Pure Science
600–699	Applied Science
700–799	Arts and Recreation
800–899	Literature
900–999	History and Geography

Every nonfiction book will fit into one of these classifications.

Because there is also an unlimited number of subdivisions, the decimal point is important in numbering the books. For example, the 550's are used only for life sciences, and 551 may be used for books about water. A specific book on water may be numbered 551.5N. (The *N* is the first letter of the author's last name. It is used in case there is more than one book on exactly the same subtopic.)

The key to finding a nonfiction book, then, is to find its call number. You can do this by looking in the *card catalogue.* The card catalogue is a series of drawers filled with cards which are arranged alphabetically. Each drawer is labeled with letters showing the cards that are in it. For example, a drawer marked *Aa-Am* would contain cards on such topics as *aardvarks, accidents,* and *agriculture.*

There are usually at least three cards in the catalogue for every nonfiction book in the library: an *author* card, a *title* card, and *subject* card. The author card is filed under the author's last name. The title card and the subject card are filed according to the first important word in the title or subject of the book. All three cards carry the book's call number, so that you can find the number if you know the author, title, or subject.

If you are gathering information for a report, you will be looking for books on your subject. Look for a subject card.

Suppose, for example, that you need information on water conservation. In the *Wa* drawer of the card catalogue, you may find cards for several books on that subject.

The subject is printed in capital letters on the top line of the card, as shown below. Study the subject card and notice the information it gives. The *J* at the beginning of the call number stands for *Juvenile.* This means that the book is suitable for readers under age fourteen.

WATER

J551.5-N   Nelson, Clifford R.

     From one drop of water. Illustrated by
Ren Patterson. Science Consultant: Stanley R.
Wachs. New York, J. Messner, 1970 32 pp.,
illus.

To Discuss

1. What is the subject of the book?
2. Who is the author of the book? What is the title?
3. Who illustrated the book?
4. What is the name of the publisher? Where was it published and when? Why is this helpful information?
5. What other information is given? How is it helpful?
6. What is the call number of the book?

● Practice

Plan a visit to your school or public library. While you are there, find the answers to the questions below.

1. Where is the big dictionary located?
2. How many sets of encyclopedias are there? Where are they located? What are the copyright dates?
3. Where is the card catalogue?
4. Where are the following publications located: biographies, books on science, poetry books, fiction, magazines, reference books?
5. Which books can you take out of the library? Which books must you read there? Can you take magazines and paperback books out of the library? How?
6. How can you get a library card?

Going Ahead

Choose a subject with which you have already had some experience or about which you have done some reading. Take the first steps toward becoming an expert. Learn all you can through interviews, books, and further experiences of your own. For this assignment, do your reading in non-fiction books rather than encyclopedia articles, since the books will develop the topic in greater detail.

Keep a diary dating your entries and recording the information or ideas you gain and the source of your information.

Preparing a Bibliography

As you use books to find information on a topic, make a list of the books from which your information comes. Such a list is called a **bibliography.**

A bibliography gives the name of the author and the title of each selection listed. For example:

Buehr, Walter. *Water, Our Vital Need*
Redlauer, Edward. *Water for Your Community*
Rothman, Joel. *At Last to the Ocean: the Story of the Endless Cycle of Water*

A complete bibliography may also give other information about the book: the place of publication, publisher, year of publication, and a brief description of contents or other material. Here is a more complete entry for Joel Rothman's book.

Rothman, Joel. *At Last to the Ocean: the Story of the Endless Cycle of Water*. New York: Crowell-Collier Press, 1971. Illustrations.

To Discuss

1. Notice that books in a bibliography are listed in alphabetical order. How are they alphabetized?
2. How is the author's name written? What punctuation mark follows the author's last name? What mark follows the author's full name?
3. How can you tell what the title of the book is in a handwritten or typewritten bibliography?

● Practice

List these books for a bibliography. Use capital letters and punctuation correctly.

1. the earth for sam, by w maxwell reed
2. soil, water, and man, by muriel deusing
3. sun, earth, and man, by george p and eunice s bischof

Taking Notes

It is necessary to take notes on what you have been reading if you wish to remember and use what you learned. Study these notes.

> _Undersea Cable_
> _Compton's Pictured Encyc. Vol. 3, pp. 5-7_
>
> _Characteristics of undersea cable:_
>   _Copper core for transmission of electric current. Core surrounded by layers of insulating materials._
>   _Cable lasts from 30-40 years._
>
> _Laying the cable:_
>   _Especially equipped cable-laying ship follows charted path._
>   _Guiding device feeds out cable._

Check the model against the guides below. Be prepared to tell whether or not the student who wrote the model followed them.

How to Take Notes

Write the topic at the top of your paper.
Give the title of the book, the author, and the page.
Use abbreviations that are easy to interpret.
Group facts under major headings.
Record facts accurately.

● Practice

Take notes on a topic of your choice from two or more sources of information. Follow the guides above.

1. Write these sentences correctly, capitalizing the proper nouns. Underline all the common and proper nouns.

1. The capital of the united states is washington, d. c.
2. The city is on the potomac river.
3. The capitol is located at the head of pennsylvania avenue.
4. The home of the president is called the white house.
5. The lincoln memorial and the jefferson memorial are points of interest.
6. The declaration of independence is housed in the national archives building.
7. Not far from our nation's capital is mount vernon, the home of george washington.
8. The smithsonian institution houses the *spirit of st. louis,* in which charles lindbergh made the first solo flight across the atlantic ocean.

2. Write the plural form of each of the following nouns.

city	bush	scarf	piano
hero	deer	tomato	party
alley	goose	dwarf	calf

3. Write sentences using the possessive forms of these nouns:

ponies	chief	Ohio	women	Mrs. March
writer	nurse	nurses	thief	thieves

Making an Outline

Your bibliography may contain several titles and you may have written notes from several sources—an interview, an encyclopedia, books, articles, and pamphlets. The next step is to organize your information so that it can be used to make a clear-cut, interesting report on your subject.

The first step in organizing your notes is to prepare an outline by topics. Decide which topics in your notes are main ideas and which subtopics help to explain the main ideas. Then decide on the order in which you will discuss the main topics, and finally the order in which you will present the subtopics under each main topic.

Study the form of the outline on the next page. Be prepared to answer the questions below.

To Discuss

1. What is the title of the outline? Which words in the title are capitalized?
2. Read the main topics. Is the wording similar?
3. How are the main topics numbered? How are subtopics indicated?
4. Are the subtopics worded in a similar way?
5. How many subtopics are divided into further details? How is each level of subtopics marked?
6. Choose examples to show that the guides below were followed.

How to Write an Outline

Mark the main topics with Roman numerals.
Mark the subtopics with capital letters.
Mark any further details with Arabic numerals.
Place periods after numerals or letters of topics.
Capitalize the first word of each topic.

How Rocks Become Soil
I. Action of weather
  A. How winds erode rocks
    1. Sand blown against rocks
    2. Boulders loosened
  B. How extreme heat and cold
     affect rocks
II. Action of water
  A. How rain wears away rock
  B. How streams and waves erode
     rock
III. Action of plants and trees
  A. How seeds split rocks
  B. How roots break cracks open

● Practice

1. Rewrite the outline below in the correct form. Use capital letters and punctuation marks correctly in the outline.

the values of a part-time job

developing different skills
    getting along with others
    making business arrangements
    doing common tasks
        keeping records and accounts
        gardening
        baby-sitting

earning money
    becoming more independent
    learning to spend wisely
    learning to save

2. In the list below, major topics and subtopics are mixed up. Write these topics in correct outline form:

> Tennis
> Swimming
> Boating
> Table games
> Quiet recreation indoors
> Checkers
> Golf
> Active outdoor recreation
> Model making
> Hiking
> Stamp collecting

COMPOSITION: A SCIENCE OR SOCIAL STUDIES PAPER

A. In class, list half a dozen topics related to work in science or social studies which you have recently done. Choose one of the topics and prepare an outline for two levels of subtopics.

B. Write the paper you have outlined. Start a new paragraph for each point listed with a Roman numeral. The subtopics labeled *A* and *B* may both be included in the paragraph, but if the explanations or examples are too long for one paragraph, start a new paragraph for the next lettered part.

Using Words Correctly: *teach* and *learn*

The meanings of the verbs *teach* and *learn* are sometimes confused. The verb *teach* means "to show how" or "to give instruction." The verb *learn* means "to gain knowledge or skill." Study the ways in which these verbs are used in the sentences below:

1. Mrs. Allan *teaches* us swimming.
2. She *taught* me the breast stroke.
3. Some of us *learn* the strokes more easily than others.
4. Have you *learned* how to tread water?

● **Practice**

> Use the verb *teach*, not *learn*, when you mean "to give instruction."

1. Write each sentence below. Choose the correct word in parentheses.

   1. I love to (teach, learn) animals new tricks.
   2. I have (taught, learned) my parrot to say, "Birds can't talk."
   3. (Teaching, Learning) seems easy for parrots.
   4. My dog Lucy has (taught, learned) to roll over.
   5. Carol and I have (taught, learned) Lucy to sit up, too.
   6. Animals (teach, learn) easily when they are rewarded.

2. Write each sentence below. Write *teach, taught, learn,* or *learned* in place of each blank.

   1. Will you _____ your parrot anything else?
   2. I hope he will _____ to say, "More peanuts."
   3. He _____ very quickly.
   4. Who _____ your dog to beg?
   5. She _____ that by herself.

HOW ABOUT SOME PISTACHIOS?

A Book to Read

TITLE: **The House of Dies Drear**
AUTHOR: Virginia Hamilton
PUBLISHER: Macmillan

On a hill outside town loomed the House of Dies Drear. A chill passed over Thomas the first time he saw it through the mist, huge, dark, and isolated. Could this house really be the one that Thomas and his family had driven such a long way for? Could this really be their new home?

Historic notes on the house told that it was once an important station on the Underground Railroad. Tunnels under the house leading to a cave, sliding walls, and secret passages had all been very useful long ago for hiding escaped slaves when danger was near. But Thomas was not at all sure that they would be useful in a house in which he was going to live.

The moment Thomas and his family arrive, peculiar things begin to happen. Is the old caretaker, Mr. Pluto, trying to drive the family away? Why do the Darrow children call him the "keeper of the fire"?

Virginia Hamilton is the author of many books for young people. She grew up in an Ohio community, very much like the one she has written about in this book. Her own ancestors, who fled from the South during the early 1800's, may have used the Underground Railroad stations hidden in many large, old houses in her town. Ms. Hamilton has drawn on her childhood curiosity and admiration for these brave people to create this suspenseful tale.

Checkup I. Writing a Bibliography

List the following books in alphabetical order by the authors' last names. Use the correct form for a bibliography.

1. the art of the old west, by shirley glubok
2. the big wave, by pearl s buck
3. the pushcart war, by jean merrill
4. harriet the spy, by louise fitzhugh
5. dragon wings, by laurence yep
6. life and times of frederick douglass, by frederick douglass

Checkup II. Outlining

Use the following jumbled items to make an outline. Supply a title and list items correctly by indenting and using numerals and letters. Capitalize words correctly.

railway, by land, by air, ship, barge, freight truck, by water, helicopter, airplane

Checkup III. Using *teach* and *learn*

Write the paragraph below. Write the correct form of *teach* or *learn* in place of each blank.

Dad has promised to _____ me to play chess. It is not an easy game to _____. Do you think he can _____ me? Sandy said she _____ to play last winter. I hope I can _____ to play well.

6

Checkup

7

Tryout
Time

In this chapter you will be studying verbs. Here is a chance to find out how much you already know.

Tryout I.   Recognizing Verbs

Copy the verb in each of the sentences below. Be sure to include the main verb and its helper or helpers.

1. The pond always freezes in January.
2. Can we build a fire on the bank?
3. Will your father skate with us?
4. I bought a new pair of gloves.
5. Have you heard the good news?
6. Snow has been forecast for tonight.
7. It has already begun.

Tryout II.   Verbs of Action or Being

Copy the verb in each of the sentences below. Next to each verb, write *action* if it expresses action, and *being* if it tells what the subject is or is like.

1. Bea worked with clay in art today.
2. First, she slammed the clay on the table.
3. This removed any air bubbles.
4. Then the clay was ready.
5. Bea made an armadillo.
6. She fired her piece in the kiln.
7. Now the clay is hard and dry.
8. Tomorrow she will paint the clay.
9. What color is an armadillo?

Tryout III.   Verbs in Contractions

Write contractions by combining these pairs of words.

does not	could not	it is	they are
she will	I am	you are	has not

Tryout IV.   Principal Parts of Verbs

Complete the following sentences with two forms of the verb — the past in the first sentence and the past participle in the second.

1. (watch)   We _____ the cook at Pizza Palace.
We _____ never _____ such a performance.

2. (toss)   The cook _____ the pizza dough above his head.
He _____ _____ it high before but never this high!

3. (wait)   He _____ for it to come down.
He _____ never _____ this long before.

4. (stay)   But the dough _____ in the air.
We _____ _____ to see it come down.

5. (reappear)   At last the dough _____.
It _____ _____ just in time to be our lunch!

Tryout V.   Irregular Verbs

1. For each verb listed below, write a sentence using the past participle form:

take   eat   drink   sing
ride   speak   freeze   steal

2. Write each sentence below. Choose the correct form of the verb in parentheses.

1. Jenny has (laid, lain) half of the bricks for the patio.
2. The rest of the job (laid, lay) before her.
3. She (lay, laid) her trowel on the ground.
4. "I'll just (lay, lie) down for a minute," she thought.

7

Learning About Verbs

Recognizing Verbs

The groups of words below are not sentences. If you add one word to each group, you can make each one a sentence.

1. Mary _____ a dollar.
2. The farmers _____ their crops.
3. The dog _____ my slipper.

Take turns reading your sentences aloud. Did you notice that all the words you chose are verbs?

Every sentence must contain a verb. The verb brings life to a sentence, as it did in the sentences above.

▶ A **verb** is a word that shows action or being.

A verb, as you know, is the key word in the predicate of a sentence. One way to tell whether a word can be used as a verb in a sentence is to test the word with *I* as the subject. If the combination of the two words makes a sentence, the word is a verb. To illustrate this, let us test some words.

I baseball.	I lose.
I piano.	I play.
I coat.	I swim.

Can *baseball*, *piano*, or *coat* be used as a verb? Can *lose*, *play*, or *swim* be used as a verb?

Practice

Test each of the following words in the way shown on page 133. Make a list of the words that can be used as verbs.

| lion | applaud | owl | howl | tell |
| write | window | giggle | trip | discover |

Verbs of Action

A verb of action often expresses action that can be seen or heard, as in these sentences:

> Jessie *mows* the lawn regularly.
> We *played* tennis all afternoon.
> They *had won* two games by three o'clock.

Name the subject of each sentence, then the verb, then the complete predicate. With action verbs, these predicates tell what the subjects do or did. Other verbs of action are *swim, walk, call, hit,* and *carry.*

A verb of action can also express action of the mind, which cannot be seen or heard. Such verbs as *think, know, doubt,* and *wonder* express action of the mind.

Verbs of Being

Some verbs express *being* rather than action. The most common are forms of *be: am, is, are, was,* and *were.* Other examples include *seem* and *become.*

Verbs of being are found in predicates that tell what or where the subject *is* or *was* or what the subject *is like* or *was like.*

Name the subject, verb, and complete predicate in the following sentences. What does each predicate tell about its subject?

> These boys are good friends.   Nino was happy.
> The girls became friends, too.   She seemed busy.

● Practice

Read aloud the verb in each sentence below. Tell whether it is a verb of action or a verb of being.

1. The home team came to bat in the last half of the ninth inning.
2. They trailed the visitors by one run.
3. The first two batters were quick strike-outs.
4. The next one got a walk.
5. Then Janowski approached the plate.
6. He seemed supremely confident.
7. The pitcher became nervous on the mound.
8. She eyed the catcher narrowly.
9. Finally, she threw her best pitch.
10. Janowski swung the bat with all his might.
11. The ball sailed deep into left field toward the stands.
12. Was it a home run?

Going Ahead

Well-chosen verbs make interesting sentences. Write the paragraph below. Choose the words in parentheses that would give the reader the more lively and interesting picture.

Three fire engines (went, tore) past our house. A neighbor (called, shouted), "The roof's on fire!" Children (ran, raced) down the street to see it. Several boys on bikes (rode, sped) by. Firefighters were already (putting out, drowning) the flames with water. Before they left, they (took away, tore out) all the blackened shingles. Amazingly, they (did, completed) their job in half an hour.

Sentence Patterns: A Third Pattern

Study the following symbols. You have already worked with two of them. Which one is new to you?

N = Noun   **V** = Action
V^{be} = Verb of being (when it is part of a predicate that tells what the subject *is* or *was*)

Now that you have studied verbs of being you can use the new symbol **V**^{be} to show a new sentence pattern.

                                   N Vbe N
PATTERN 3: N V^{be} **N** The trees are oaks.

                                   N Vbe   N
                              Leslie is a nurse.

Here are the sentence parts which make up each of the three patterns you have studied so far:

                                   N   V
PATTERN 1: N V (Noun — Verb) Hyenas laugh.

PATTERN 2: N V N (Noun — Action verb — Noun)

                       N   V   N
                The sailor scrubbed the deck.

PATTERN 3: N V^{be} **N** (Noun — Verb of being — Noun)

                   N Vbe   N
               The bird is an oriole.

Notice that in Pattern 2 the two **N**'s stand for different things: *sailor* and *deck*. In Pattern 3, the two **N**'s refer to the same thing: *bird* and *oriole*.

Try building sentences of your own, using the following combinations of symbols as guides. Write sensible sentences and vary your sentence ideas.

1. N V	4. A N V N	7. The N V N
2. The N V	5. N V^{be} the N	8. The N V^{be} a N
3. N V a N	6. A N V the N	9. A N V^{be} the N

How Our Language Grows

Ups and Downs

Just as people change all during their lives, words frequently change in meaning over a period of time.

Often these changes are simple alterations of a word's original meaning. *Hospital* once meant a "guest room" or "inn." *Host, hospitality,* and *hospitable* still show that meaning.

In the course of change, however, many words have become more dignified. *Nice,* an often overworked compliment today, wasn't always such. It originally meant "foolish or ignorant." *Minister* once meant "servant." The word still carries the meaning that a minister serves the people. However, over the centuries the word has moved up in status. So has *respect,* which at one time meant "to spy."

Many other words have taken on less respectable meanings. When we refer to someone today as being *sly,* we're hardly paying a compliment. At one time we would have been, however, for *sly* once meant "wise." The word *bribe* once simply meant "a piece of bread." How might its original meaning be related to what it means today?

Our language is constantly changing. Even words we take for granted have been involved in the process.

1. Look up the words below in a college dictionary. Write the original meaning of each one and tell whether it has moved up or down in status.

     brave   silly   villain   paradise   pioneer

2. Look up the words below. Tell how each has changed in meaning.

     dandelion   candidate   clever   cute   lady

Helping Verbs

Examine the three sentences below carefully.

1. Barbara *earned* six dollars.
2. She *is working* on Saturdays.
3. She *has been earning* money each Saturday.

How many words does the verb in each sentence contain? When a verb contains more than one word, the last word is called the **main verb.** The others are called **helping verbs.** What is the main verb in sentence 2? In sentence 3? What are the helping verbs?

Name each main verb listed below. Then name the helpers.

are spoken	have frozen	shall hear
is hoping	has sung	should have run
was done	had broken	may have been chosen

Among the most frequently used helping verbs are forms of the verbs *have*, *be*, and *do*.

have	be	are	do
has	am	was	does
had	is	were	did

However, these verbs are not used only as helping verbs. They can also be used as main verbs.

AS MAIN VERBS

1. I *am* fond of all pets.
2. My dog Flash *is* a Dalmatian.
3. He *has* spots.
4. Flash *did* a new trick.

AS HELPING VERBS

1. I *am reading* about dogs.
2. He *is seen* all over town.
3. Flash *has chased* his own tail.
4. He *did perform* very well.

When the main verb and its helpers are used next to each other in a sentence, it is easy to find the entire verb.

The pond *has been frozen* all winter.

Sometimes, though, the main verb and its helpers are separated by other words in the sentence. The word *not* and words that tell *when* and *how* may come between verb parts.

We *shall* not *rehearse* our play again.
I *have* never *seen* a dress rehearsal.
She *was* quietly *humming* a song from the third act.

In a question, the subject often comes between verb parts.

Where *have* you *been staying?*

● **Practice**

1. Read aloud each sentence below and name the verbs. Include the main verb and its helper or helpers.

1. We have always worked on the farm.
2. Len did not find the eggs.
3. Lara was happily feeding her goats.
4. Am I going with you to milk the cows?

Now go back and name the words that separate the verb parts.

2. In each sentence below, tell whether the verb in italics is used as a helping verb or a main verb.

1. The golfer *has* driven the ball onto the green.
2. *Did* she leave her clubs with the caddy?
3. The huge crowd *was* led by reporters.
4. She *has* a number nine iron in her golf bag.

3. Write two sentences for each verb listed below. In one sentence, use the verb as a main verb. In the other, use it as a helping verb.

am   is   have   does   was

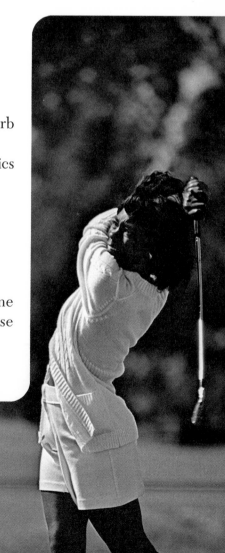

Verbs in Contractions

Sometimes verbs are combined with the word *not* to make contractions such as those italicized below.

aren't	= are not	*hasn't*	= has not
isn't	= is not	*didn't*	= did not
haven't	= have not	*doesn't*	= does not

A verb can also be combined with the words *I, he, she, it, we, you,* and *they* to form contractions.

I'm	= I am	*we're*	= we are
he's	= he is	*they've*	= they have
she'd	= she would	*you'll*	= you will
it's	= it is		

Notice the apostrophe in each contraction above. An apostrophe is used in a contraction to show that a letter or letters have been omitted.

Do not let contractions confuse you when you are looking for the verb in a sentence. Remember that *n't* is never a part of the verb. The words *I, he, she, it, we, you,* and *they* are never part of the verb. Look for the verb in each of these sentences:

1. I've heard that speaker before.
2. You'll not be hearing from me again.
3. Jill didn't come in time for the first speech.
4. She hasn't arrived yet.

The verb in sentence 1 is *have heard.* In sentence 2, it is *will be hearing.* What are the verbs in 3 and 4?

● Practice

1. Name the verb in each of these contractions:

you'll	I'm	isn't	we're
didn't	aren't	you're	I've

2. Make contractions by combining each of the verbs below with the word *not*. Remember to use an apostrophe.

could	is	had	do
have	was	did	are

3. Name the verb in each of the following sentences.

1. We're on our way to the band concert.
2. The band members haven't tuned their instruments yet.
3. Don't you play the flute?
4. Isn't that your sister with the tuba?

Trifle

Against the day of sorrow
Lay by some trifling thing
A smile, a kiss, a flower
For sweet remembering.

Then when the day is darkest
Without one rift of blue
Take out your little trifle
And dream your dream anew.

GEORGIA DOUGLAS JOHNSON

What sort of "trifle" have you saved up for a "rainy day"? How does such a trifle help to make a dark day brighter?

Sentence Patterns: Helping Verbs

Now that you have studied helping verbs, you can add a new verb symbol to your growing list.

N = Noun $\qquad$ V^{be} = Verb of being

V = Action verb $\qquad$ V^h = Helping verb

Study the three basic sentence patterns listed below, as well as the sentences that illustrate them. Notice that the V or V^{be} in each pattern can stand for more than one word. They can include helping verbs as well as main verbs. For example, the symbols V^h and V are represented by either the V symbol or the V^{be} in the basic pattern.

$$\begin{array}{ll} & \quad\; N \quad\; V^h \quad\; V \\ \text{PATTERN 1: } N\ V & \text{Justice has triumphed.} \end{array}$$

$$\begin{array}{ll} & \quad\; N \quad V^h \quad V \quad\; N \\ \text{PATTERN 2: } N\ V\ N & \text{Tony will cook spaghetti.} \end{array}$$

$$\begin{array}{ll} & \quad\; N \quad\; V^h \quad V^h \quad V^{be} \quad\; N \\ \text{PATTERN 3: } N\ V^{be}\ N & \text{Sandy could have been president.} \end{array}$$

Study the combinations of symbols listed below. Match each one with the sentences that follow the pattern.

1. $N\ V^h\ V\ N$	a. Snow has fallen.
2. $N\ V^h\ V^h\ V\ N$	b. Peter will build forts.
3. $N\ V^h\ V$	c. Lisa can be captain.
4. $N\ V^h\ V^{be}\ N$	d. Lee should have been treasurer.
5. $N\ V^h\ V^h\ V^{be}\ N$	e. Ruth may have seen Brownie.
6. $N\ V^{be}\ N$	f. Bobbie has been crying.
7. $N\ V^h\ V^h\ V$	g. Mr. Seelie was president.

Using the symbols below, build a variety of sensible sentences of your own. Identify each sentence as Pattern 1, 2, or 3.

1. $N\ V^h\ V$	4. The $N\ V^h\ V^h\ V$ a N
2. A $N\ V^h\ V$ the N	5. A $N\ V^h\ V^{be}$ the N
3. $N\ V^h\ V^h\ V$	6. $N\ V^h\ V^h\ V^{be}$ the N

How Verbs Show Time

Verbs change their forms to express time. These forms are called **tenses.** The three most common tenses are *present, past,* and *future.*

PRESENT: I *hear* music. PAST: I *heard* music.
FUTURE: I *shall hear* music.

In the first statement above, the verb *hear* describes something that is happening right now. The verb *hear* is called the *present tense.* The present tense may also be written *hears,* as in "Tina hears the music."

In the second statement, the verb *hear* expresses what happened in past time. It is therefore called *past tense.* The change in written form consists of adding a *d.*

In the third sentence, *hear* has a helping verb which shows that something will happen in the future. The verb *shall hear* is the future tense. The helping verb *will* also shows future time when it is used with a main verb, as in "Tina will hear the music."

Yesterday you stayed home. Tomorrow you will travel.

● Practice

1. Tell whether each verb below is the present tense, past tense, or future tense.

    dances   shall arrive   walks   will travel
    learned   will move   listen   turned

2. Use each of the verbs below in three sentences. In the first sentence, show the present tense; in the second, the past tense; and in the third, the future tense.

    pack   burn   admire

Form the past tense of most verbs by adding *ed* or *d.*
Form the future tense of most verbs by using *shall* or *will* as helping verbs.

Principal Parts of Verbs

There are three important forms of a verb. They are called the **principal parts.**

PRESENT		PAST	PAST PARTICIPLE
race	races	raced	(*has, have, had*) raced
help	helps	helped	(*has, have, had*) helped

Notice that the present tense of a verb includes a form with an *s* ending. Study the examples below. Note that the *s* ending is used only when the subject is singular and refers to someone or something being talked about besides the people who are talking.

I race.	Carol races.
You race.	We race.
He, she, or it races.	They race.

Notice the two ways that a verb can show past time. In the past tense form, the ending *d* or *ed* is added to the present tense of the verb. In the past participle form, the helping verb *has, have,* or *had* is used.

● Practice

1. Write five original sentences, using the subjects and verbs below. Change the verb ending if necessary to fit the subject.

	SUBJECTS	VERBS
1.	She	laugh
2.	My friends	collect
3.	We	try
4.	You	see
5.	It	fall

2. Complete the sentences below with two forms of a verb that show past time. Use the verbs in parentheses.

1. (sprinkle)   Cindy _____ her plants this morning.
   She _____ _____ them every day.

2. (help)   Marsha and Tom _____ her.
   They _____ _____ to keep the plants healthy.

3. (talk)   Cindy _____ quietly to the spider plants.
   She _____ _____ to them since they were tiny sprouts.

4. (play)   She even _____ music for them.
   She _____ _____ mostly classical music.

Proofread the paragraph below to find the errors. Then rewrite the paragraph making the necessary corrections.

Have you read *The Black Stallion's Filly* it is an exciting story about a horse named Black Minx. She was Black Stallion's foal Henry Dailey bought the filly. To train her for racing. The training was difficult. Because she was so stubborn. Finally Black Minx ran in a great race. The book is by Walter Farley.

Review Practice

Punctuation
Capitalization

Irregular Verbs

Some verbs in our language do not add *d* or *ed* to form their past tense. These are called **irregular verbs.** Study the principal parts of the four irregular verbs below.

PRESENT	PAST	PAST PARTICIPLE
freeze	froze	(*has, have, had*) frozen
ride	rode	(*has, have, had*) ridden
speak	spoke	(*has, have, had*) spoken
steal	stole	(*has, have, had*) stolen

Notice that each principal part of an irregular verb is spelled differently. Therefore, the only way to learn to use irregular verbs correctly is to memorize their principal parts and to practice using them.

The second and third principal parts of the verbs *freeze, ride, speak,* and *steal* are used correctly in the sentences below.

Mother *froze* the chicken.

I *rode* my bike.

She *spoke* of her trip.

He *stole* second base.

The river *had frozen.*

The cowboys *have ridden* the steer.

The mayor *has spoken* to our class.

Has someone *stolen* your pen?

In these examples, you can see that the second principal part of an irregular verb does not use a helping verb. The third principal part always requires one.

146

● Practice

1. Read each sentence aloud. Use the correct form of the verb in parentheses. Each sentence should express past action.

   1. (steal)   The bandits _____ the silver.
   2. (ride)   The posse _____ after them.
   3. (speak) The sheriff has _____ to the bandits.
   4. (freeze) Their blood _____ in fear.
   5. (ride)   The bandits have _____ into town and surrendered.

2. The irregular verbs listed below are ones that you have studied earlier in this book. Prepare to present two sentences orally for each verb. In one sentence, use the past tense; in the other, the past participle and a helping verb.

      take   write   eat
      grow   drink   sing

Using Words Correctly: *lie* and *lay*

Study the three forms of the verbs below:

PRESENT		PAST	PAST PARTICIPLE
lie	lies	lay	(*has, have, had*) lain
lay	lays	laid	(*has, have, had*) laid

The verbs *lie* and *lay* are often confused, even though they have different meanings. The sentences below show these verbs used correctly.

To lie — to rest or recline

1. The tiger *lies* on the grass. (present)
2. He *lay* there for a long time. (past)
3. He *has lain* there since dinner. (past participle)

To lay (something) — to put or place something

1. Please *lay* the book on the counter. (present)
2. She *laid* her magazine on my desk. (past)
3. I *had laid* mine on the shelf. (past participle)

Use a form of the verb *lie* when you mean "to rest" or "to recline." Use a form of the verb *lay* when you mean "to put" or "to place" something.

● **Practice**

1. Read each sentence aloud. Use the form of the verb *lie* that is called for in parentheses.

   1. I _____ on the sun deck every day. (present)
   2. The tree _____ directly in our path. (past)
   3. We had _____ in bed until ten. (past participle)

2. Read each sentence aloud. Use the form of the verb *lay* that is called for in parentheses.

   1. _____ those cards on the table. (present)
   2. The woman _____ the rug on the floor. (past)
   3. They have _____ the package here. (past participle)

Choice of Verbs in Composition

Which sentence gives the sharper image?

The car *stopped.*   The car *screeched* to a stop.

When you write, use verbs that give your readers a lively mental image.

The sentences that follow are from *The Wheel on the School*, by Meindert DeJong. Read them and notice how the author's choice of words adds vividness to his writing.

Lina slept alone in the attic, directly under the roof tiles. A sweep of wind slashing under the tiles lifted some of the heavy tiles and tossed them like paper. They crashed back down on the roof, smashed, and went slithering down the steep roof to shatter into a thousand pieces on the cobble-stone street. The attic beams groaned. A moaning, wolfish howl of wind ran down the chimney and through the trembling house.

To Discuss

1. Name the vivid verbs and descriptive words in the sentences you have just read.
2. To how many of the five senses does the author's description appeal? Explain your answer. Which one receives most attention?

● **Practice**

Compose sentences by adding a predicate to each of the subjects below. Choose verbs that give a vivid impression. Make the predicates appeal to a reader's senses of hearing, sight, and taste.

1. A jet plane . . .
2. The lion in the cage . . .
3. The hamburgers on the grill . . .
4. Mountains in the distance . . .

A Book to Read

TITLE: The Lion, the Witch and the Wardrobe
AUTHOR: C. S. Lewis
ARTIST: Pauline Baynes
PUBLISHER: Macmillan

Sent to the country home of an aged professor for safety during air-raids in London, Peter, Susan, Edmund, and Lucy decide to explore their new surroundings. Lucy steps into a clothes closet, or wardrobe, and is surprised to feel a second row of coats behind the first. She steps back, back, back into the wardrobe and suddenly finds herself outdoors on a snowy night. She has accidentally discovered the door to the Kingdom of Narnia.

Narnia is a magical kingdom populated with giants, fawns, helpful beavers, enchanted leopards, good dwarves, and Aslan, a noble lion. But the kingdom is spellbound by the icy White Witch. Forces of evil are gathering in Narnia when the four children arrive. Soon, they are swept up in extraordinary adventures which result in thawing the frozen kingdom.

If you think that fantasy is fantastic, you will be happy to know that *The Lion, the Witch and the Wardrobe* is the first book in a series of seven, called the *Chronicles of Narnia*. Later, you may want to read about Prince Caspian, the Emerald Witch's underground kingdom, a talking horse, and many more exciting characters in the books that follow.

Checkup I. Recognizing Verbs

1. Copy the verbs in these sentences.

1. I must rake the leaves today.
2. They are always blowing around the house.
3. Did Mom bring home boxes for the leaves?
4. The city truck doesn't collect until tomorrow.
5. Will you help me?
6. We'll finish before lunch.
7. Don't you want an autumn bonfire?
8. No, the gardeners may have the leaves for compost heaps.

2. Underline the main verb in your list of verbs for section 1 above.

Checkup II. Verbs of Action or Being

Write these two headings on your paper: *Action Verbs* and *Verbs of Being*. Write the verb in each of the following sentences under the proper heading.

1. Autumn seems the best time of year to me.
2. The leaves are so colorful.
3. Pumpkins are everywhere.
4. We ate pumpkin bread for lunch.
5. Terry baked it early this morning.
6. I roasted some pumpkin seeds.
7. They became a bit too brown.
8. But they tasted good anyway.

Checkup III. Verbs in Contractions

Make contractions from these words.

I am	have not	we have
you are	he is	would not
we will	did not	they are

7

Checkup

Checkup IV. Principal Parts of Verbs

Write each sentence below. Use the form of the verb called for in parentheses.

1. (mend; *past*)   We _____ the tennis net in the park.
2. (work; *past participle*)   Mother _____ _____ on her serve all morning.
3. (practice; *present*)   I _____ my backhand every day.
4. (play; *past participle*)   I _____ _____ tennis since I was six.

Checkup V. Irregular Verbs

1. Write the paragraph below. Write the correct verb form in place of each blank.

The squirrels have (steal) _____ the food from the bird feeder. Now the birds have (take) _____ flight. They (grow) _____ tired of getting no food. The suet we tied on a tree has (freeze) _____, but the squirrels have (eat) _____ it, anyway.

2. Write the correct form of the verb in parentheses. Each should express past action.

   1. (write)   Lori and Ike have _____ a play.
   2. (take)   Michael has _____ the part of the villain.
   3. (speak)   He _____ his lines like a pro.
   4. (do)   I _____ some painting on the scenery.

3. Write each sentence below. Choose the correct form of the verb in parentheses.

   1. The big tom cat (lay, laid) on the table.
   2. He (has laid, has lain) there all morning.
   3. I wouldn't (lay, lie) a finger on him.
   4. My sister picked him up and (lay, laid) him on the floor.

In this chapter you will be studying how to improve the way you express yourself, both in writing and orally. Here is your chance to find out how much you already know.

Tryout I. Using Negatives Correctly

Read each sentence below. Choose the correct word in parentheses.

1. I didn't do (nothing, anything) right today.
2. I couldn't find (no, any) socks that matched.
3. I had (no, any) homework to hand in.
4. I forgot to bring (any, no) clean gym clothes.
5. Maybe tomorrow (nothing, anything) will go wrong.

Tryout II. Expressing Yourself Well

Read this paragraph. Decide how it could be improved. Then rewrite the paragraph, correcting its faults.

Paul Revere was a silversmith and he lived in Boston and he rode through the colony to warn the people that the British were going to attack by land. He was caught before he got to Concord, but two other riders went on to Concord. I like the story of Paul Revere's ride.

Tryout III. Capitalizing and Punctuating Correctly

1. Write these book and magazine titles correctly.

   dynamite   seventeen   wind in the willows

2. Write the titles of these articles correctly.

   making a movie   all about white mice

3. Write these sentences correctly.

   1. Horace Greeley said go west.
   2. Greeley was a newspaper man in the east.

Tryout Time

8

Written and Oral Reports

Choosing a Topic

Many of the reports that you will prepare during your school career will be on assigned subjects. Sometimes, however, you may be asked to choose your own topic. Here are three things to consider in choosing a topic for an informational report:

Can you find enough solid information on the topic? Try putting your topic in the form of a question. If the question can be answered very briefly, the topic is not a good one for an informational report. If the answer depends mainly on opinion, then the topic is also not a good one.

Choose a topic of interest to you and to others. The problem of *energy conservation* concerns citizens today and therefore is a good topic. People want to help solve such a problem, and to do their part, they must have information. There are many similar problems which are important for citizens to understand. Think of some of the current problems in your community or in your school.

Choose a topic that is limited enough so that you can cover it in an interesting way. In a single report on electricity, you can only hope to scratch the topic's surface. You can, however, think of one aspect of this subject that would make an interesting report. Here are some examples. See if you can add to the list.

The Story of the Electric Light
Sources of Electric Power
How Electricity Has Changed the Kitchen
Conductors of Electricity
The Inventions of Thomas A. Edison

To Discuss

Each of the topics below is probably too broad for one report. Too much about the subject would necessarily be left uncovered. Choose a single part of the topic which you think would make an interesting report. See how many topics you and your classmates can suggest.

Sports	The Oil Industry
How to Garden	Conservation
Ham Radio Operation	Safety
Helicopters	Birds
Sanitation	Physical Fitness

As topics are suggested, have someone write them on the board. See if you can narrow some of the topics still further.

● Practice

1. List five topics which you believe would make interesting informational reports. For ideas, consider your current interests, studies, reading, discussions, conversations, or recent events.

   If the first topic that comes to mind seems too broad for one report, think of a part of it that you could cover in an interesting way.

2. Read your topics to the class. Ask your classmates to judge whether your topics are limited enough for a report.

Making Your Report Interesting and Clear

A good report should have an interesting beginning, a well-organized body, and a clear-cut conclusion. The title, too, is important in making a successful report.

Planning the Title and Introduction

Choose a title that tells as briefly as possible what your subject is. Then begin your report in a way that interests others and shows the importance of your subject.

This is the way Gina introduced her topic. Notice how she kept her listeners in mind.

Our Town's Watershed

You may think watersheds are buildings of some kind. I did before I began reading about them. I learned that a watershed is land, a little like a huge sloping roof. The streams on one side of the highest land flow in different directions from those on the other side. As I tell you how the land absorbs and releases moisture, you will learn how it supplies water for our town.

To Discuss

1. Is Gina's title brief and to the point?

2. How did she attract interest in her topic?

3. Which term did Gina explain? Did this help make her subject clear?

4. Did she show the importance of her topic?

5. Is her introduction brief and to the point?

6. On the basis of the questions above, offer and discuss suggestions for introducing a topic. Make a list of those your class agrees are worthwhile.

Developing a Topic from an Outline

You have learned to make an outline of a topic. Such an outline contains the major ideas you want to present, and you can use it as a guide in developing the body of your report.

Read this part of the outline that Gina prepared for her report on her town's watershed.

Our Town's Watershed

I. Why a watershed is important
   A. What it is
   B. What it controls
      1. Direction of flow
      2. Rate of flow

II. Where our watershed is
   A. Size
      1. About 360 square kilometers
      2. About 12 kilometers wide by 30 kilometers long
   B. Extent
      1. Starting in Bristol Hills
      2. Including Harper Creek and tributaries
      3. Draining into Headley Reservoir

You have read Gina's first paragraph, in which she developed the first main topic in her outline. Now read how she developed the second main topic.

You have all visited Headley Reservoir and so you know where our water supply is stored. The water in that reservoir comes from rainfall over a large area—360 square kilometers of farms, hills, and forests. This area is about twelve kilometers wide at its widest place and thirty kilometers long.

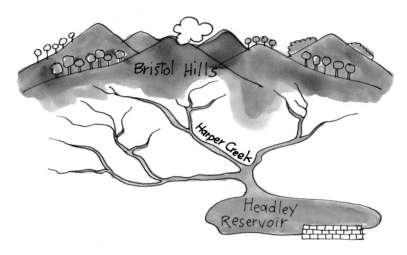

As you can see from the map, the top of the "roof" is Bristol Hills. These hills rise to 500 meters above sea level. Rain falls in the watershed. Raindrops become trickles, the trickles flow into rivulets, the rivulets into brooks, and the brooks drain into Harper Creek. Finally, the water of Harper Creek backs up behind the dam of Headley Reservoir.

To Discuss

1. Did Gina follow her outline?
2. How did she make her report more interesting than her outline?
3. What did she use to show clearly the location of the watershed?

Concluding a Report

A concluding statement is not always necessary. Usually, though, it is useful to sum up the main ideas or to restate the major theme.

Here is how Gina concluded her report.

Our town's watershed is truly priceless to us. Because of the way in which it supplies our reservoir, we are lucky enough to have all the water that we need.

How to Prepare a Report

Choose a limited subject.
Choose a good title.
Write a careful outline.
Plan an interesting introduction.
Explain every main topic in your outline, using facts and ideas in the subtopics.
Refer to your notes or the references you have studied for interesting details that may not be in your outline.
Use maps, charts, and other helpful aids.
Conclude your report by summarizing the main ideas or restating the major theme.

● Practice

Following the guides above on how to plan a report, choose a subject you have been studying. Write an outline; then plan the title, introduction, body of the report, and conclusion. Save your outline and other plans for later use.

Using Negatives Correctly

Words that mean *no* are called **negatives.** *No, not, never, none, nothing,* and words ending in *n't* are examples. Never use more than one of these words in a sentence.

RIGHT: I *don't* know any of the answers.
RIGHT: I know *none* of the answers.

RIGHT: The lookout *didn't* see anything.
RIGHT: The lookout saw *nothing*.

● Practice

Read each sentence. Choose the correct word in parentheses.

1. There is (nothing, anything) in my hat.
2. I haven't (nothing, anything) up my sleeve.
3. Poof! Now I haven't (any, no) sleeve . . . except in my hat!
4. Weren't (any, none) of you watching?
5. Haven't you (never, ever) seen the disappearing sleeve trick before?

There are no gains without pains.

POOR RICHARD

Benjamin Franklin wrote and published *Poor Richard's Almanac* for twenty-five years. Poor Richard gets the credit for many witty and wise statements that Franklin made about how to lead a good life. Franklin especially emphasized thrift and the value of hard work. What is Poor Richard promoting in the statement above? Would you agree with him? Why or why not?

Expressing Yourself Well

In expressing yourself, remember that there are certain things you should *not* say, as well as certain things you should say.

Avoiding Common Faults

There are three faults that can make interesting material seem very dull. You should recognize them and avoid using them.

1. beginning too many sentences with the same word
2. using *I* too often
3. joining too many sentences with *and*

To Discuss

Read this paragraph aloud. Decide what faults the writer did not avoid and what might be done to get rid of them.

> Last year I visited Sturbridge Village in Massachusetts. It is made up of old buildings that have been moved there from all over New England and it looks like a town in colonial times. It has a large village green in the center where I went and I saw sheep grazing, and I went into the buildings and I saw people working at crafts that were important during colonial times—pottery making, barrel making, candle dipping, and weaving. It is a place that I would like to visit again.

● Practice

Rewrite and improve the paragraph above.

Using Guiding Words and Phrases

Try to use words and phrases that will help your reader to follow your ideas. Some examples are *first, second, in the first place, in addition, then, therefore,* and *finally.*

Read the following paragraphs and find the guiding words and phrases. Be prepared to read them aloud.

Later on, when darkness fell, the young dog moved over and stretched out closely at his side and the cat stalked over to lie between his paws; and so, warmed and comforted by their closeness, the old dog slept, momentarily unconscious of his aching, tired body or his hunger. . . .

—From *The Incredible Journey,*
by Sheila Burnford

Many small-boat voyagers had stated in their books that size has little or no bearing on a boat's seaworthiness, and . . . I was inclined to believe they were right. A small boat, first of all, is a great deal stronger, pound for pound, than a big ship. Secondly, a small boat, being light and buoyant, will recoil before waves and tend to ride over them, whereas a big ship will offer immense resistance.

—From *Tinkerbelle,*
by Robert Manry

● **Practice**

Read the sentences in the paragraph below and think of a way to relate the thoughts to each other. Then rewrite the paragraph, adding words, such as those at the top of this page, to guide the reader from one point to another.

In its present state, our basement is untidy and dangerous. Several things must be done. The stacks of old papers must be removed. The empty cartons must go. We must sweep the floor.

Giving Credit to Sources of Information

Sometimes a report you prepare may contain a great deal of information from one source. Sometimes you may use the ideas or exact words from another source. In such cases, it is necessary and fair to name your source. To give credit, name the person whose ideas or words you are using and tell where you found the information.

Notice how credit for information is given in the examples below.

1. Mrs. Emma Staver, who lived in England until five years ago, gave me these picture postcards of London.
2. Ralph Sutter made this point about the gold rush in "A Cabin on the Yukon." The article appeared in *Boys' Life.*

> Underline the names of books, magazines, and newspapers. Place the titles of articles in books and magazines in quotation marks.

To Discuss

1. In the first sentence above, how is credit for information given?
2. In the second example, how is credit for information given?

Notice that the title of the magazine article is placed in quotation marks. Notice also that the name of the magazine is in italics. Like the titles of books, the names of magazines are printed in italics, but are underlined in handwriting or typewriting.

Using Direct and Indirect Quotations

When you repeat another person's exact words, you are making a *direct quotation*. In oral reports, simply tell your listeners whom you are quoting. In written reports, put quotation marks around direct quotations.

When you refer to a person's ideas without using his or her exact words, you are using an *indirect quotation*. Do not put quotation marks around indirect quotations.

Notice how credit for information is given in this selection.

Did you know that bats have a kind of radar system that keeps them from bumping into things? I learned about this ability in *The Personality of Animals*, by Munro Fox. He explained that bats in flight make shrill squeaks that set up vibrations or waves in the air. When the waves strike an object, they bounce back to the bat. Mr. Fox said, "Bats emit supersonic sound waves, and the time taken for their echo to return to the bat's ear gives the distance away of the obstacle."

To Discuss

1. How is credit given in the selection on page 165? Where did the writer find the information?
2. Find and read aloud a direct quotation in the passage on page 165.
3. Find and read aloud an indirect quotation from page 165.

● **Practice**

Place quotation marks around direct quotations.
Separate the quotation from the rest of the sentence by some mark of punctuation.
Begin a quotation with a capital letter.
Place a period that follows a quoted statement within the quotation marks.

Write the following sentences correctly.

1. In her lecture Dr. Costa said my interest in plants started right in my own backyard.
2. The earthquake was one of the most disastrous, according to an article in the times.
3. I found most of this information in an article by franklin folsom, which appeared in junior scholastic. The name of the article was lewis and clark.
4. Marian McMurphy researched the subject and wrote a report for our changing society, a monthly magazine.

Review Practice

Verbs

1. Read aloud the verb in each sentence below. Be prepared to tell whether it is a verb of action or a verb of being.

   1. My aunt and uncle are film-makers.
   2. They travel frequently.
   3. They shoot many animal pictures.
   4. My aunt is now busy in Australia.

2. Write a sentence for each of these action verbs.

   screamed.   was lost
   had been broken slipped

3. Write a sentence for each of these verbs of being.

   was   have been   are   is being   am

How Our Language Grows

Shortcuts

One way language changes is by the creation of short words from longer ones. Sometimes both words remain in active use. *Attend* was shortened to *tend* and *amend* was shortened to *mend*. Both words in each pair are used today, but they aren't often thought of as being related.

In other cases, the longer word has disappeared or nearly disappeared as the shortened one has become popular. *Cab* has come from *cabriolet* and *piano* from *pianoforte* in this way.

Some shortened words are at first considered to be slang terms. *Ad* once belonged to this group. However, today most people would consider it an acceptable short form of *advertisement*. Other shortened terms, however, remain slang. While *professor* is considered conventional English, *prof* is not. The same holds true for the pair *doctor* and *doc*. Perhaps, in time, *prof* and *doc* will be accepted as standard English just as *ad* has been.

1. Look up the words below. What does each one mean? From what longer word or words did it come?

   mob   curio   bus   zoo   ruff

2. Phrases and sentences are often shortened, too. Check your dictionary to find the origins of *good-by* and *farewell*.

Naming Sections of a Country

You have already learned to capitalize proper nouns. The italicized words below name a particular section of the country. They are proper nouns, too.

1. What are the largest cities in the *East*?
2. Many states in the *South* produce cotton.

Now read this sentence.

3. We say that the sun rises in the *east* and sets in the *west*.

The italicized words in sentence 3 name a direction. They do not name a particular place. Therefore, they should not be capitalized.

● **Practice**

Write the sentences below, using capital letters correctly. Study each sentence. What words mean a section of the country? What words indicate a direction?

1. New mexico is in the southwest.
2. Turn north at jackson boulevard.
3. Corn is the major crop in many states in the midwest.
4. During our vacation in the south, we toured georgia.
5. The trail goes west through the underbrush.
6. Walk three blocks north to the library.
7. The pioneers left the east in covered wagons.
8. The sky toward the north was getting dark.

> Begin a word with a capital letter if it names a particular section of a country: for example, *South, East,* or *Southwest.* Do not begin a word with a capital letter if it merely indicates a direction.

Proofreading and Revising Your Work

Form habits of neatness and accuracy in all written work. Once you are satisfied with the content, proofread your paper to see that it is written correctly, in good English. Use these questions as a check list.

1. Are words used correctly?
2. Are words spelled correctly?
3. Are the paragraphs indented?
4. Are capital letters and punctuation marks used correctly?
5. Is the general arrangement, including margins and the placement of the title, good?

After you have proofread your paper, read it aloud. You may catch additional errors. Then copy it neatly in ink.

● Practice

1. Read each of the following selections from reports. Discuss the faults of each in class.

Yesterday we seen a movie about making flour. The movie began with a picture of a wheat field in harvest time. Machines were cutting and sacking the wheat. the trucks carried beg loads of sacks to the mill where the wheet would be made into flour.

A pioneer had to learn many trades to survive in the wilderness. A pioneer women she had to make cloth and had to sew and a pioneer man he had to be a blacksmith and carpenter?

2. Write each paragraph above correctly.

COMPOSITION: WRITING A REPORT

On page 160 you were asked to choose a good subject for a report. Then you were to write an outline for the report, plan the title, introduction, body, and conclusion, and save your plans for later use. You then studied and practiced skills necessary to write a report well, such as avoiding faults of expression and giving credit to sources of information.

Now you are ready to prepare a written report on a topic of your choice. If you have kept the plans you made earlier, you can use them as the basis for the report. If you wish, you may select a new topic, outline it, and write your report on that instead.

Use the guides under "How to Prepare a Report" on page 160. Also, try your best to express yourself well and credit your sources of information correctly.

After you have written your report, proofread your paper for errors, using the questions on page 169 as a check list. Read the report aloud; then copy it neatly in ink.

Giving an Oral Report

Many of the techniques you learned to help you develop written reports are also useful in preparing oral reports. There are differences, however. For example, for an oral report you need not write out every word. Instead you should speak from an outline that contains the ideas you want to present.

Preparing to Speak from an Outline

Study your outline and decide what you are going to say about each major topic. If necessary, return to your notes for details that will add interest to the discussion. Some exact figures or a direct quotation might help you to develop a particular topic in an interesting way.

Write each major topic of your outline on a note card, leaving space between topics for any details which you must report exactly, such as direct quotations. Be sure to copy your facts correctly.

Practicing the Report

After you have prepared note cards, practice your report, beginning with an interesting introduction. Then talk about each of the major ideas in the order you have outlined them. Finally, summarize the main ideas.

Practice your report aloud, until you can give it well. Refer only occasionally to your note cards for exact quotations or other details.

Speaking Distinctly

As you practice, try to achieve these four goals:

1. Speak loudly enough to be heard.
2. Speak slowly enough to be understood.
3. Pronounce your words distinctly.
4. Speak with expression.

If possible, deliver your report aloud at home to a willing listener. Let that person criticize your volume, rate, articulation, and expression.

Giving Your Oral Report

When the time comes to give your report, take your place confidently. Look at your audience. Wait until the members of the audience are ready to give you their attention. Then begin. Follow these guides.

How to Give an Oral Report

Speak directly to your audience, referring to your notes for details.

Speak distinctly, loudly enough, and with expression.

Give an introduction that will capture the attention of your audience.

Discuss each major topic of your outline in order.

Present enough facts and report them correctly.

Throughout your oral report, try to make "eye-contact" with members of your audience.

Summarize the main ideas.

● **Practice**

1. Give your oral report, following the guides above.
2. Listen carefully to the reports your classmates give. After a report has been given, see if you can remember the main points and suggest improvements if you can.

172

Round-Table Discussions

Now that you have had some practice in presenting oral reports singly, you are ready to present an oral report as part of a group. One way to do it is to have a round-table discussion in class.

In a round-table discussion, four or five people familiar with a subject discuss it before an audience. In the classroom, this means that four or five students become "experts" on a subject and discuss it before the rest of the class. For example, one class decided to have a round-table discussion about the book *The Secret of the Andes*, by Ann Nolan Clark. It is the story of a lonely Peruvian boy, Cusi, whose llama leads him down a hidden trail to an ancient temple. It is a tale of suspense and adventure.

Here is how the group of "experts" on the book planned to organize the discussion.

1. They decided that the purpose of the discussion would be to point out what makes *The Secret of the Andes* a good book.

2. They decided to answer these questions.

   1. Where did Cusi start his journey? Where did he go?
   2. What was the country like?
   3. What kind of people did he meet?
   4. What were interesting parts of the story?
   5. Does the story have any weak points? For example, was some useful information left out?

3. They decided to make a map of Cusi's journey.

4. They chose a discussion leader to introduce the topic, keep the discussion moving, and give a summary.

5. They decided to invite class members to ask questions and make comments.

To Discuss

1. Why is it important for the group to agree on the purpose of the discussion?
2. Why is it important for the discussion group to agree on the questions to be answered?
3. How would a map help this discussion? Can you think of other things the group could show or do to add interest to the discussion?
4. What background information should the leader supply?
5. Why is a summary helpful?
6. Can you offer some helpful suggestions to follow in planning round-table discussions?

● Practice

Get together in groups of four or five. Decide on a subject for a group report that you will present in the form of a round-table discussion. You might choose as a subject a book you all will read or a community problem you all will study.

Work together to plan your discussion. Decide which group member will report on each major part of the subject. Choose a chairperson to introduce the subject and to conduct the discussion. Finally, agree on the main topics for discussion and the order in which you will present them.

A Book to Read

TITLE: **Philip Hall likes me. I reckon maybe.**
AUTHOR: Bette Greene
ARTIST: Charles Lilly
PUBLISHER: Dial

Philip Hall was number one in just about everything. Beth Lambert always seemed to come in second. But could it be that Beth *let* Philip come out first?

Beth knew that Philip was her friend. After all, he let her come over and brush down his cows after she finished the chores on her own farm. Beth's mother thought Beth was smart about almost everything, except . . . Philip Hall.

When Beth Lambert got tired of being number two and decided to be a winner, there was no stopping her. She did everything from nabbing turkey thieves to forming a picket line with the Pretty Pennies Girls' Club of Pocahontas, Arkansas. She even changed the policy of the Tiger Hunters Boys' Club. But Beth found that there were problems she hadn't counted on in becoming a winner. The way she solves them makes Beth number one with her readers.

Checkup

Checkup I.   Using Negatives Correctly

Rewrite this paragraph, choosing the correct word in parentheses.

Joey doesn't have (any, no) idea how to make a kite. He has (no, any) string. None of Joey's friends (never, ever) made a kite, so they aren't (no, any) help. Since there isn't even (any, no) wind today, maybe Joey should make something else.

Checkup II.   Expressing Yourself Well

Rewrite these groups of sentences so that they form good paragraphs.

1. My dog Pixie is three years old. My dog can do tricks. My dog is learning a new trick now.
2. We are going to decorate the gym and we will use the school colors. We will bring plants from home and these will make it more attractive.
3. I should have written before, but I have been busy and I am studying hard, and I am taking trumpet lessons, too, which I like very much. I hope to play in the school band someday.

Checkup III.   Capitalizing and Punctuating Correctly

1. Write this paragraph correctly.

My friend gets the magazine science digest. Sometimes I find an article I like. This month I read one called look out mars, here we come.

2. Write these sentences correctly.

    1. The writer ralph waldo emerson said hitch your wagon to a star.
    2. Emerson lived in the northeast.

In this chapter you will learn more about pronouns. Here is a chance to find out how much you already know.

Tryout I. Singular and Plural Pronouns

List each of the pronouns in the following sentences under the heading *Singular* or *Plural*. Beside each pronoun, write the noun for which it stands.

1. Diana paid for the ski boots and took them home.
2. Angela showed her how to fasten them.
3. She got a parka and had her try it on.
4. It fit except for the sleeves, and they were long.

Tryout II. Possessive Pronouns

Supply the correct possessive pronouns.

1. Do these masks belong to you and Jay? Yes, those masks are _____.
2. Is this Janet's costume? Yes, it is _____.

Tryout III. Writing Pronouns Correctly

Write each sentence below. Choose the correct word in parentheses.

1. Is that (their, there, they're) lunchbox?
2. (Its, It's) lid is open.
3. (Its, It's) a fine day for a picnic.
4. (Their, There, They're) planning to eat later.

Tryout IV. Pronoun Forms

Write each sentence below. Choose the correct word in parentheses.

1. (We, Us) girls are going to the concert.
2. Gerry met Renee and (he, him) on the way.
3. Peg and (I, me) had to leave early.

Tryout
Time

9

Learning About Pronouns

The Useful Pronoun

You have been using such words as *I, he, she, it, we, you,* and *they* for a long time. These words are called **pronouns,** and they are very useful. To see what our language would be without them, read the sentence below aloud.

Annamarie laid down the scuba-diving equipment after Annamarie had cleaned the scuba-diving equipment and had taken the scuba-diving equipment off the boat.

Notice how long and awkward this sentence is because the nouns have been repeated so often. Now read aloud this version of the same sentence.

Annamarie laid down the scuba-diving equipment after *she* had cleaned *it* and had taken *it* off the boat.

As you can see, in this version pronouns have been used in place of several of the nouns. What are the pronouns? What do they do? How do they improve the sentence?

▶ A **pronoun** is a word that is used in place of a noun.

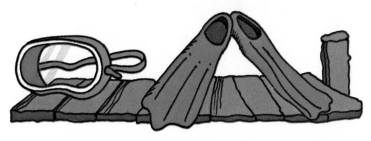

● Practice

1. Read the paragraph below silently. Think of the correct pronoun to use in place of each italicized noun or noun and its signal. Then read the paragraph aloud.

Penny was not very good with *Penny's* skis. *Penny* just never seemed able to keep *the skis* in a straight line beneath *Penny*. Usually when *Penny* put *the skis* on and started down a hill, *Penny* found one ski traveling east and one west. The result? You guessed *the result!* A tumble.

2. Read each sentence below. Tell what noun each italicized pronoun stands for.

1. A lioness was returning to *her* den.
2. *She* left *her* tracks on the sand.
3. The hunter saw *them* plainly.
4. *He* hastened along the river bank with *his* guide.

Singular and Plural Pronouns

Just as nouns can be singular and plural, so can pronouns. Pronouns do not form their plurals as nouns do, though. They have special singular and plural forms.

At the top of page 181 are the pronouns that are used to stand for the person or persons speaking or writing.

SINGULAR	PLURAL
I, me, my	we, us, our
mine, myself	ours, ourselves

Now look at the pronouns that are used to stand for the person or persons spoken or written to.

SINGULAR	PLURAL
you, your, yours	you, your, yours
yourself	yourselves

The pronouns listed below stand for other persons, places, or things.

SINGULAR	PLURAL
he, she, him, her	they, them
his, her, hers	their, theirs
himself, herself	themselves
it, its, itself	

● **Practice**

1. Study the italicized pronouns in this selection. Name the noun (or nouns) each pronoun stands for.

> Have *you* ever heard the legend of Annie Christmas? *She* was so strong that *she* could carry a barrel of oats under each arm and one on *her* head. *She* was a keelboat pilot on the Mississippi River, but *her* chief claim to fame was that *she* could lick any bully that crossed *her* path. Even evil Mike Fink was afraid of Annie. *She* said that if *he* ever showed up in *her* territory, *she* would pole *him* home tied to the bottom of *her* boat. *She* believed that bullies ought to behave *themselves*, and if *they* didn't, then *they* deserved what was coming to *them*.

2. On the board, write the headings *Singular* and *Plural*. List the pronouns from the paragraph above under the correct heading.

Possessive Pronouns

Nouns show possession by adding an apostrophe and *s* or simply an apostrophe. Pronouns can show possession, too. Unlike nouns, however, they never use an apostrophe and *s* or an apostrophe alone. Pronouns have special forms that show possession. We call these special forms **possessive pronouns.** Study the list of possessive pronouns below.

my	our	your	his	her	their
mine	ours	yours	its	hers	theirs

Note that there are two pronouns showing ownership by the speaker or writer.

> I already have *my* ticket.
> That ticket is *mine*.

Which of the other possessive pronouns have two forms? Make up a sentence for each of them. Be prepared to tell your sentences to the class.

Two possessive pronouns need particular attention because they are often used incorrectly. One of them is *its*. This possessive pronoun is frequently confused with the contraction *it's*. Study the difference between *it's* and *its* in these sentences.

> *It's* a beautiful fish. (contraction for *it is*)
> The fish injured *its* fin. (possessive pronoun)

What part does *It's* play in the first sentence? What part does *its* play in the second sentence?

The other troublesome possessive pronoun is *their. Their* is frequently confused with the adverb *there* and with the contraction *they're.* Study the differences among the three words in these sentences.

The scouts inspected *their* cabins. (possessive pronoun)
Over *there* is a grill for cooking. (adverb telling *where*)
They're cooking supper on it now. (contraction for *They are*)

What part does each italicized word play in its sentence?

● Practice

1. Choose the correct possessive pronoun to complete each sentence below. Write the sentences. Be prepared to read your sentences aloud in class.

   1. Is this (you, your) favorite camping spot?
   2. It is one of (my, me) favorites.
   3. Ruth and Kim have put up (their, they) tents. Shall we put up (us, ours)?
   4. No, let's make a fire first and use (it's, its) light to work by.

2. Write each sentence below. Choose the correct word in parentheses.

   1. I believe (its, it's) going to rain.
   2. The hikers are returning to (their, there, they're) camp.
   3. The brook may overflow (its, it's) banks.
   4. (Their, There, They're) cabin is built on a ledge near the stream.

How Our Language Grows

Internationalese Spoken Here

As people travel and move from place to place, their languages travel, too. English is always changing and growing with additions of foreign words. Do you know the origins of words that you use every day?

If you described a girl who was dressed in a khaki shirt, denim pants, and moccasins, and who poured ketchup on her macaroni, you would use words from all over the world. *Khaki* is a Hindustani word meaning "dust-colored." *Denim* was first manufactured in France. It was called *serge* (the name of the cloth) *de Nimes* (the name of the town). Can you tell how the word *denim* came to be? *Moccasin* is an Algonquin word, and *ketchup* is a Malay word for a sauce. *Macaroni*, of course, is Italian.

1. Here is another "international description." Use your dictionary to find the origins of the seven italicized words.

   Carl is sitting in the *garage,* eating *hominy* grits, sipping *orange tea,* and working on *algebra* problems. He was supposed to go to a *jubilee,* but he has to complete some *dittos*.

2. Make up your own international person or situation using the words below. Look them up in your dictionary to see where they originated.

   coffee   sofa   orangutan   bungalow   plaid

1. Read the sentences below and name the verb in each one. Be prepared to tell whether it is an *action verb* or a *verb of being.*

    1. Have you read any books by the great naturalist, William Beebe?
    2. A naturalist is an authority on animals and plants.
    3. I have just read about one of Beebe's expeditions to tropical seas.
    4. The name of his ship was the *Arcturus.*
    5. Every day, Beebe left the *Arcturus* in a flat-bottomed boat.
    6. Through the windows in his helmet, the explorer studied undersea creatures.

2. In the sentences below, words or the contraction *n't* (or both) separate the parts of the verb. Copy each sentence. Then underline the main verb and its helpers.

    1. Haven't you ever tried scuba diving?
    2. No, I don't swim well enough.
    3. Carlo has often explored this coral reef.
    4. Have you seen his underwater photographs?

Pronouns as Subjects

Pronouns are used in sentences in the same way as nouns. This means that they are often used as subjects. Unlike nouns, however, pronouns have special subject forms. Here is a list of **subject pronouns.**

I   he   she   they   we   it   you

Note how these subject pronouns are used in sentences.

1. *He* entered the room.
2. *She* saw the movie.
3. *They* sold newspapers.
4. *We* can form a new team.
5. *I* will help the committee.
6. *It* will be a small group.
7. *You* can come along.

Now look at these sentences when another subject is added to them. Is the subject form of the pronoun still used?

1. *Lynn* and *he* entered the room.
2. *She* and *I* saw the movie.
3. *Carla* and *they* sold newspapers.
4. *You* and *we* can form a new team.
5. *Judy* or *I* will help the committee.

As you can see, whether there is one subject or more than one, the subject form of the pronoun is used. Sometimes people get confused and use another form of the pronoun when there is more than one subject. To guard against doing this, test each pronoun alone with the verb. For example, in the sentence "Edie and (I, me) left," try the pronoun alone with the verb. As you say "I left," you will realize that *I* is the correct pronoun. You would never say "Me left."

Pronoun Subjects in Questions

Do you remember how to find the subject in a question? If so, you should have no difficulty in choosing the correct pronoun forms for subjects in a question. Read the following sentences.

1. Will *Elena* and *he* make the report?
2. Can *Kim* and *they* explain their actions?

How can you know that *he* and *they* are correct? Turn the questions above into statements. This will help you tell whether the pronouns are used as subjects.

1. *Elena* and *he* will make the report.
2. *Kim* and *they* can explain their actions.

Since *he* and *they* are the subject forms of pronouns, they are used correctly in the questions.

● **Practice**

> Use the subject form of a pronoun when it is the subject of a sentence.

1. Read the sentences below aloud. Use a subject pronoun in place of each blank.

   1. _____ and I went to a square dance.
   2. Are Eddie and _____ partners?
   3. Terry and _____ are good callers.
   4. Korie and _____ love to do the Virginia Reel.
   5. What dance would Sara and _____ like to do next?

2. Read the sentences below aloud. Use a subject pronoun in place of the person or persons named in parentheses.

   1. (*Pam*) My sister and _____ visited the aquarium.
   2. (*Joyce*) _____ and I met them at the entrance.
   3. (*Ron and Joyce*) Have _____ ever been there before?
   4. (*My brother and I*) No, but _____ have visited it many times.

187

Subject Pronouns After Verbs of Being

You have often been asked questions like "Who was here?" or "Who was that?" These might be the answers:

It wasn't *he.*   That was *she.*

Notice that the verbs in these sentences are *verbs of being.* Verbs of being help to tell who or what the subject is. Review these forms of the verb *be.*

am   is   are   was   were

Because these verbs tell what or who the subject is in a sentence, any pronouns that follow should be in the subject form. Read these sentences.

1. The culprit is *I.*
2. The winners are *they.*
3. Your mysterious callers were *we.*

Notice that in sentence 1, the pronoun *I* refers to the same person as the subject *culprit.* In sentence 2, what is the subject and what is the pronoun? Are they the same persons? What are the subject and pronoun in sentence 3? Why are subject pronouns used in all these sentences?

Sometimes more than one pronoun or a noun and a pronoun follow a verb of being in a sentence. Again, the pronouns should be in the subject form.

The finalists were *he* and *I.*
The fastest runners were Maggie and *she.*

To test pronouns in a sentence with a verb of being, reverse the order of the subject and the pronoun that follows the verb. You should be able to use the subject pronoun in both places.

The winner was *she.*
She was the winner.

● Practice

Use the subject pronouns *I, she, he, we,* and *they* when they follow a verb of being and mean the same person or persons as the subject.

1. Read each of the sentences below aloud. Supply the correct pronoun in place of the person or persons named in parentheses.

    1. It was (the girl) who led the parade.
    2. It had always been (Jim) who was the leader before.
    3. The clowns were Lucy and (person speaking).
    4. Wasn't it (two students) who sold popcorn?

2. Write each sentence below. Choose the correct word in parentheses.

    1. Yes, it was (they, them).
    2. The best flute players in our class are Bill and (her, she).
    3. It was (he, him) who played the drum.
    4. The marchers were (they, them).
    5. It was (she, her) who decorated that float.

Humans always . . . fear an unknown situation—this is normal. The important thing is what we do about it. If fear is permitted to become a paralyzing thing that interferes with proper action, then it is harmful. The best antidote to fear is to know all we can about a situation.

JOHN H. GLENN, JR.

Why would John Glenn be a good person to give advice on facing the unknown? What is an *antidote*? Can this advice be applied to unknown experiences that we face every day?

Pronouns After Action Verbs

Look at the following sentences:

1. *Sue* found the wallet.
2. Mother found *Sue*.

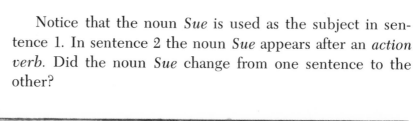

Notice that the noun *Sue* is used as the subject in sentence 1. In sentence 2 the noun *Sue* appears after an *action verb*. Did the noun *Sue* change from one sentence to the other?

Now use a pronoun in place of the noun *Sue*.

1. *She* found the wallet.
2. Mother found *her*.

Notice that the pronoun form changed in sentence 2. Unlike nouns, pronouns change their forms according to their use in a sentence. In sentence 2 the pronoun *her* follows an action verb. Because it receives the action of the verb, it is called the **object of the verb.** The pronoun *her* is an **object pronoun.** Study the forms of the object pronouns:

me   us   him   her   them

The pronouns *you* and *it* are also used as objects of verbs. However, they do not have different forms for subject and object, and so are not listed here.

Often an action verb has more than one object. An object pronoun must be used after an action verb whether there is one object or more, as in these sentences:

1. Lisa called *me*.
2. Lisa called *Marty, Sue,* and *me*.
3. Frank invited *her*.
4. Frank invited *them*.

190

● **Practice**

Use the object form of a pronoun when it is the object of an action verb.

1. Read the sentences below aloud. Choose the correct word in parentheses.

   1. Have you seen Dave and (they, them)?
   2. They promised Jean and (I, me) that they would meet (we, us) at the ski lift.
   3. Dave told (she, her) and (I, me) that they would be here by 3:00.
   4. We can meet (he, him) and (they, them) at the top.

2. Read the sentences below aloud. Choose the correct pronoun in parentheses. Tell whether it is a subject or object pronoun and why you chose that form.

   1. Janette and (I, me) are learning to ski.
   2. Last week, (she, her) and (I, me) did well for beginners.
   3. Today the instructor showed Bob and (we, us) how to stop quickly.
   4. Eva and Olga saw Dad and (we, us) and waved.
   5. Katy and (they, them) were on snowshoes.

COMPOSITION: WRITING A SHORT NARRATIVE

A. Tell about an incident that happened to you or another person either in or out of school—for example, when you were engaged in some game or sport or on a trip. Make your opening sentence attract attention, and keep the reader's interest alive.

B. Describe an imaginary incident that might have occurred at a time and place about which you know through reading or study. Help your readers to feel that the person or persons you are telling about acted as people did who lived (or will live) in that place and at that time.

Review Practice

Punctuation

Correct Verb Forms

1. Write these sentences, punctuating them correctly.

   1. A fox saw a crow with a bit of cheese in its beak
   2. How fine you are looking today said the fox
   3. Your feathers are so glossy the fox added
   4. Is your voice as fine as your feathers the fox asked
   5. As the vain crow began to caw, the cheese fell to the ground
   6. The fox gulped down the cheese and said to the crow never trust a flatterer

2. Read the sentences below aloud. Choose the correct form of the verb in parentheses.

   1. (ride)   Cathie _____ Rocky in the horse show yesterday.
   2. (do)   She has _____ a good job.
   3. (know)   I _____ she would win!
   4. (ride)   She has _____ in many shows.
   5. (choose)   Cathie has been _____ to ride in the rodeo.
   6. (grow)   Do you think they will have it tomorrow since it has _____ so cold?
   7. (freeze)   The ground has _____ solid.
   8. (speak)   I _____ to Cathie's father about that.
   9. (ride)   He said last year the performers _____ inside the arena.

Pronouns After Prepositions

Such words as *to, in, for, at, by,* and *with* are called **prepositions.** Notice the prepositions in the following sentences.

1. I got a chemistry set *for* my birthday.
2. I made a foamy drink *with* it.
3. My sister was sitting *in* the den.
4. I took the drink *to* her.
5. But she said that she never drinks anything *without* a label.

Every preposition is followed by a noun or pronoun which is called the **object of the preposition.**

Pass the sandwiches   to   Sally.
                 preposition   *object*
                             of preposition

1. What is the preposition in sentence 1 above?
2. What is the object of the preposition in sentence 1?
3. Name the prepositions and their objects in sentences 2, 3, 4, and 5.

Notice that when a pronoun is the object of a preposition, it is an *object pronoun.*

They took the keys   with   them.
                preposition   *object*
                             pronoun

Sometimes a preposition is followed by more than one object, as shown in these sentences.

1. Did you speak to *Roger* and *her?*
2. We gave your message to *Pauline* and *him.*
3. Don will go with *Jack* and *me.*
4. There are many surprises in store for *you* and your *family.*

193

Do you remember the subject forms of pronouns and the object forms? Review them now before you do the practice exercises below.

SUBJECT PRONOUNS	OBJECT PRONOUNS
I	me
we	us
she	her
he	him
they	them

Use the object form of a pronoun when it is the object of a preposition.

● **Practice**

1. Read aloud each sentence below. Supply the correct pronoun for the person or persons referred to in parentheses.

1. Sally and (person speaking) reported the fire to the fire marshall.
2. We received letters of thanks from (the fire marshall) and the city government.
3. A firefighter came to speak to (persons speaking).
4. He gave Smoky the Bear T-shirts to Sally and (person speaking).
5. We wrote a story about it for (classmates and persons speaking) to read.

2. Write each sentence below. Choose the correct word in parentheses.

1. Pat tossed the frisbee to (her, she).
2. (She, Her) threw it to (me, I).
3. (I, Me) threw it to (he, him).
4. (He, Him) didn't catch it.
5. It landed in a tree near (they, them).
6. (They, Them) offered to get it for (we, us).
7. (We, Us) finally got it back.
8. Pat tossed the frisbee very carefully to (her, she).

Using *we* and *us* Correctly

Study the expressions *we girls, we boys, us girls,* and *us boys* as they are used in these sentences.

1. *We girls* are planning a science project. (as subject of a sentence)
2. The fastest were *we boys.* (after a verb of being)
3. Mrs. DeSanto has invited *us girls* to lunch on Saturday. (as object of an action verb)
4. Your cousin can come with *us boys.* (as object of a preposition)

In the sentences above, when is the subject pronoun *we* used? When is the object pronoun *us* used? Which of these two pronouns would you use in this sentence: "The final winners were (we, us) girls." Why did you use that pronoun? Which one would you use in this sentence: "The photographer took a picture of (we, us) boys for the newspaper"? Why?

● **Practice**

Choose the correct pronoun in parentheses.

1. (We, Us) swimmers were ready for the meet.
2. (We, Us) Sharks were hoping to win.
3. For weeks, (us, we) divers had been practicing.
4. The first race was for (we, us) girls.
5. The winners were (us, we) Sharks.
6. (We, Us) boys were in the next race.
7. Trophies were given to (us, we) winners.
8. (Us, We) champions had our pictures taken.
9. Mom drove (we, us) girls home.
10. (We, Us) tired swimmers went right to bed.

> Use the expressions *we girls* and *we boys* as subjects or after a verb of being.
> Use the expressions *us girls* and *us boys* after an action verb or a preposition.

Sentence Patterns: Pronouns

What new symbol do you see below? Study it and review the others you already know.

N = Noun V^h = Helping verb

Np = Pronoun V^{be} = Verb of being (when it is part

V = Action verb   of a predicate that tells what

                           the subject is or was)

Because pronouns are words that are used in place of nouns, they appear in sentences in the same places that nouns do.

PATTERN 1: N V

$$\overset{N}{\text{The books}} \overset{V}{\text{arrived.}}$$

$$\overset{Np}{\text{They}} \overset{V}{\text{arrived.}}$$

PATTERN 2: N V N

$$\overset{N}{\text{Marie}} \overset{V^h}{\text{has}} \overset{V}{\text{fed}} \overset{N}{\text{the puppy.}}$$

$$\overset{Np}{\text{She}} \overset{V^h}{\text{has}} \overset{V}{\text{fed}} \overset{Np}{\text{him.}}$$

PATTERN 3: N V^{be} N

$$\overset{N}{\text{The intruder}} \overset{V^{be}}{\text{was}} \overset{N}{\text{Mr. Carl.}}$$

$$\overset{N}{\text{The intruder}} \overset{V^{be}}{\text{was}} \overset{Np}{\text{he.}}$$

Remember that noun signals and helping verbs do not change the basic pattern of a sentence.

● Practice

Build sentences of your own, using the following symbols. Try to vary the ideas in your sentences.

1. N V
2. Np V^h V
3. The N V^h V Np
4. The N V^h V^{be} Np
5. Np V^h V^h V a N
6. N V^h V Np
7. Np V^h V^h V Np
8. A N V^{be} the N
9. Np V^h V^h V^{be} a N
10. The N V^h V^{be} Np

A Book to Read

TITLE: **Julie of the Wolves**
AUTHOR: Jean Craighead George
ARTIST: John Schoenherr
PUBLISHER: Harper & Row

Miyax had not had anything to eat for many days. Alone and lost in the vast, uninhabited Alaskan tundra, she thought of her desperate situation. She thought about her father who had told her that he had once been without food on an unlucky hunting trip. He had told the leader of a wolf pack that he was hungry, and the wolves had killed a caribou for him. But *what* had he said to the wolves? *How* had he said it?

Miyax watched the regal wolf she had named Amaroq and his gentle, playful pack, struggling to survive in a permanently frozen land. She observed their communication with one another. How did a wolf show friendly intentions? How did a wolf say, "I'm hungry"?

Julie of the Wolves is a story of conflict. Is it possible for Miyax to think of herself as Julie, citizen of the United States and a part of the civilization of helicopters, guns, and theaters with velvet seats? Must that "American way of life" destroy the beauty and natural harmony of the Eskimos' world? Whether you call her Julie or Miyax, she is a character who will touch everyone who reads her tale.

Checkup

Checkup I. Singular and Plural Pronouns

List the pronouns in the following conversation under the headings *Singular* and *Plural*. Beside each pronoun, write the noun for which it stands.

Rachel turned to Joe. "Did you know," she asked, "that raccoons make good pets? My brother found a raccoon in our garden and we tamed him."

"Don't raccoons bite and scratch?" he asked.

"Raccoons won't hurt you unless they are threatened," she replied. "I bought a leash and put it on ours and he didn't object."

Checkup II. Possessive Pronouns

Write each sentence substituting a possessive pronoun for the possessive noun in parentheses.

1. The exhibit is (the girl's).
2. This one is not mine; it is (the boys').
3. The first prize is (Mark's) and mine.

Checkup III. Writing Pronouns Correctly

Write a sentence for each of these words: *their, there, they're, its,* and *it's.*

Checkup IV. Pronoun Forms

Write each sentence below. Choose the correct word in parentheses.

1. Alan asked Priscilla and (she, her) to the party.
2. The party was given by Les and (they, them).
3. (We, Us) girls will arrive ahead of the others.
4. Please wait for (us, we) boys.
5. The guest of honor was (she, her).

In this chapter you will be improving your letter-writing techniques and verb usage. Use the Tryouts below to find out how much you already know.

Tryout I.   Writing a Friendly Letter

Arrange and write these parts of a friendly letter correctly.

fairfield maine   with love
april 6 19___   debbie
dear theresa

Tryout II.   Using *sit* and *set*

Write each sentence below. Choose the correct word in parentheses.

1. Marla (sat, set) on the bow of the sailboat.
2. She watched the sun (set, sit).
3. "Come (set, sit) down," she called to her dad.
4. Her father (set, sit) the sails.
5. Marla took his place at the wheel while he (set, sat) down.

Tryout III.   Interjections

Begin each sentence below with an interjection and put the correct mark of punctuation after it.

1. _____ I made a goal.
2. _____ It was so close.
3. _____ try again.
4. _____ You made it.

Tryout IV.   Writing Business Letters

Write the heading, inside address, greeting, closing, and signature of a letter to the Radio City Music Hall, 1260 Avenue of the Americas, New York, New York 10019.

10

Tryout
Time

10

217 Hunter Avenue
Hartford, CT 06105
March 7, 19___

Dear Sandy,

You shouldn't live so far away. We need you here on Saturday for the playoff. That's right. We've made it through to the soccer finals. Everyone thinks our chances are very good, but they'd be better if we could count on you as our goalie.

Mom made me stay home Monday because I had a cold, but luckily I had a good book. I laughed all the way through. Maybe you have read it. The title is <u>Henry and Beezus</u>.

As soon as the weather warms up a little, Jim, Terry, and I are going to build a tree house in our backyard. If you are planning to visit your grandmother during spring vacation, you can help us.

Please write and tell me what you are doing and when I will see you again.

Your friend,
Pat

The Appearance of a Letter

Sending a letter that is easy to read is a courtesy. Your handwriting should be legible and neat. Whether you are using lined or unlined paper, you should write as evenly as possible.

Always write letters in ink. A letter in pencil is hard to read and is likely to become smudged.

Place your letter on the page so that the margins make a frame for it. Keep the left-hand margin straight, but indent each paragraph. The right-hand margin should be as straight as possible.

● **Practice**

1. Show that you know how to write the parts of a friendly letter. Correctly and neatly write on your paper the parts listed below. Use capital letters and punctuation marks where needed.

   1. *Headings:*

      1. 342 east 40 street new york new york 10016 july 18 19__
      2. 643 northeast widener street portland oregon 97214 november 11 19__

   2. *Greetings, closings,* and *signatures:*

      1. dear mrs albert   sincerely yours   helen
      2. dearest fran   your cousin   john

2. Write a friendly letter in reply to Henry Van Dyke. Use the notes you made, and follow the guides on page 202. Be prepared to read your letter to the class. Write the first draft of your letter in pencil. Then read it over to see if you can improve any of the paragraphs. Make sure that its parts are written correctly and in good form. Then copy the letter neatly in ink.

Addressing an Envelope

Study the envelope which Pat prepared for her letter to Sandy. There are two addresses on it. Notice the form in which they are written.

Pat Clark
217 Hunter Avenue
Hartford, CT 06105

Sandy Harron
644 Sheridan Avenue
Columbus, Ohio 43209

Write the receiver's address a little below the middle of the envelope, and to the right of center, unless it is unusually long. If you do not have room to write the address out, you may abbreviate words like *Street* (St.) and *Avenue* (Ave.) and also names of states.

To Discuss

1. Why is the Zip Code necessary? Is it set off by any punctuation mark?
2. Why is the return address important?
3. What rules for punctuation and capitalization are followed in both addresses? Notice that the names of cities and states are usually spelled out. Why is this helpful? Where are the Zip Codes written?

● Practice

1. Study the model envelope. Then close your book. On paper, draw a rectangle the size of an envelope. As your teacher dictates, write the addresses correctly.
2. Prepare an envelope for the friendly letter which you wrote to Henry Van Dyke. (Make up a home address for him.)

  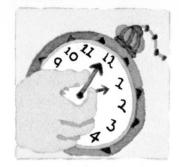

Using Words Correctly: *sit* and *set*

The verbs *sit* and *set* are easily confused. As you read the following sentences, think about the differences in their meanings.

1. *Sit* here, please. (to rest, to stay)
2. *Set* the plant on the windowsill. (to place)
3. *Set* your watch. (to put in a certain position, place, or condition)

Before you can use a verb correctly, you must know its correct forms as well as its meaning. Study the correct forms of *sit* and *set* in the sentences that follow.

Sit

1. They *sit* in the last row. (present)
2. Sharon *sat* on the porch. (past)
3. She *has sat* there for hours. (past participle)

Set

1. Please *set* the table. (present)
2. The workers *set* the girders in place. (past)
3. They *have set* the chair on the porch. (past participle)

What is the past tense form of *sit*? What is the past participle form of *sit*?

What do you notice about the three forms of *set*?

The three correct forms of *sit* and the three correct forms of *set* are as follows.

PRESENT	PAST	PAST PARTICIPLE
sit	sat	(*has, have, had*) sat
set	set	(*has, have, had*) set

● **Practice**

Write each sentence below. Choose the correct word in parentheses.

1. I (sat, set) on a rock to tie my new hiking boots.
2. Arnold (sit, set) his canteen next to me.
3. He (sat, set) down to have a drink before we started.
4. After an hour of hiking, I was ready to (set, sit) down.
5. At the top, we (set, sat) our packs down.
6. Arnold and I (set, sat) under a tree.
7. We watched the sun (sit, set).

> Use a form of the verb *sit* when you mean "to rest."
> Use *set* when you mean "to place" or "to put in order."

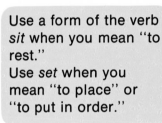

Little things make perfection but perfection is no little thing.

MICHELANGELO

Michelangelo Buonarroti was an Italian sculptor, painter, poet, and architect. He was born seventeen years before another famous Italian, Christopher Columbus, made his voyage to America. Michelangelo's paintings and sculptures are considered to be some of the most magnificent works ever achieved. He concentrated hard on the tiniest details in his works of art. What is he saying in the quotation above about the relationship between attention to little things and accomplishing something close to perfection?

Using Interjections

Certain words are used only to express feelings. They are not really a part of the sentence pattern. Such words are called **interjections.** Look up *interject* in a large dictionary to find the meanings of *inter* and *ject.* How do these meanings help to explain the word *interjection*?

Read each sentence below and find the interjection. Decide whether it expresses a strong feeling or a mild feeling. Notice the mark of punctuation that follows the interjection.

1. Whew! That was a close call.
2. Well, the joke was on me.
3. Oh, I'm sorry about that.
4. Whee! That was some toboggan ride.

Which sentences begin with strong interjections? Mild ones?

What mark of punctuation follows a strong interjection? A mild interjection?

▶ A word that is used to express a feeling is called an **interjection.**

Put an exclamation point after a strong interjection.
Place a comma after a mild interjection.

● **Practice**

1. Write each sentence below. Use the proper marks of punctuation after the interjections.

1. Wow What a great ride.
2. Oh Look out for that tree.
3. Ouch My foot's caught in the chain.
4. Hurry Help me get it out.
5. Oh no just look at my bike.
6. Well at least you're not hurt.

2. Write six sentences using different interjections. Punctuate your sentences correctly.

Notes for Special Purposes

Sincere friends remember to say *thank you, please, I am sorry*, or *congratulations*. When they cannot express these words of thoughtfulness in person, they write courtesy notes.

Courtesy notes are a kind of friendly letter and are therefore written in the form of a friendly letter.

A Note of Appreciation

There are many occasions for writing a letter of appreciation or a thank-you note. If someone sends you a gift or does something for you, you will want to express your appreciation. It is also courteous to write a note of thanks after visiting or staying at the home of a friend or relative.

Read this note of appreciation. Be ready to discuss the questions that follow.

72 Oscar Street
Paula, CA 95451
October 3, 19__

Dear Mrs. Herrera,

Our class felt very lucky to have you visit us last Friday. The pictures of Mexico you showed helped us to feel better acquainted with the country and its people. We especially liked your description of the fiesta and the wedding.

After we have studied more about Mexico, we plan to give a program for our parents. We will let you know when it will be. If you can come, Mr. Baum and our class will be very pleased.

Yours sincerely,
Sandy Meyer

To Discuss

1. Why did Sandy write Mrs. Herrera a note of thanks?
2. How did Sandy show the class's appreciation?
3. Was the note written promptly? How can you tell?
4. Did Sandy follow the correct form for all parts of a friendly letter? What rules for capital letters and punctuation did she follow?
5. Why did she use both her first and last name in the signature?
6. Prepare a list of suggestions to follow in writing courtesy notes.

Practice

1. Pretend that Mr. Han talked to your class about airplanes and that he used pictures and models to illustrate his talk. Write him a letter of thanks for the class. In your letter, mention some features of his talk that made it especially interesting.
2. Write a thank-you note for a gift, real or imaginary.

An Invitation

A good invitation is clear, interesting, and friendly in tone. It must contain all the necessary information — date, time, place, and occasion.

Read this invitation. Discuss the questions that follow it.

2830 Brown Street
Conroy, Iowa 52220
April 12, 19____

Dear Joan,

Can you come next Saturday morning and stay until Sunday afternoon? Mother says your parents may attend the conference. If so, they could leave you here and call for you on their way home.

Right now the farm is very busy. Three calves have just been born, and there is a litter of piglets, too.

If you can come, bring an extra sweater and boots or heavy shoes for outdoors. We can have fun indoors, too. I have a new game to show you.

With love,
Ruth

To Discuss

1. How did Ruth make her letter interesting?
2. What arrangements did Ruth suggest? Did she state them clearly?
3. What sentence shows that Ruth is a thoughtful person?
4. Why should invitations be answered promptly?

● Practice

Write a letter inviting a friend to be your guest for a weekend or on a camping trip or at a picnic. Follow the suggestions for writing courtesy notes which you have prepared. Try to mention in your note some reasons why your friend would enjoy the occasion.

Divide the class into writing teams of two members each. Number 1 in each team is to write Number 2 a friendly letter expressing appreciation for a recent action of Number 2 in which he or she showed unusual courage or kindness or originality. Number 2 is to write to Number 1 thanking him or her for a gift. Both writers should use their imagination to supply the facts. Have fun with this assignment. Read some of the letters to the class.

Review Practice

Correct Form for Friendly Letters

Study the note of congratulation below. Notice the placement of the parts, the punctuation, and the spelling. Then close your book and write the letter as your teacher dictates it.

21 Stanton Road
Sandy, Idaho 82374
March 24, 19___

Dear John,

Mother just read me the part of Aunt Emma's letter about your robot winning first prize at the state science fair. Congratulations! We are proud of you. When we come to visit you this summer, I hope you will show me how it works.

Your cousin,
Al

Business Letters

Business letters differ from friendly letters. In business letters, the message should be stated in a businesslike way. It should be clear and as brief as possible.

The business letter has six parts (a friendly letter has five). Study the form of the business letter on the next page.

To Discuss

1. *The heading:* What information does it give? What rules for capital letters and punctuation are followed? What is the Zip Code? Why is it important?

2. *The inside address:* Whose address is it? Note the use of capital letters and punctuation. If a business letter is addressed to an individual, the person's name comes first in the inside address.

3. *The greeting:* Why is this greeting used? What other greetings may be used in business letters? What punctuation follows the greeting?

4. *The body of the letter:* Is the request stated clearly and courteously? Is it brief and to the point? Are punctuation marks and capital letters used correctly? Why does the word *Northwest* have a capital letter?

5. *The closing:* What rules for capital letters and punctuation are followed? What other closing phrases may be used for business letters?

6. *The signature:* Whose signature is it? How is the signature placed in relation to the heading and closing? Why do you think Rex Allen wrote the letter?

Choose and be ready to read aloud parts of a letter which show the writer followed the guides on the next page that applied to his letter.

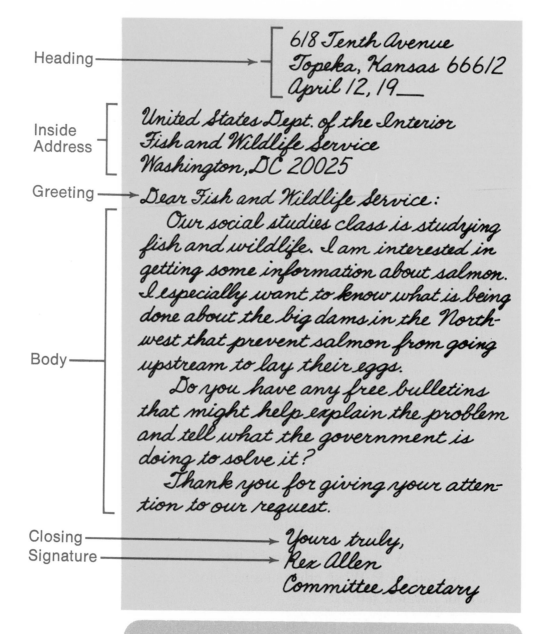

Heading

618 Tenth Avenue
Topeka, Kansas 66612
April 12, 19___

Inside Address

United States Dept. of the Interior
Fish and Wildlife Service
Washington, DC 20025

Greeting

Dear Fish and Wildlife Service:

Body

Our social studies class is studying fish and wildlife. I am interested in getting some information about salmon. I especially want to know what is being done about the big dams in the Northwest that prevent salmon from going upstream to lay their eggs.

Do you have any free bulletins that might help explain the problem and tell what the government is doing to solve it?

Thank you for giving your attention to our request.

Closing
Signature

Yours truly,
Rex Allen
Committee Secretary

How to Write a Business Letter

Explain exactly what you want.
Give all the information that your reader will need.
Be courteous.
Be brief and to the point.

Practice

1. Write the heading, inside address, greeting, closing, and signature for two business letters. Use the following information.

    1. A letter from you to mrs r c davis   the davis book store   816 foster avenue   halsey oregon 97809
    2. A letter from you to the charleston public library circulation department   416 tenth avenue charleston nevada 89702

2. Write a business letter to order something you have seen advertised in a paper or magazine. Follow the guides on page 216. Use the correct form for business letters.

Addressing the Envelope for a Business Letter

On the envelope for a business letter, write the *receiver's address,* which is also the inside address of the letter. Then write the *return address.* Follow the form you used in addressing an envelope for a friendly letter.

Practice

1. Draw and address the envelope for the business letter you wrote for section 2 above.
2. Draw an envelope and address it correctly to your principal. Use your home address for the return address.

TITLE: **The Search for Delicious**
AUTHOR/ARTIST: Natalie Babbitt
PUBLISHER: Farrar, Straus & Giroux

Prime Minister DeCree was writing a dictionary. The King had been delighted with A, B, and C. "*Annoying* is a loose boot in a muddy place. *Bulky* is a big bag of boxes. *Calamitous* is saying 'no' to the King." But when the Prime Minister came to "*Delicious* is fried fish," there was disagreement. The King said that *Delicious* was an apple. The Queen knew that *Delicious* was Christmas pudding. There was just one thing to do: send Gaylen to the four corners of the kingdom to take a poll. Whatever the majority decided upon would be the dictionary entry.

So Gaylen began the search for *Delicious*. Mayors, dwarves, a woldweller (who is 900 years old and lives in a tree), a minstrel, and a mermaid are some of the creatures that help Gaylen in his quest. But Hemlock, the Queen's evil brother, wants to hinder Gaylen's search. He rides ahead of Gaylen spreading rumors that whatever wins the vote for *Delicious* will be the only food that the King will allow the people to eat. The search for *Delicious* takes Gaylen into many unexpected adventures and is a quest that you won't want to miss.

Checkup I. Writing a Friendly Letter

Write the following parts of a friendly letter correctly.

18 gaines avenue   your friend
larson montana 59989   kim
september 8 19—

Checkup II. Using *sit* and *set*

1. Write each sentence below. Choose the correct word in parentheses.

    1. Let's (sit, set) these picnic things down near that tree.
    2. Then we should (sit, set) down too; I'm tired.
    3. Let's (sit, set) the barbecue grill here.

2. Write four sentences, using forms of *sit* and *set* correctly.

Checkup III. Interjections

1. Write these sentences correctly, using the proper punctuation after the interjections.

    1. Hey let's play dodgeball.
    2. O.K. you can be in the circle.
    3. Ha I got you.

2. Write sentences of your own, using these interjections:

    ouch   help   oh   well

Checkup IV. Writing Business Letters

Write the heading, inside address, greeting, closing, and signature of a letter to Geographia Map Co., Inc., 15 Bloomfield Street, Hoboken, New Jersey 07030.

10

Checkup

You probably know a good deal about adjectives and adverbs. Here is your chance to find out how much.

Tryout I. Adjectives

Make a list of the adjectives in the sentences below. Next to each adjective, write the noun it modifies. (Do not include *a, an,* and *the.*)

1. Have you seen the performing dogs?
2. Two silver poodles walked on their hind legs carrying tiny chihuahuas in their front paws.
3. A cute boxer does several tricks.
4. A spotted puppy does the "Canine Can-can."
5. The talented trainer loves the loud applause.

Tryout II. Making Comparisons with Adjectives

Write each sentence below. Change the adjectives in parentheses to the comparative or superlative degree.

1. (fast)   John is the _____ runner in our class.
2. (fast)   But Tina says she is _____ than John.
3. (easy)   The _____ way to tell is with a race.
4. (new)   John has _____ track shoes than Tina.
5. (good)   The winner will be the _____ runner in our school.

Tryout III. Proper Adjectives

List the names below on your paper. Opposite each, write a proper adjective made from it.

Mexico	Canada
Japan	Spain
America	France

Tryout Time

Tryout IV. The Adverb

Copy each sentence below. Underline the adverbs in each one.

1. Angela displays her stamp collection carefully.
2. She never loses any stamps.
3. She pastes each stamp slowly and neatly in place.
4. Angela often buys new stamps.

Tryout V. Making Comparisons with Adverbs

Write each sentence below. Change the adverbs in parentheses to the comparative or superlative degree, as required.

1. (early)   Sally arrived _____ than I for the game.
2. (well)   Of all the team members, she bats _____ .
3. (fast)   Jim runs _____ than Tom.
4. (slowly)   Sometimes our pitcher will pitch the ball _____ than the batter expects.
5. (well)   We do _____ than most other teams.

Tryout VI. Using Words Correctly

Write each sentence below. Choose the correct word in parentheses.

1. (good, well)   Drake plays the trumpet _____ .
2. (those, them)   He knows many songs and plays _____ well.
3. (those, them)   He is in the band with _____ two girls.
4. (good, well)   Jan and Pat play the clarinet quite _____ .
5. (good, well)   They are _____ players.
6. (those, them)   Let's listen to _____ play.

Using Adjectives and Adverbs

Here are two paragraphs from *The Secret in the Wall* by Jean Bothwell, a book about a boy named Fin who lives in Nassau. Read the paragraphs and see how clear and vivid a picture comes to your mind.

Fin liked the smell of dawn. Water and fish and wet sand were in it and just now sound was added. He stood close to the shore of the inner channel of Nassau Harbor and listened to the rush of miniature waves as they lapped gently against the rough sand that bordered the ruin of little old Fort Montagu. A small fishing boat was passing, a scarcely seen shadow against the faintly paling sky on the low horizon.

Perhaps he had given himself more time than he needed to ride his bicycle in from Cable Beach and along silent Bay Street to this now quiet spot.

Good writers make you see the people, places, or things about which they write. They use words that help you to see, hear, smell, taste, and feel what they are describing.

Two kinds of words that add to writers' word pictures are **adjectives** and **adverbs.** These two parts of speech help to make our language lively and colorful. An adjective or an adverb can change a dull sentence to one that is bright and interesting. Look at the two sentences below. Which creates a clearer picture in your mind?

The monkey stole our lunch.
The mischievous, chattering monkey slyly stole our lunch.

The Adjective

Take another look on page 223 at the description of the harbor and find the words below. What word comes after each one of them in the selection?

wet _____   miniature _____   quiet _____

What do the words above tell about the nouns that follow them? How do they change the meaning of those nouns or add to their meanings?

Look at the italicized words below. Notice how each one tells something different about the noun *place*.

horrible place   *ugly* place
familiar place   *empty* place
beautiful place   *crowded* place

We call such words **adjectives.** They *modify* the nouns or pronouns with which they are used. Find the adjectives that modify these words on page 223.

_____ _____ boat   _____ sky   _____ Bay Street

Show how a different adjective in each blank above would give the reader an entirely different idea. Read the phrases aloud, substituting other adjectives that could modify the nouns.

▶ An **adjective** is a word that modifies a noun or a pronoun.

As you know, other parts of speech may be used like adjectives to modify nouns. Nouns and pronouns that show possession may be used like adjectives.

ADJECTIVES	POSSESSIVE NOUNS AND PRONOUNS
delicious fudge	*brother's* fudge
hot biscuits	*our* biscuits

● Practice

Read the following description of Paul Bunyan from *Paul Bunyan and His Great Blue Ox,* by Wallace Wadsworth. Try to spot the adjectives in it. Then answer the questions about adjectives that follow it.

Paul Bunyan was of tremendous size and strength, the strongest man that ever swung an ax. He had curly black hair which he used to comb every morning with a great crosscut saw, after first parting it nicely with a broadax. He also had a big black beard that was as long as it was wide and as wide as it was long. He was rather proud of this beard and took great care of it. Several times every day he would pull up a young pine tree by the roots and use its stiff branches in combing and brushing it smooth.

1. What adjective describes Paul Bunyan's size and strength?
2. Which two adjectives describe Paul's hair?
3. Which adjectives modify the following nouns?

    _____ man   _____ times

    _____ morning   _____ _____ tree

    _____ care   _____ branches

Position of Adjectives

Did you notice that all the adjectives discussed on pages 223 and 224 were placed directly before the words they modified? This is the most common position for adjectives. However, they can appear elsewhere in sentences. Look at these possibilities.

1. Ann is a *musical* girl.
2. Ann, *musical* and *artistic*, leads the band.
3. Ann is *musical*.
4. She is *artistic*.

What does the adjective in sentence 1 modify? Who or what is described by the adjectives in sentence 2?

Notice that the adjectives in sentences 3 and 4 each follow a verb of being. When you studied verbs of being, like *am, is, are, was,* and *were,* you learned that the predicate tells what the subject *is* or *is like.* The verb of being may be completed by either a noun or an adjective.

In the sentence *Ann is a musician,* the words *musician* and *Ann* name the same person. *Musician* is a noun, like *Ann.* Did the noun signal *a* before *musician* also help you to know it was a noun? Try placing a noun signal — *a, an,* or *the* — before *musical* in sentence 3: *Ann is musical. Musical* is not a noun; it is an adjective that tells what Ann is like. Try placing a noun signal before *artistic* in sentence 4: *She is artistic.* Is *artistic* a noun? Why not?

● Practice

The sentences below call for you to supply different adjectives in a variety of positions. Choose interesting adjectives that make sense. Read your sentences aloud.

1. Hansel and Gretel lived near a _____, _____ forest.
2. Their parents were _____.
3. They were also _____.
4. The children, _____ and _____, were lost in the woods.
5. _____ and _____ was the forest.
6. Coming upon a _____ house, they knocked, and a _____ witch appeared.

The best way to cheer yourself is to try to cheer somebody else up.

MARK TWAIN

Sometimes when we feel sorry for ourselves, we begin thinking our problems are much more serious and important than they really are. Think about times when you needed cheering up. Do the worries you had then seem so important now? Why would cheering someone else up be a good way to cheer yourself?

227

Making Comparisons with Adjectives

Suppose that you were talking about three brothers and you wanted to tell someone how they compared in age. You might say:

1. Jack is *young*.
2. Bud is *younger* than Jack.
3. Charles is the *youngest* of the brothers.

What part do adjectives play in this comparison? How has the word *young* been changed to show how their ages compare?

Suppose that you wanted to compare the three boys' talents in music. You might say:

1. Charles is *talented*.
2. Jack is *more talented* than Charles.
3. Bud is the *most talented* of the three.

What words have been used to make this comparison? How has the word *talented* been changed?

Both of the comparisons above show that adjectives have three **degrees of comparison.** They are called the **positive, comparative,** and **superlative** degrees.

POSITIVE	COMPARATIVE	SUPERLATIVE
large	larger	largest
difficult	more difficult	most difficult
difficult	less difficult	least difficult

▶ The **positive degree** is the simple form of the adjective.
▶ The **comparative degree** is the form used to compare two persons or things.
▶ The **superlative degree** is the form used to compare three or more persons or things.

Rules for Making Comparisons

How do you determine which adjectives can be compared by using the *-er* and *-est* endings, and which should be compared by using *more* and *most* or *less* and *least*? The number of syllables in the adjective will usually tell you.

1. Most adjectives of one syllable form the comparative degree by adding *-er*, and the superlative by adding *-est*.

   small   smaller   smallest

   If a one-syllable adjective ends in *e*, it adds only *-r* or *-st*.

   fine   finer   finest

   Some one-syllable adjectives double the last letter before adding *-er* and *-est*.

   big   bigger   biggest

2. Most two-syllable adjectives use *more* or *less*, *most* or *least*, to form comparisons.

   careless   more careless   most careless
                less careless   least careless

   A few adjectives of two syllables add *-er* and *-est*.

   happy   happier   happiest

   Notice that in *happy*, the *y* is preceded by a consonant. Therefore, *y* changes to *i* before *-er* or *-est* is added.

3. Adjectives of three or more syllables use *more* or *less*, *most* or *least*.

   wonderful   more wonderful   most wonderful
                 less wonderful   least wonderful

There are exceptions to these rules. Some adjectives, such as *good, bad,* and *little,* form their degrees of comparison in a different, or irregular, way.

a good circus	a better circus	the best circus
a bad act	a worse act	the worst act
a little practice	less practice	the least practice

Form the comparative degree of most one-syllable adjectives by adding -er, and the superlative degree by adding -est.
Form the comparative degree of most two- and three-syllable adjectives by using *more* or *less,* and the superlative by using *most* or *least.*

● **Practice**

1. On the board, write the comparative and superlative forms of the words given below.

flat   funny   lean   gay
sad   wet   dry   lovely

2. Read each sentence below aloud. Use the correct comparative or superlative form of the adjective in parentheses.

1. (deep)   The water in Polliwog Pond is _____ than it is in Tadpole Pool.
2. (green)   The _____ lily pads I have ever seen grow here.
3. (small)   One frog that is _____ than the others has a fine voice.
4. (good)   A big bullfrog is the _____ croaker of all.
5. (beautiful)   The frog chorus gives the _____ twilight concert you have ever heard.

3. Write four sentences, using adjectives to compare (1) two girls, (2) two boys, (3) two dogs, and (4) two sports. Use forms of these adjectives: *strong, lively, thoughtful, dangerous.*

4. Write three sentences comparing more than two persons or objects. Use forms of these adjectives: *good, distant, busy.*

How Our Language Grows

Are You a Lingu*ist*?

An ending that changes the meaning of a word is called a *suffix*. Suffixes are useful in describing people.

What do act*or*, auction*eer*, and teach*er* have in common? Each word has a suffix meaning "one who." The suffixes *-ist* and *-ster* have similar meanings. A young*ster* is "one who is young." A pian*ist* is "one who plays the piano." You can see from the last example that sometimes the root word has to be changed slightly when a suffix is added.

A person from Canada is a Canad*ian*, a person from Rome is Rom*an*, while someone from Alaska is an Alaska*n*. These last three suffixes can mean "one who belongs to." They are used to express a connection with a place, person, belief, or profession. Words like veteri-nar*ian* and vegetar*ian* are other examples.

A person who is the object of some action might have the suffix *-ee* attached to her or his title. One to whom a letter is addressed is called an address*ee*.

Since linguistics is the study of language, you must be a lingu*ist*!

Add the suffixes in the right-hand column below to words in the left-hand columns to form "person words." You may need to change some of the root words slightly. To which word may two suffixes be added? You may consult your dictionary.

conduct	employ	govern	-er, -or, -eer
trick	cartoon	sculpt	-ster
climb	motor	engine	-ist
violin	guard	New York	-ee
edit	Texas	America	-ian, -an, -n
prank	Paris	mob	

Using Adjectives Correctly

The words *this, that, these,* and *those* are often used as adjectives to answer the question *Which one?* They point out someone or something, as shown in these sentences.

1. *This* game requires only two players.
2. Did you buy the game from *that* store?
3. *These* instructions are useful.
4. *Those* pieces are in the box.

In the sentences above, which nouns do the italicized adjectives modify? Notice that these adjectives can do their own work; they do not need the words *here* and *there.* "This here boat" is incorrect. Say *This boat.*

those and *them*

Once you learn what work each part of speech does in a sentence, you can avoid many errors. You have studied the word *them* as an object pronoun. It can never be used to modify a noun as an adjective can.

In these sentences, *those* and *them* are used correctly. Read the sentences carefully.

1. *Those* paintings will be framed soon. (*Those* is an adjective.)
2. I have separated *them* from the others. (*Them* is an object pronoun. It takes the place of the noun *painting.*)

● **Practice**

1. Write four sentences, using *this, that, these,* and *those* as adjectives. Read your sentences aloud.
2. Write each sentence below. Use *those* or *them* in place of each blank.

    1. Did you take _____ pictures?
    2. We can use _____ in the exhibit.
    3. _____ photographs belong to _____.
    4. Ask _____ if we can borrow one.

> Never join "here" and "there" to the words *this, that, these,* and *those.*
> Never use *them* as an adjective to point out someone or something.

Proper Adjectives

Study the italicized words in the sentences below.

1. A *Dutch* fur trader discovered the lake.
2. Nora showed us her *Mexican* pottery.
3. Last summer we saw an *Indian* art show.

Each of the italicized words above is an adjective that has been made from a proper noun. Such adjectives are called **proper adjectives.** Like proper nouns, proper adjectives are capitalized.

● **Practice**

Write each sentence below correctly, capitalizing every proper adjective. Be prepared to read your sentences aloud, naming the proper adjectives.

1. I went with my spanish friend to an international restaurant.
2. She had chinese food.
3. I ordered matzoh ball soup from the jewish menu.
4. A violinist played hungarian music.
5. For dessert we ate italian ice cream.

233

The Adverb

Turn back to the paragraphs from *The Secret in the Wall* on page 223. Find the verb *lapped*. Which word tells *how* the waves lapped against the sand? Find the verb *was added*. Which words tell *when* the sound was added? Find the verb *stood*. Which word tells *where* Fin stood?

The words that you named are called **adverbs.** Each one answered the question *How?*, *When?*, or *Where?* These adverbs all *modify*, or add to the meaning of, verbs.

Name the verbs in the sentences below, and name the adverbs that modify them. Which question does each adverb answer: *How?*, *When?*, or *Where?*

1. The two boys called *loudly.*
2. Fred *soon* came to the window.
3. He looked *down.*
4. The boys *quickly* hid behind the hedge.
5. They *then* decided to leave.

One adverb that modifies a verb but does not tell *how*, *when*, or *where* is the word *not.*

Do not eat that piece of cake.

In the sentence above, *not* modifies the verb *eat.*

Many adverbs end in *-ly*: *suddenly, happily, sadly, kindly.* Can you think of other adverbs that end in *-ly*?

Some adverbs do not have an *-ly* ending: *soon, often, too, up, down.* Can you think of others?

English sentence patterns allow adverbs a greater variety of positions than other classes (groups) of words. Most adverbs can be placed in any of these positions.

> *Angrily* she left the party.
> She *angrily* left the party.
> She left the party *angrily.*

Adverbs That Modify Other Adverbs
and Adjectives

Most of the adverbs in our language answer the questions *How?*, *When?*, or *Where?* and modify verbs. A small number of adverbs, however, act differently from the others.

EXAMPLES:

1. Patricia works very carefully.
2. We arrived too late.

Find the adverb in sentence 1 that tells *how* Patricia works. Find the adverb in sentence 2 that tells *when* we arrived. Both *carefully* and *late* modify the verbs in the sentences, as most adverbs do. Now which word in sentence 1 tells *how carefully* Patricia works? Which word in sentence 2 tells *how late* we arrived? The words *very* and *too* are also adverbs. They answer the questions *How much?* or *To what degree?* by modifying the adverbs *carefully* and *late*.

Adverbs can also modify adjectives, as shown in the sentences below. In them, each italicized adverb modifies an adjective. Each answers the question *How much?* about the adjective it modifies.

1. Sue was *somewhat* thoughtful.
2. A *very* sad story was told.

Name the adjective in each of the sentences above.

▶ An **adverb** is a word that modifies a verb, an adjective, or another adverb.

Write this list of adverbs in your notebook. As you discuss adverbs in class, keep adding to your list.

HOW?	WHEN?	WHERE?	HOW MUCH?
slowly	soon	down	very
quickly	then	here	too

235

● Practice

1. Read this paragraph from *Lad: A Dog* by Albert Payson Terhune. Study the italicized adverbs. Be prepared to read aloud each italicized adverb and name the word it modifies. Tell whether the adverb tells *where, how, when,* or *how much.*

There were other people at The Place—people to whom a dog must be courteous, as becomes a thoroughbred, and whose caresses he must accept. *Very often,* there were guests, too. And from puppyhood, Lad had been taught the sacredness of the Guest Law. *Civilly,* he would endure the pettings of these visiting outlanders. *Gravely* he would shake hands with them, on request. He would permit them to paw him or haul him *about,* if they were of the obnoxious, dog-mauling breed. But the moment politeness would permit, he *always* withdrew, *very quietly,* from their reach and, if possible, from their sight as well.

2. Use one or more adverbs to add to the meaning of each sentence below. Use an adverb that answers the question in parentheses. Then read the sentence aloud.

1. The skier glided _____ to the lodge. (Where?)
2. She stopped _____. (How?)
3. _____, she took her skis off. (How?)
4. She walked home _____ slowly through the snow. (To what degree?)

Review Practice

Correct Verb Forms

Write each sentence below. Choose the correct word in parentheses.

1. Phil (set, sat) his hat and gloves on the table.
2. He (sat, set) by the fire to get warm.
3. His cat (laid, lay) down beside him and purred.
4. Winter had (sat, set) in at last.

Sentence Patterns: Adjectives and Adverbs

Here are two symbols to add to your collection:

Adj = Adjective (including *a*, *an*, and *the*)
Adv = Adverb

With an adjective you can show the fourth sentence pattern. In sentences of this type an adjective comes after a verb of being and describes the subject.

PATTERN 4: **N V^{be} Adj**   Venice is beautiful.

You can also use the new symbols **Adj** and **Adv** to expand the sentence patterns you have learned.

PATTERN 1: **N V**
Adj   N   V   Adv
Hungry soldiers marched slowly.

PATTERN 2: **N V N**
Adj   N   Adv   V   Adj   N
White clouds almost hid the mountaintop.

PATTERN 3: **N V^{be} N**
N^p   V^h   V^{be}   Adj   N
We were becoming good players
Adv
quickly.

Notice, however, that the addition of adjectives and adverbs does not change Patterns 1, 2, or 3.

● Practice

Build sentences from the following combinations of symbols. Avoid using the same words over and over.

1. **Adj N V**
2. **Adj Adj N V Adj N**
3. **Adj N V Adv**
4. **N V^h Adv V**
5. **N V^h V Adv**
6. **N^p V^{be} Adj**
7. **Adj Adj N V Adv**
8. **N V^h V^{be} Adj Adj N**
9. **Adj N V^h V Adj Adj N**
10. **Adj N V^h V^h V Adv**

Making Comparisons with Adverbs

Adverbs are used to compare actions as to time or manner in such sentences as these.

time: late   later   latest

1. Pat walked into the meeting *late.*
2. Did she arrive *later* than Tony?
3. Of all the members, Ted arrived *latest.*

manner: gracefully   more gracefully   most gracefully

4. Swans swim *gracefully.*
5. Do swans swim *more gracefully* than seagulls?
6. Of all water birds, swans swim the *most gracefully.*

Like adjectives, adverbs have three degrees of comparison.

POSITIVE	COMPARATIVE	SUPERLATIVE
soon	sooner	soonest
late	later	latest
loudly	more / less } loudly	most / least } loudly
silently	more / less } silently	most / least } silently

1. Adverbs of one syllable usually add -er and -est to make the comparative and superlative forms.

fast   faster   fastest

2. Most two-syllable adverbs use *more* or *less,* or *most* or *least.*

calmly ${more \atop less}$ calmly ${most \atop least}$ calmly

A few two-syllable adverbs add -*er* or *est.*

3. Three-syllable adverbs use *more* or *less,* or *most* or *least.*

quietly ${more \atop less}$ quietly ${most \atop least}$ quietly

4. There are some exceptions. A few adverbs have irregular comparative and superlative forms.

well	better	best
far	farther	farthest
little	less	least
much	more	most

5. Some adverbs cannot be used in making comparisons. These include:

not	here	now	up
never	there	again	down

● **Practice**

1. Read each sentence below aloud. Use the correct form of the adverb in parentheses.

    1. (soon)   The play will open _____ than you think.
    2. (well)   Of all the actors, Sue speaks _____.
    3. (loudly)   Jack speaks _____ than Sherry.
    4. (quickly)   Amy learned her lines _____ than Ted.

2. Write six sentences. Make comparisons of two and more than two persons. Use these adverbs: *well, calmly, far.*

Form the comparative degree of most one-syllable adverbs by adding -*er* and the superlative by adding -*est.*
Form the comparative degree of most two- and three-syllable adverbs by using *more* or *less,* and the superlative by using *most* and *least.*

Do you have some favorite poems? Borrow a variety of poetry books from the library for your room. Find a short poem or lines from a long poem that you can memorize.

Organize a poetry period. Have a program chairperson who can arrange the order in which the poems will be given and who will introduce each person in turn. Before presenting your poem, practice reading it aloud in an expressive voice.

COMPOSITION: ADJECTIVES AND ADVERBS

A. Study the picture below. Then, write six sentences in which you tell what is happening in the picture. Use a variety of adjectives and adverbs in your description, and position them in different places in your sentences.

B. Write an account of an action that you recently observed. Include adjectives and adverbs in your description.

Using *good* and *well*

The word *good* is always an adjective. You may never use it to modify a verb.

1. I made a *good* grade. (adjective)
2. This pie is *good*. (adjective)

Well may be either an adjective or an adverb.

3. Carmen is *well*. (adjective)
4. Ed speaks *well*. (adverb)

Which noun does the adjective *good* describe in the first sentence? In the second sentence?

In sentence 3, *well* is an adjective meaning "in good health." Which noun does it describe?

In sentence 4, *well* is an adverb because it modifies the verb *speaks*. It tells *how* the action is performed.

> Use the adjective *good* to describe or modify a noun.
> Use the adjective *well* to describe health or appearance.
> Use the adverb *well* to express how an action was performed.

● **Practice**

Read each sentence below aloud. Choose the correct word in parentheses. Tell whether the word is used as an adjective or an adverb.

1. Harry is a (good, well) dancer.
2. He and Rosa make (well, good) partners.
3. I hope Harry feels (good, well) enough to dance in the assembly.
4. My little sister tap dances (well, good).
5. Doesn't Nancy dance (well, good), too?
6. She doesn't dance as (good, well) as Tony.
7. The teacher said that you do ballet quite (good, well).
8. I have been (well, good) about practicing every day.

Sentence Patterns: Adjectives and Adverbs

With the exception of the adjective in Sentence Pattern 4, adjectives and adverbs do not change the basic sentence pattern.

    Adj   **Adj**   **N**   **Adv**   **V**
1. Tall majestic trees suddenly toppled.

    Adj   **Adj** **N**   **Adv**   **V**   **Adj**   **N**
2. Two heavy storms soon destroyed the crops.

    Adj   **N**   **V**^{be}   **Adv**   **N**
3. Both storms were surely tornados.

    Adj   **N**   **V**^{be}   **Adv**   **Adj**
4. The villagers were very courageous.

Examine the sentence parts that make up the basic patterns of the sentences above.

    PATTERN 1: N V (Noun–Verb) Trees toppled.

    PATTERN 2: N V N (Noun–Action verb–Noun) Storms destroyed crops.

    PATTERN 3: N V^{be} **N** (Noun–Verb of being–Noun) Storms were tornados.

    PATTERN 4: N V^{be} **Adj** (Noun–Verb of being–Adjective) Villagers were courageous.

● Practice

Copy the sentences below, leaving a blank line above each. Above each word, write its symbol. Then, identify the pattern of each sentence by writing 1, 2, 3, or 4.

1. The crocodiles slowly raised their heads.
2. They listened intently.
3. Their cold eyes grew alert.
4. Two swimmers were passing nearby.
5. They would be easy prey.
6. The swimmers spotted the moving crocodiles.
7. Madly they swam away.
8. Luckily they were safe.

A Book to Read

TITLE: **Shadow of a Bull**
AUTHOR: Maia Wojciechowska
ARTIST: Alvin Smith
PUBLISHER: Atheneum

It was one thing to have had a father who was famed as the greatest of bullfighters, but quite another to be expected to repeat the glory of that father's life.

Because Manolo looked so much like his father, everyone expected him to follow in the footsteps of their hero. People who had almost worshiped his father's skill and courage undertook to train Manolo. They brought him to see his first bullfight when he was nine, and thereafter prepared him steadily for the day when, at twelve, he would be ready to step into the ring to face the bull that was already chosen for him.

From the first, Manolo felt that his life was in the hands of others. His own wishes seemed to make no difference. What others expected him to be determined his fate, and the fact that he wanted to live another kind of life seemed to be of no importance at all. He was destined to carry on the reputation of his father in the bull ring.

Courage was always Manolo's watchword. In the end, he proved his courage in more ways than one. Perhaps the greatest proof of courage came when he made an important decision for himself.

Checkup

Checkup I. Adjectives

List the adjectives in the following sentences. Next to each one, write the noun it modifies.

1. The small child could not hold the wild soaring kite.
2. Several people saw the huge kite sail toward the gray clouds.
3. The bright golden kite shone briefly in the fading light and disappeared into the threatening sky.

Checkup II. Making Comparisons with Adjectives

List the following words on your paper. Opposite each, write the comparative and superlative forms.

1. slow
2. funny
3. beautiful
4. important
5. good
6. bad

Checkup III. Proper Adjectives

Write each sentence below. Choose a proper adjective for each blank.

1. St. Patrick's Day is an _____ holiday.
2. The bagpipe is a _____ musical instrument.
3. Spaghetti is often served in _____ restaurants.
4. Chow mein is a _____ dish.

Checkup IV. The Adverb

Copy each sentence below. Underline the adverbs.

1. Yesterday Tina found a small stone.
2. She had never seen one like it.
3. Tina took the stone to her teacher immediately.
4. Her teacher examined the stone carefully.

Checkup V.   Making Comparisons with Adverbs

Write each sentence below, choosing the correct word in parentheses.

1. That girl was the (better, best) high jumper at the track meet.

2. Ellen jumped high but Ann jumped (higher, highest) than she.

3. Eva did (best, better) in the fifty-meter dash than I.

4. Don did (good, better) than Eva.

5. Angela ran very well but Al ran (best, better) of all.

6. Next time, I plan to practice (more, most) than this time.

Checkup VI.   Using Words Correctly

1. Write each sentence below. Choose the correct word in parentheses.

  1. (good, well)   Marty planned the party very _____.
  2. (those, them)   Peg made _____ cookies.
  3. (those, them)   What did she put in _____?
  4. (good, well)   She used _____ fresh ingredients.
  5. (good, well)   Who brought this _____ fudge?
  6. (those, them)   Carl brought that and _____ coconut bars.

2. Write four sentences, using these words as adjectives: *this, that, these,* and *those.*

How good are you at writing and telling stories? Use these Tryouts to find out how much you already know.

Tryout I. Improving Your Word Choice

One of the words in parentheses in each sentence below is often overworked. Write each sentence using the more vivid word.

1. The conceited young reporter (swaggered, went) into the newspaper office.
2. "Stop the presses!" he (said, shouted).
3. He (dashed, went) into the editor's office.
4. "Look at this (brilliant, fine) scoop I've gotten!" he demanded.
5. The editor (glanced at, looked at) the story and replied, "Yes, I enjoyed reading about this in last night's *Post*."

Tryout II. Using the Correct Expression

Write each sentence below. Choose the correct word in parentheses.

1. John might (of, have) eaten the rest of the cake.
2. You could (of, have) had a piece, too.
3. I couldn't (of, have) eaten any because I wasn't here.
4. Who would (of, have) finished the whole thing?

Tryout III. Writing Conversation

Write the conversation below correctly.

When is your cousin from Dallas coming I asked Tina. She wrote that she would arrive on Thursday said Tina. Then tomorrow I said you will have to meet her at the station. When does her train arrive? Oh Tina replied I haven't looked it up yet.

Tryout IV.   Using Commas

Review each sentence below. Insert commas where they are needed.

1. "Have you bathed the dog yet Sid?" Mom asked.
2. "Yes he is all clean Mom" Sid replied.
3. "Well he doesn't look it" said Mom.

Tryout V.   Using *say, says,* and *said*

Write each sentence below. Choose the correct word in parentheses.

1. Yesterday Beth (says, said) the fish weren't biting.
2. I'll bet today she (says, said) she caught a dozen!
3. I (say, says) she just doesn't want any competition.

Tryout VI.   Writing Stories

Complete each statement below. Choose the correct group of words.

1. The opening of a story usually (a) gives a preview of what is going to happen, (b) gives the time and place of action and introduces the characters.
2. A strong chain of events is one in which (a) one incident leads to another, (b) something fantastic is always happening.
3. One way to have well-developed characters is to have them (a) doing things all the time, (b) say and do things that reveal their traits.
4. In most stories the characters get involved in (a) funny situations, (b) unexpected situations.
5. A climax usually (a) shows what happens to the characters as a result of the unexpected development, (b) shocks the reader.

12

Writing for Fun

Making an Experience Seem Real

You often write to share an experience or to express your personal ideas and feelings. Much of the pleasure you find in this kind of writing comes from making your experiences and moods seem real to others. It is fun to help your readers see what you have seen and to put them in the same mood you remember or imagine.

A good writer makes us feel what is happening. Often the setting of the place where events are about to take place is made very real. This gives readers a feeling of taking part in whatever the writer wishes to share with them.

Read the selection below, which is from *The Cheerful Heart*, by Elizabeth Janet Gray. See how this writer makes you feel a part of the scene that she is describing in this paragraph.

The rainy season came early. Every day when they woke up they knew that the sky would be gray, the air cool and damp, and the rain falling steadily. Sometimes it was a fine mist; sometimes it slanted in white lines through the air; sometimes it poured straight down as if a huge faucet had been turned on. At night they heard it pattering on the roof or lashing against the shutters.

To Discuss

1. Notice the details. What does the author tell us about the rainy season? Find an interesting detail and read it aloud.

2. Notice the order in which the details are presented. What part of a rainy day did the author describe first? Last?

3. What three things did "they" expect to find every morning of the rainy season? Which words appeal to the sense of sight? The sense of touch?

4. Read the sentence that brings out the differences or contrasts in the rainfall from time to time. Does this kind of comparison make the description seem more true to life?

5. Notice that the author compares pouring rain to an open faucet. What is the resemblance? How can you make the scene more valid?

6. What words in the last sentence does the author use to appeal to the reader's sense of hearing?

COMPOSITION: USING DETAILS

A. Write your answers to questions 2 and 3 above.

B. Write a paragraph, making one of the situations below seem real. Use specific details and words that appeal to the senses.

> a sunny day at the beach
> a windstorm at a camp in the woods
> a traffic jam
> waiting for a thunderstorm to end
> a hot day on a city street
> signs of spring where you live

Appealing to the Sense of Sight

Many words and expressions can be used to help the reader "see" the scene being described. In Elizabeth Enright's *The Saturdays,* the Melendy children have a playroom which they call their office. Read the description of it below. Notice how the author shows you its outstanding characteristics.

The floor was covered with scarred red linoleum that didn't matter, and the yellow walls were encrusted with hundreds of indispensable objects: bookcases bursting with books, pictures both by the Melendy children and less important grown-up artists, dusty Indian war bonnets. . . . In one corner of the room stood an old upright piano that always looked offended, for some reason, and whose rack was littered with music all patched and held together with Scotch tape.

To Discuss

1. What does the adjective *indispensable* mean? (Use your dictionary to check the meaning.)
2. In the selection above, what indispensable objects did the office contain?
3. What is "scarred" linoleum? What does "encrusted with objects" look like?
4. Did the children have many books? Read the words that answer this question.
5. How could a piano look "offended"?
6. In the selection above, find and read some more vivid word pictures.

In order to help your readers know just how something looks to you, you must sharpen your own skills of observation. Look around the classroom for one minute. Then, without looking at it again, list all of the things you saw that you can remember.

Appealing to Other Senses

The senses of hearing, smell, taste, and touch, as well as the sense of sight, can also be appealed to by skillful writers to add vividness to a scene. Read the description of a barn from *Charlotte's Web,* by E. B. White. Notice how the author appeals to your sense of smell by telling about the things to be found in the old barn.

The barn was very large. It was very old. It smelled of manure. It smelled of the perspiration of tired horses and the wonderful sweet breath of patient cows. It often had a sort of peaceful smell—as though nothing bad could happen ever again in the world. It smelled of grain and of harness dressing and of axle grease and of rubber boots and of new rope. And whenever the cat was given a fish-head to eat, the barn would smell of fish. But mostly it smelled of hay, for there was always hay in the great loft overhead. And there was hay being pitched down to the cows and the horses and the sheep.

To Discuss

1. What did the barn smell of mainly? How does the author make this stand out?
2. Notice the words that appeal to your sense of smell. Give an example and read it aloud. What words help you to see things in the barn as the author tells of the barn's odors? What is a "peaceful smell"?
3. Suppose the author had wanted to appeal to your sense of hearing. What sounds might you hear in a barn? What words might the author have used?
4. Can you think of words to describe how some of the objects in a barn feel to the touch—for example, hay, rope, harnesses, milk pails?

● Practice

Before you can describe anything, you must have a sharp picture of it in your own mind. How closely do you observe the shapes, colors, sounds, odors, flavors, and textures of things? Think of a room in your home — the kitchen, for example. How many of the following details can you recall?

1. *Appearance:* What is its shape? What are the colors of the walls? What are the furnishings? How does the kitchen look at different times of the day?
2. *Sounds:* What sounds come from there?
3. *Textures:* How do the appliances feel — for example, the top of the stove, the sink, or the water tap? Are they cold, hard, soft, warm, smooth, rough?
4. *Smells:* What are some of the aromas in the kitchen? What foods have pleasing aromas? How would you describe the smell of something burning?

COMPOSITION: APPEALING TO THE SENSES

A. In good sentences, answer one of the four groups of questions above.
B. Write a paragraph describing a place that has made a strong impression on you. It may be a garage, a bakery, a schoolroom, a cafeteria, or something else. Include sentences that refer to sounds as well as sights, and, if appropriate, to smells and textures.

Write in your notebook, for your own information only, the impression you tried to give your readers.

Divide the class into groups of four and pass the compositions around within the groups. Let each reader sign the back of your paper and write the word that best tells his or her impression of the place you described. When your paper comes back to you, tell whether your readers received the impression you tried to give.

Speaking Distinctly

1. Read aloud the questions below. Say the italicized words and letters correctly and clearly.

1. Don'*t* you wan*t* to ea*t* now?
2. Di*dn't* you br*ing* *your* raincoat?
3. Wha*t* time does the li*b*rary open?
4. Woul*dn't* you like a six*th* candle on tha*t* cake?
5. Wha*t* are the fa*cts* tha*t* you learne*d*?

2. Read aloud the sentences below. Say the italicized letters correctly and clearly.

1. Eva liv*ed* in Canad*a*.
2. Dictionari*es* have gui*de* word*s*.
3. The princip*al* speaker yes*ter*day was the pre*s*iden*t* of our organ*i*zation.
4. The car need*s* *oi*l and *r*adiator wa*ter*.
5. Banan*as* grow *wh*ere *th*ere is a ho*t*, moist clima*te*.

3. Study each word below. Think of the sound that the italicized letters spell. Say each word correctly.

twe*nty*	fi*sts*
mi*lli*on	roo*fs*

Find descriptive passages in books you have read and prepare to read them as examples for the class.

Have someone listen to you as you practice reading. Ask your listener if every word was clearly understood. Did you drop your voice at the end of a sentence or a thought? Did you pause when necessary for the best effect? Did you have a pleasant variation in tone of voice?

Introduce your selection to the class by naming the author and title. Tell your audience the kind of description they may expect and let them tell the senses to which the author appealed.

Improving Your Word Choice

Using the same words over and over makes conversation or writing dull. Using synonyms, however, can add variety. **Synonyms** are words that have the same, or nearly the same, meaning. For example, the words *bathe* and *wash* are synonyms.

Look for the overworked word in these sentences:

A *little* old man lives in that *little* white cottage. He has a parakeet which can ring a *little* silver bell.

When you notice an overworked word such as *little* in your writing, add variety by using synonyms.

A *little* old man lives in that *small* white cottage. He has a parakeet which can ring a *tiny* silver bell.

To Discuss

List these words on the board: *clean, good, pretty, go,* and *big.* Take turns naming synonyms for these words until there are five for each word. Then look up each set of synonyms in a large dictionary and discuss the differences in their meanings.

● Practice

1. Rewrite each of the following quotations, using a different word for *said* each time.

1. Sheila *said,* "Look out for that bike!"
2. "Are you all right?" Sheila *said.*
3. "It just startled me," I *said* to Sheila.

2. Write two or more words you could use instead of each of the following words to put variety into your writing.

came   nice   thing   liked   walked

Using Vivid and Specific Words

The following sentence contains a verb so general in meaning that it leaves very little impression.

The girl went to school.

More specific and interesting verbs can be used instead of went. Say the sentence substituting each of these words: skipped, sauntered, swaggered, dashed. On the board, list other specific words that could be used.

The next sentence contains an adjective that is not specific enough to create a vivid picture.

A big executive came to our room.

More exact and interesting adjectives give the readers a better clue to your idea. Say the sentence substituting each of these words: large, tall, well-known, important. On the board, list other interesting words that you might substitute for big.

To Discuss

1. How did the words substituted for the verb went in the sentences above change the picture you had of the girl going to school?
2. How did the words substituted for big change the picture you had of the executive?
3. Why are the suggested substitute words more effective?

● Practice

Rewrite the sentences below, substituting a more specific or vivid word for the verb or adjective in italics.

1. The elves ate the food the cobbler left for them.
2. Then they ran into the workshop.
3. They quickly began their hard work.
4. Soon a nice pair of shoes was finished.

COMPOSITION: USING VIVID AND SPECIFIC WORDS

A. Write sentences using these words: *shrill, rare, brilliant, tottered, pathetic.*

B. Select one of the pairs of contrasting scenes listed below. Describe the scenes vividly, using one paragraph for each. You may choose one of these pairs or think of topics for yourself.

1. a wild animal free in its natural setting and one that is caged in a zoo
2. a country scene in summer and in winter
3. a city street on a busy weekday and the same street on a Sunday afternoon
4. the kitchen in your house on a schoolday morning and at midnight

Going Ahead

Make a bridge of words from *bad* to *good*. First find as many words as you can that suggest some degree of badness. Arrange them in order from those meaning most to least bad. Then continue the bridge by finding and arranging words that suggest goodness, from the least to the best. You may wish to arrange them on the page to look like an arched bridge, like this.

Using Words Correctly: *could have*

Study the sentence below. One word is used incorrectly. What word is it?

Jill could of warned us.

In the sentence, *of* is used incorrectly. It is used as a verb, but it is not a verb. Perhaps the writer was thinking of *could've*, which is a contraction for *could have*. The sentences below are correct.

Jill *could have* warned us.
Jill *could've* warned us.

Now study the verbs and their contractions in the sentences below.

Lois *should have* gone home.
Lois *should've* gone home.

Al *would have* played ball.
Al *would've* played ball.

Notice that *should've* is a contraction for *should have*. *Would've* is a contraction for *would have*. The word *of* is not used.

Read aloud the following sentences, pronouncing each word distinctly.

1. Robert should have seen this detective movie.
2. He would have loved it.
3. The butler couldn't have done it.
4. But I wouldn't have blamed him for trying.

● **Practice**

Use each of the following phrases correctly in a sentence: *could have, would have, couldn't have,* and *wouldn't have.* Be ready to read your sentences aloud.

How Our Language Grows

Scandinavian Influences

Late in the eighth century, people from Denmark invaded England. The Anglo-Saxons living in England during this time spoke what we today call Old English, a Germanic language. Danish is also a Germanic language, and the Anglo-Saxons and the Danes lived and worked side by side, using the same kinds of everyday words. It is difficult, therefore, to tell exactly how much Danish influenced English.

We do know, however, that many words we use with the /sh/ sound, such as *ship* and *fish* came from Old English, while many of those with an /sk/ sound, like *skull, ski, scare,* and *bask,* came from Danish. Also, if it had not been for this Scandinavian influence on our language, we might still be saying *yive* for *give.* The use of both *g* and *k,* as in *egg* and *kid,* can often be traced to Scandinavian origins. Perhaps the biggest Scandinavian contribution to Modern English is that of the pronouns *their, they,* and *them.*

The words in the left-hand column below are Modern English words that long ago were borrowed from Scandinavia. Their original meanings are shown on the right. Write each word on the left. Find the meaning that matches each one and write it across from that word.

law	acid, tart
sky	fearful, dreadful
window	layer, that which is laid down
skirt	to lack
want	cloud, mist, fog
meek	wind-eye
wrong	shirt
ugly	soft, mild

Writing Conversation

In your stories, plan to let the characters talk. Let them speak as naturally as you can.

Study this conversation. Notice that the quotations are divided.

"Hi," said Karen breathlessly, "want to help?"

"Sure," said Alan, looking at her warily. "What's going on?"

"It's a dog," said Karen. "I found him with his paw caught in this hole. We've got to get him loose."

To Discuss

1. In which paragraphs above is the second part of the divided quotation the beginning of a new sentence? How are capital letters and punctuation used?

2. Read the paragraph in which the second part of the quotation is not the beginning of a sentence. How are capital letters and punctuation marks used?

3. Below are other rules for writing conversations. Find an example of each rule in the above model.

   1. Begin a new paragraph for each speaker.
   2. Enclose each quotation in quotation marks.
   3. Separate the quotation from the rest of the sentence by some mark of punctuation.
   4. Capitalize the first word in a quotation.
   5. Put the punctuation mark that ends the quotation inside the quotation marks.

Other Uses for Commas in Conversation

Conversation often includes words that refer directly to the person spoken to. These are called words of **direct address.**

1. "Where are you going, Angela?" asked Mrs. Epstein.
2. "I'm going to the movies, Mom," Angela replied.
3. "John," their mother asked, "are you going, too?"
4. "I don't think so, Mom," answered John.

Name the words of direct address in the sentences above.

Words such as *yes, no,* and *well* may appear at the beginning of a quotation or a sentence. Study these examples.

"Yes, I hope so," she said.
"Well, he won't do that," René informed me.

What mark of punctuation follows words such as *yes, no,* or *well* when they appear at the beginning of a sentence?

● **Practice**

1. Look again at the model conversation on page 260. Study the spelling, punctuation, and form. Then close your book and write the conversation as your teacher dictates it.
2. Rewrite the following sentences, using punctuation marks correctly.

   1. Isn't Tim's birthday on April Fool's Day Eddie asked.
   2. Yes I think it is answered Juanita.
   3. Let's bake an April Fool's birthday cake Juanita Eddie suggested.
   4. That's a good idea agreed Juanita.

COMPOSITION: WRITING CONVERSATION

A. The following conversation is from *Alice's Adventures in Wonderland* by Lewis Carroll. Rewrite it correctly.

Take off your hat the King said to the Hatter. It isn't mine said the Hatter. Stolen the King exclaimed, turning to the jury, who instantly made a memorandum of the fact. I keep them to sell, the Hatter added as an explanation. I've none of my own. I'm a Hatter.

B. Write an imaginary conversation between two characters who have different traits. What they say should reveal their traits. Choose one of these situations or use one of your own.

1. A rabbit scolds a turtle for being so slow.
2. A peacock brags about its beauty to a monkey.
3. A talkative person asks a quiet person to tell about her or his vacation.
4. A sales clerk tries to please a shopper who cannot make up his or her mind.

 It is what befits you
that gives you dignity.

This is a line from a traditional poem of the Yoruba tribe of Africa. *Befit* means "to be fitting or appropriate." How can you tell what "befits" you? Can you restate this line another way?

Using Words Correctly: *say, says, said*

When you talk or write about something that has already happened, use the past tense of the verb. Study the correct use of *say* and *said* in the sentences below.

> "Did you *say* when to expect Lisa?" asked Carla.
> "I *said* next Thursday," John answered. "Lisa *said* she'd like to see the boat your uncle built."
> "It's a masterpiece," *said* Carla.

● **Practice**

Read each sentence below aloud. Choose the correct word in parentheses.

1. Melba arrived and (says, said), "I'm hungry."
2. I (says, said), "We'll have dinner soon."
3. Yesterday, she (says, said) she'd like a ham sandwich, but now she (says, said) she wants two!
4. I (say, says) that at this rate we will run out of food by Sunday!

Review Practice

Adjectives and Adverbs

Write each sentence below. Use the correct form of the adjective or the adverb in parentheses. Consult your dictionary when in doubt.

1. (old)   Gawain was the _____ of the knights.
2. (early)   He was also the _____ riser.
3. (well)   And he rode a horse _____ than most.
4. (lively)   He was the _____ of all the knights.
5. (beautiful)   His shield was once _____ than words could tell.
6. (bad)   But now it was covered with the _____ dents you have ever seen.
7. (good)   To tell the truth, Gawain was _____ with his shield than he was with his sword.

Writing Stories

All good stories capture and hold the readers' and listeners' interest. They keep you wondering what is going to happen next.

Planning a Story

A story's power to keep the reader or listener in suspense has something to do with the order in which it is put together or told. In most stories, you will find this development.

1. The *opening of the story* sets the stage for what is going to happen. It usually gives the time of action and tells *who* the characters are, *where* they are, and *what* they are doing.
2. From the beginning there is a strong *chain of events.* In other words, one incident leads to another.
3. The action leads to an unexpected problem or difficulty for one or more of the characters. This is the turning point, or *crisis,* of the story.
4. Something interesting happens to the characters as a result of the difficult situation. For example, they may show unusual courage, strength, or cleverness. Someone may find a friend or learn a lesson. What happens as a result of the crisis provides the *climax* of the story.
5. The *ending* follows soon after the climax.

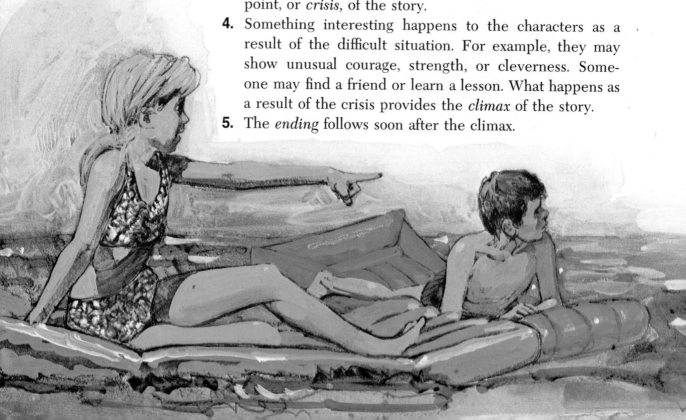

Here are some situations that could be the subjects of interesting stories.

1. Two characters set out to find a treasure which they believe is buried in a cave. When they approach the cave, they see a strange creature sitting on a box.
2. Two characters are hiking along a marked trail in the woods. They leave the trail to wade in a creek. When they return, they lose their way.
3. Two characters are caught in a sudden downpour. The only shelter nearby is a house which one of them believes is haunted.
4. Two characters are sunbathing on a raft. Suddenly one notices that they have drifted far away from shore.
5. A young woman suddenly discovers, as her train travels speedily past her home station, that she is on an express train headed for the next county before it is due to stop.

To Discuss

Discuss each of the situations above and think how you might develop an adventure story from it. Use these questions and suggestions to help you plan the characters, setting, and chain of events.

1. Think of two characters with contrasting traits.
2. How will you set the stage or describe the scene of action?
3. How important is the time of action?
4. What will be the outcome of the story? Will the characters learn a lesson? Will they do something clever or brave? Will something funny happen?
5. By working together in class, plan a chain of events for one of the situations above.

COMPOSITION: WRITING STORIES

A. Read situation 1 at the top of page 265 again. Study the picture on page 266. Write a short story about it. Think about what the strange creature did. Maybe it was somebody in disguise. Did it disappear or speak to the other characters?

B. Write a story about some experience you have had. The questions below may help you think of a possible experience.

1. Have you ever been lost or in danger?
2. Has an animal ever helped you?
3. Have you succeeded at something difficult?
4. What is the hardest work you have ever done?
5. Have you ever had an amusing or frightening experience while baby-sitting?

Sharing Your Stories

Half the fun of writing a story comes from sharing it with others. Before you give your story to others to read, proofread your paper carefully. Correct errors in spelling, capitalization, and punctuation. Check to see that you have used words correctly. Then copy your story neatly in ink.

Reading Stories Aloud

If you are going to read your story to the class, practice beforehand at home. Here are some goals to aim for as you practice.

1. Read slowly enough to be understood.
2. Pronounce words distinctly and correctly.
3. Adjust your tone of voice and rate of speech to fit the mood of the story.
4. Emphasize important words.
5. Let your voice show your interest in the story.

If you have written several stories, prepare your own book of stories. Ask two or three people to read the stories and select those which they like best. Then prepare the manuscripts carefully and place them in an attractive cover with an interesting title.

A committee can prepare a class booklet with the best work from each pupil. Arrange the selections, write a table of contents and a foreword, and bind them attractively.

Review Practice

Choosing the Correct Verb

1. Write each sentence below. Choose the correct word in parentheses.

   1. The snake charmer (set, sat) his basket down.
   2. He (lay, laid) his flute beside the basket.
   3. The old man (set, sat) on the ground while people gathered around him.
   4. "(Let, Leave) the show begin!" someone shouted.
   5. The snake charmer took the lid off the basket and (sat, set) it on the ground.
   6. The people (set, sat) very still and watched.
   7. The old man (leave, let) his music work its magic.

2. Write each sentence below. Choose the correct past form of the verb in parentheses.

   1. (teach)   Who _____ Olga to ski?
   2. (learn)   She _____ from me when she was very young.
   3. (break)   Yesterday she _____ the record for the jump.
   4. (drink)   We _____ hot chocolate to celebrate.
   5. (break)   Then she saw that she had _____ the tip of one ski.
   6. (ride)   She just _____ into town to have it fixed.

A Book to Read

TITLE: **Sunrise Island**
AUTHOR: Carella Alden
PUBLISHER: Parents Magazine Press

Between the Pacific Ocean and the Sea of Japan lies Sunrise Island. Actually, there are four main islands and many smaller ones that form Sunrise Island, or the country we know as Japan. One way to discover how a country has developed and grown is to take a look at its art. In this book, history is the story, and art is the teller of the tale.

Sunrise Island begins with the "birth" of Japan and moves into its early history with the use of bronze and clay for sculpture. Shōtoku, who was responsible for bringing Buddhism to Japan, is honored in many works of art. Scrolls, delicately lettered with Japanese ideographs, are shown along with many lovely lacquered pieces. Bold art depicts the members of the samurai, the hereditary warrior class in feudal society. The ancient tea ceremony and the Imperial Palace, home of the Emperor, show other forms of Japanese art. The gardens give us a glimpse into a fascinating aspect of Japanese culture.

Sunrise Island traces the progress of one of the world's great cultures by showing us its art.

Checkup I. Improving Your Word Choice

1. Write two or more synonyms for each of the italicized words below. Be specific.

> an *interesting* story   a *difficult* thing
> a *poor* road   an *old* car

2. Suggest a synonym for each italicized word below.

> 1. He was *afraid*.
> 2. Let us *rest* for a moment.
> 3. The man *said*, "Hey! Come back here!"

Checkup II. Using the Correct Expression

1. Write four sentences using *could have, wouldn't have, should have*, and *couldn't have*.
2. Read your sentences aloud. Be sure to pronounce every word distinctly.

Checkup III. Writing Conversation

Write this conversation correctly.

> My home said Tom is the white one up the hill. Do you have a basketball court in the back asked Jim. No Tom replied. We have a rose garden there. Yesterday he added our roses won a prize at the garden show.

Checkup IV. Using Commas

Write these sentences. Use commas correctly.

1. Well I cannot decide.
2. Yes I remember the picnic Dana.
3. No George jumping that brook is impossible.

Checkup V. Using *say, says,* and *said*

Write three sentences using *say, says,* and *said* correctly.

Checkup VI. Writing Stories

Write the answers to these questions.

1. What three goals should you try to achieve in the opening part of your story?
2. How do the individuals you meet reveal their traits? Is it possible for characters in a story to reveal theirs in the same way?
3. What is a chain of events? (Think of the meaning of the word *chain*.)
4. Would a strong chain of events alone make a good story? Why is an *unexpected event* important?

Tryout Time

In this chapter you will meet two new parts of speech — prepositions and conjunctions. Here is a chance to find out how much you already know.

Tryout I. Recognizing Prepositions

List the prepositions in these sentences.

1. We inflated the hot air balloons in the park after lunch.
2. The passengers climbed into the baskets.
3. All at once we let go of the baskets.
4. The balloons floated over the trees.

Tryout II. Prepositional Phrases

Copy each sentence below. Underline each prepositional phrase.

1. The house around the corner is being painted.
2. We help with the painting after school.
3. Marla dips her brush into the paint with care.
4. I plunge my brush to the bottom of the can.
5. Somehow I get covered with paint from head to toe.

Tryout III. Using Words Correctly

Write each sentence below. Choose the correct word in parentheses.

1. Were you (at, to) school yesterday?
2. There was a contest (among, between) Sheila and me for water polo champ.
3. We jumped (in, into) the pool.
4. The ball was lost (among, between) the splashes.
5. Finally Sheila got the ball and threw it (among, between) the two goal markers.

272

Tryout IV.   Words in a Series

Write each sentence below and punctuate it correctly.

1. Copper silver and gold were mined in the area.
2. The miners dug scraped and blasted.
3. The ore can be high-grade low-grade or worthless.
4. One prospector studied the gold slowly patiently and thoroughly.
5. An old mule plodded up the hill through the desert and into the town.

Tryout V.   Writing Sentences with Conjunctions Correctly

Make one sentence out of each pair of sentences below, using the conjunction in parentheses. Punctuate each sentence correctly.

1. (but)   The Saint Bernard searched everywhere. He could not find the missing climbers.
2. (and)   The ski patrol had been called out. Helicopters circled overhead.
3. (and)   We had to find them before dark. It was getting late.
4. (but)   When we found them, they were frightened and half frozen. They had never been so happy.

Tryout IV.   Subject and Verb Agreement

Write each sentence below. Choose the correct word in parentheses.

1. Dan and I (has, have) returned to camp.
2. (Don't, Doesn't) the deer or the elk come to this watering hole now?
3. It (doesn't, don't) seem like the same place now.
4. The eagles, coyotes, and wildcats (is, are) disappearing, too.

273

13

Prepositions and Conjunctions

The Preposition

Look at this list of words. Are they words that you use frequently?

about	behind	down	inside	over
across	below	during	into	to
among	beside	for	near	under
around	between	from	of	up
at	by	in	on	with

When the words above are used with nouns and pronouns, they are called **prepositions**. Read the following sentences aloud, filling the blanks with prepositions.

1. The book _____ the desk is not mine.
2. The plane flew _____ the airport.

A preposition is followed by a noun or pronoun, which is called the *object of the preposition*. In sentence 1 above, the noun *desk* follows the preposition you chose; for example, *in the desk, on the desk, behind the desk.* The noun *desk* is the object of the preposition. (A noun signal or modifier may appear between a preposition and its object.) Complete sentence 2 above and name the preposition and the object of the preposition.

▶ A **preposition** is a word that is used to relate nouns or pronouns to other words.

Study the following sentences:

1. The rehearsal will be held at my house.
2. Play the record for Teresa and me.
3. Can you pirouette across the room?
4. The ticket inside the envelope is yours.

In sentence 1 above, which word is the preposition? Which word is the object of the preposition?

In sentence 2, which word is the preposition? A preposition may be followed by more than one object. Name the objects of the preposition in sentence 2.

Now name the prepositions and their objects in sentences 3 and 4.

● **Practice**

1. Read the sentences below and name the prepositions and their objects. Tell whether the object is a noun or pronoun.

    1. Tod accidentally knocked the perfume bottle to the floor.
    2. It shattered into a million pieces.
    3. He wiped the floor with a rag.
    4. Now he smells of Purple Delight.
    5. His friends make jokes to him about it.

2. Write sentences of your own, using the prepositions below. Underline the noun or pronoun used as the object of the preposition.

with	around	during	under
across	below	near	for

Prepositional Phrases

In the previous lesson you identified prepositions and their objects. Each preposition and its object forms a unit called a **prepositional phrase.** Look for the prepositional phrases in these sentences.

1. The junk in this basement is a fire hazard.
2. Let's carry it to the incinerator.
3. The neighbors from that apartment will help us with it.

What is the preposition in sentence 1? What is its object? Notice that this object has a modifier. It, too, is part of the prepositional phrase.

What is the prepositional phrase in sentence 2? There are two phrases in sentence 3. Name the preposition that starts each phrase. Name the object of each preposition.

▶ A preposition and its object or objects, along with any modifiers, form a **prepositional phrase.**

In a prepositional phrase, the preposition connects its object to another word in the sentence. To see how this works, study what the prepositional phrases below do.

The mosquito flew . . .

under the table.	*near* the table.
over the table.	*to* the table.
beside the table.	*behind* the table.
around the table.	*across* the table.

Each preposition above connects the noun *table* to the verb *flew.* Notice how each phrase adds to the meaning of the verb. The phrase modifies the verb in the same way that an adverb does.

Now look at these examples. Each prepositional phrase adds to the meaning of the noun *dog*. It modifies a noun in the same way that an adjective does.

The dog
$\begin{cases} \textit{near} \text{ the kennel} \\ \textit{in} \text{ the kennel} \\ \textit{behind} \text{ the kennel} \\ \textit{inside} \text{ the kennel} \end{cases}$
has been sold.

● **Practice**

1. Find and read aloud the prepositional phrases in the sentences below. Name the word that each phrase modifies.

1. The path near the lake wound through the bushes.
2. Mara ran around us, over the hill, and out of sight.
3. We looked for her for several minutes.
4. Suddenly she appeared behind us.

2. Rewrite the sentences below, adding a prepositional phrase to modify the italicized noun in each one. Use a different preposition in each sentence.

1. The *girl* ran away.
2. The *chest* was empty.
3. The *road* was bumpy.
4. We explored the *cave*.

3. Rewrite the sentences below, adding a prepositional phrase to modify the italicized verb in each sentence. Use a different preposition in each sentence.

1. Luis *ran* swiftly.
2. Nobody *left* the room.
3. The lamp *flickered*.
4. Everybody *jumped*.

278

How Our Language Grows

What's New?

One way languages change and keep up to date is by adopting new words for inventions. But, just how new are these words?

Though today we usually associate the word *rocket* with space travel, the word's original meaning described the shape of a stick used in spinning wool or flax. With inventions and discoveries, old words like *rocket* may be used in new ways.

Sometimes prefixes, root words, and suffixes from ancient Greek and Latin are combined in words to name inventions. *Airplane, locomotive, submarine*, and *astronaut* are all combinations of such word parts. Knowing the meanings of a few word parts can let you discover the meanings of many new words.

Various parts and types of inventions also require names. With the invention of the *automobile*, came the words *windshield, dashboard, convertible*, and *station wagon*. These four terms are coined from very common words. Their meanings are easy to decipher.

1. Below is a list of prefixes used frequently to describe inventions. Write each prefix and then, after it, write its meaning. Use your dictionary.

1. tele-	6. stereo-	four	solid
2. auto-	7. quadri-	distant	self
3. astro-	8. phono-	under	spiral
4. sub-	9. helio-	two	star
5. bi-	10. hydro-	water	sound

2. Using the list above, what can you tell about the meaning of the following names?

astrodome	automat	television
helicopter	subway	hydrofoil

Preposition or Adverb?

Some words can be used as a preposition in one sentence but as an adverb in another. Read these sentences.

1. Stan looked *down* the road.
2. I was also looking *down* at my feet.

To test whether a word is a preposition or not, look for the object of the preposition.

Down is a preposition in sentence 1 above. How do you know? Look at sentence 2 above. Does *down* have an object? What question does it answer about the verb? Therefore, what part of speech is it? What is the preposition in sentence 2?

● **Practice**

1. Read the pairs of sentences below. Tell whether the italicized word in each sentence is used as a preposition or as an adverb.

  1. James fell *off* the springboard.
  2. Why did he fall *off*?
  3. We looked *inside* the cabin.
  4. *Inside* stood an old scarecrow.
  5. Karen bounded *up* the stairs.
  6. She looked *up* and saw her sister.
  7. Angie remained *behind*.
  8. She stood *behind* the screen.
  9. Margarita walked *near* the barn.
 10. Several cows came *near*.

2. Write two sentences for each word listed below. In one sentence, use the word as a preposition. In the other use it as an adverb.

    behind   down   above   about   near

Sentence Patterns: Prepositions

Review all the symbols you have studied so far. Notice the new symbol below, **P,** for preposition.

N = Noun   **Adj** = Adjective (including *a,*
Nᵖ = Pronoun   *an,* and *the*)
V = Action verb   **Adv** = Adverb
Vᵇᵉ = Verb of being   **P** = Preposition
Vʰ = Helping verb

You can now expand the sentences you are writing by adding prepositional phrases. Here are some examples:

P N   to school
P Nᵖ   for you
P Adj N   with a paintbrush

1. **N V P N**   Roger rushed to school.
2. **Adj N V P Nᵖ**   Many members voted for you.
3. **Adj N P Adj N Vᵇᵉ Adj**   That boy with a paintbrush is messy.

Build sentences of your own, using the symbols below and *a, an,* or *the.* Write your sentences, leaving space above each one. Write the correct symbol above each word.

1. **Adj N P Adj N Vᵇᵉ Adj**
2. **N V P Adj N**
3. **Adj N P Nᵖ Vᵇᵉ Adj N**
4. **Adj N P Adj N Vʰ V Adj N**
5. **Adj N P Adj Adj N Vᵇᵉ Adj**

Now review the four basic sentence patterns you studied on page 242. Underline the words in each of your sentences that make up the basic sentence pattern. Then identify the pattern as **N V, N V N, N Vᵇᵉ N,** or **N Vᵇᵉ Adj.**

Using Prepositions Correctly

Some prepositions can cause you difficulty if you confuse their meanings. Compare the meanings of the prepositions in these three pairs.

1. *at* and *to*

The preposition *at* should be used when you mean that someone or something is "already there."

> We are *at* school.   The boys are *at* the lake.

The preposition *to* shows movement. It should be used when you mean "going toward."

> We went *to* school.   The boys are going *to* the lake.

2. *between* and *among*

The preposition *between* should be used when you want to refer to *only two* persons, places, or things.

> We divided the flowers *between* Liz and Ben.
> I sat *between* two empty seats.

The preposition *among* should be used when you want to refer to *three or more* persons, places, or things.

> We divided the flowers *among* all the guests.
> I sat *among* the members of our baseball team.

3. *in* and *into*

The preposition *in* should be used when you mean "within" or "already inside."

> I am *in* the garage.   Donna is *in* the pasture.

The preposition *into* should be used when you mean "movement from the outside to the inside."

> I am going *into* town.   Donna is going *into* the barn.

Practice

Read the sentences below aloud. Choose the correct word in parentheses.

1. Sal, Tex, and Pat drove the cattle (in, into) the corral.
2. Then they went (in, into) the house.
3. The cook was waiting (in, into) the kitchen.
4. The cowhands sat down (at, to) the table.
5. The cook divided the beans (among, between) the three cowhands.
6. After lunch, the cowhands went back (to, at) the corral.
7. They divided the cows (among, between) Sal and Tex.
8. Tex took his cattle (in, into) the barn.
9. He searched (among, between) them to find the cows with brands.

Use *at* when you mean "already there." Use *to* when you mean "going toward."
Use *between* when you refer to only two persons, places, or things. Use *among* when you refer to three or more persons, places, or things.
Use *in* when you mean "within" or "inside."
Use *into* when you mean "movement from the outside to the inside."

Hold Fast Your Dreams

Within your heart
Keep one still, secret spot
Where dreams may go,
May thrive and grow—
Where doubt and fear are not.
Oh, keep a place apart
Within your heart,
For little dreams to go.

LOUISE DRISCOLL

What might happen to dreams if doubt and fear were allowed to enter their secret place? Do you think it is important for people to dream? Why or why not?

The Conjunction

In sentences, you very often need to connect words or groups of words that are equal in importance.

Connecting Words and Phrases

Look at these sentences:

1. Laura *and* Robbie are on the same team.
2. He should tape *or* tie the basket together.
3. She gave orders quietly *but* firmly.
4. They *and* I joined the others.

The italicized words above are connecting words. They are called **conjunctions.** Look at the word directly before the conjunction *and* in sentence 1. Then look at the word on the right after the conjunction. Notice that *and* connects two subjects. Name them. What part of speech are they?

In sentence 2, which words are connected by the conjunction *or*? What part of speech are they? In sentence 3, which words are connected by the conjunction *but*? What part of speech are they? In sentence 4, name the conjunction. Which words does it connect? What part of speech are they?

You have just seen how conjunctions can connect single words that are equal in importance. Now read these sentences.

1. The car rolled off the road *and* into a ditch.
2. Girls in the chorus *or* on the team may go.
3. Everything on desks *and* in drawers disappeared.

The conjunctions *and* and *or* connect two prepositional phrases in the sentences above. Name the two phrases in each sentence.

Connecting Sentences

Conjunctions frequently join two sentences that are related to each other in thought.

1. Janet left a few minutes ago. Lynn is still home.
2. Janet left a few minutes ago, *but* Lynn is still home.
3. Al took these pictures. I put them into the album.
4. Al took these pictures, *and* I put them into the album.
5. We may go to the movies. We may come back here.
6. We may go to the movies, *or* we may come back here.

Notice the comma before each conjunction in sentences 2, 4, and 6 above. If you read the sentences aloud, you will notice that you pause slightly before the conjunction. The comma indicates this pause and makes the longer sentence easier to read. A comma is not needed when the sentence is very short, as in the sentence below.

You can but I can't.

▶ A **conjunction** is a word that connects words, phrases, or sentences.

● **Practice**

1. Name the conjunction in each sentence below. Then tell whether the conjunction joins single words, prepositional phrases, or sentences.

> Use a comma before a conjunction that connects two sentences, unless the sentences are very short.

1. Mail once traveled across the U.S. by stagecoach, but this was very slow.
2. In 1860 the Pony Express was formed, and it improved the mail service.
3. The riders galloped over and around hills.
4. In this way, mail sped from Missouri to California in eight or ten days.

2. Combine each pair of sentences below by connecting the sentences with the conjunction given in parentheses. Write each new sentence correctly.

1. (and) Mike Fink would stand on his boat. He would boast for all to hear.
2. (or) He'd yell that he could win any race. He'd challenge anyone to a shooting match.
3. (but) To tell the truth, he could win any contest. This was the ruin of Mike Fink.

Review Practice

Pronouns

1. Write four sentences using *we girls, we boys, us girls,* and *us boys.*
2. Write sentences using pronouns as the objects of these prepositions: *in, with, around, for,* and *to.*
3. Write each sentence below, using a possessive pronoun in place of the blank. Do not use the same pronoun twice.

   1. Which cat is _____?   3. Is this kitten _____?
   2. That big one is _____.   4. No, it is _____.

4. Read your sentences aloud several times so that your ear will become accustomed to hearing the correct pronoun.

Compound Subjects

You know that conjunctions connect words that are equal in importance. The equal parts below are subjects.

1. The cider *and* doughnuts are delicious.
2. June *and* July are my favorite months.

The sentences above have **compound subjects.** Name the compound subject in sentence 1. Name the compound subject in sentence 2.

Now study these examples of compound subjects.

3. Meg, Susie, *or* I will be at the door.
4. Hats, coats, *and* sweaters are in that pile.

Name the compound subjects in sentences 3 and 4. What mark of punctuation do you see? When you join three or more items in a compound subject, use commas to separate the items.

▶ Two or more subjects (nouns or pronouns) joined by a conjunction form a **compound subject.**

● **Practice**

1. Name the compound subject in each sentence.

    1. Max, Tim, and Grace are at the zoo.
    2. Penguins, otters, and seals live in the Aqua House.
    3. Lions and tigers stay in that building.
    4. Tim and Grace want to visit both houses.

2. In each of the sentences below, more than two items are joined by a conjunction. Write the sentences and place commas where needed.

    1. Pam Rita and Chris want contributions for the newspaper.
    2. Poems jingles or jokes are acceptable.
    3. Diane Mr. Lackey and I wrote poems.

Compound Predicates

Sometimes predicates may be joined by a conjunction, as in these sentences.

1. The old fence sagged *and* tilted.
2. The wind stirred the grass *and* bent the trees.
3. You can follow the fence *or* find a path.
4. The deer stood, listened, *and* dashed away.

The verbs in the sentences above are called **compound predicates.** Name the compound predicate in each sentence. Can you explain why there are commas in sentence 4?

▶ Two or more predicates joined by a conjunction form a **compound predicate.**

● **Practice**

1. Name the compound predicate in each of the following sentences.

   1. Some campers fished or swam all day.
   2. Others hiked and collected insects.
   3. At night they all sang songs, told stories, and played games.

2. Write five sentences, using compound predicates. In at least two of your sentences, join more than two items by conjunctions.

Punctuating Words in a Series

Three or more items joined by a conjunction form a **series.** Study the following sentences.

1. *News stories, poems,* and *anecdotes* make up our school newspaper.
2. We dusted *chairs, tables, desks,* and *books.*
3. Howie ran *from the school, through the yard,* and *into the street.*

Notice the commas in the sentences above. They separate the items in a series.

● **Practice**

Use commas to separate words or phrases in a series.

1. Write each sentence and punctuate it correctly.

    1. Jan ran up the stairs down the hall and into her room.
    2. She grabbed a suitcase and threw in her jeans a T-shirt and a pair of socks.
    3. She packed her toothbrush her toothpaste and her water gun.
    4. Then she sped down the stairs out the door and into the waiting station wagon.

2. Write four sentences of your own, joining in a series each group of items below. Use the correct punctuation.

    GROUP 1
    whales
    sharks
    dolphins

    GROUP 2
    under the chair
    behind the door
    near the sofa

    GROUP 3
    glue
    tape
    ruler

    GROUP 4
    brown bear
    grizzly bear
    polar bear

Subject and Verb Agreement

A verb must agree with its subject in number. A singular subject names one person, place, or thing. A plural subject names more than one.

Study the sentences below. Notice the number of persons, places, or things named in each compound subject.

1. Athens and Babylon have left their mark.
2. The art, music, and theater of Greece are still famous.
3. Bill and she will study the history of Japan.

Which conjunction is used in the compound subjects above? Are the subjects singular or plural? Are the verbs singular or plural?

Now study these sentences, in which the compound subjects are connected by the conjunction *or*.

1. A Red or a Blue has a chance to win.
2. The Reds or the Blues have a chance to win.
3. Peppers or an onion has been added.
4. A pepper or onions have been added.

Read aloud the nouns in the compound subjects of sentences 1 and 2 above. Notice that in sentence 1 each noun is singular. Therefore, the verb must be singular. In sentence 2 each noun is plural. Therefore, the verb must be plural.

Read aloud the compound subject in sentence 3. Notice that the first item is plural but the second is singular. Now look at the compound subject in sentence 4. The first item is singular, but the second one is plural. Is the verb singular or plural in sentence 3? In sentence 4?

In order to know whether to use a singular or plural verb in these sentences, look at the last item of the compound subject. If the last item is singular, the verb must be singular. If the last item is plural, the verb must be plural.

● Practice

1. Read the sentences below aloud. Choose the correct word in parentheses.

   1. "The Tinder Box" or "The Ugly Duckling" (is, are) my favorite story.

   2. Gina and she (doesn't, don't) know those stories.

   3. My brother, my sister, and I (have, has) heard them many times.

   4. Hans Christian Anderson or the Brothers Grimm (have, has) recorded many fairy tales.

2. Write each sentence below. Choose the correct word in parentheses.

   1. Sol and she (don't, doesn't) belong to the club.

   2. Jennie and I (was, were) invited to join.

   3. The club outing and its cost (have, has) been discussed.

   4. A bus, a driver, and a club sponsor (is, are) needed.

   5. The president, the treasurer, or the secretaries (have, has) the information.

> A compound subject connected by the conjunction *and* is plural and must be used with a plural verb.
> When each noun or pronoun in a compound subject connected by *or* is singular, use a singular verb.
> When each noun or pronoun is plural, use a plural verb.
> When a singular and a plural subject are connected by *or*, the verb must agree in number with the last item of the compound subject.

Review Practice

Quotations

Write these quotations correctly.

1. Those trucks make such a noise Paula complained.

2. That's because they shift gears on the hill said Olga.

3. Well Paula answered I wish they would stay away from our hill.

4. But then how would our groceries get to the supermarket asked Olga.

5. How would our gasoline get to the service station she added.

A Book to Read

TITLE: **A Wrinkle in Time**
AUTHOR: Madeleine L'Engle
PUBLISHER: Farrar, Straus & Giroux

Meg Murry had problems. All of her "faults" seemed so much more apparent than her good qualities when she was at school. Meg's friend Calvin was the only one at school who understood Meg. He was popular and good at sports, but he had his share of trouble at home.

Things at the Murry household were not going any too smoothly either. Meg worried about her missing father and about her younger brother, Charles Wallace. Brilliant though he was, Charles Wallace could not seem to get home from school without being roughed up by other kids. Life, for Meg, seemed full of worries.

But when Mrs. Whatsit made her mysterious appearance, strange events started to happen, and Meg began to find solutions to some of her problems. Meg, Calvin, and Charles Wallace were suddenly transported out of the familiar world into worlds beyond. Mrs. Who and Mrs. Which joined them as guides to the outer planets. As they searched for Meg's father, they met creatures stranger than they could ever have imagined, like Aunt Beast, who enchanted Meg with her music, and IT, a giant, pulsating brain which sought control of Charles Wallace. They even learned the terrible secret of the Dark Planet. School frustrations and problems at home no longer seemed so great.

If science fiction is for you, then you will want to TESSERACT with Meg into the worlds of outer—and inner—space.

Checkup I. Recognizing Prepositions

List the prepositions in these sentences.

1. We looked behind the barn for the first clue to the hidden treasure.
2. These words were written on the piece of paper, "Under a tree with branches few, beneath a rock is the second clue."
3. The third clue was in the middle of a patch of poison ivy.
4. I hung by my knees from a branch for this one.
5. It said, "In the garage behind the crates on top of a shelf your treasure waits."

Checkup II. Prepositional Phrases

1. Copy each sentence below. Underline each prepositional phrase.

   1. The bus trip to the city was slow.
   2. We took a seat for two by the window.
   3. Through the rain I looked at the countryside.

2. Write two sentences. In one, use a prepositional phrase that modifies a noun; in the other, a verb.

Checkup III. Using Words Correctly

Write each sentence below. Choose the correct word in parentheses.

1. I stayed (at, to) school to watch a hockey game.
2. There was a disagreement (among, between) the two goalkeepers.
3. An argument began (among, between) all the players.
4. The coach and the goalkeepers went (in, into) the locker room.

Checkup

Checkup IV.   Words in a Series

Write these two sentences correctly.

1. When an earthquake occurs, the earth's crust cracks slips or folds.
2. Earthquakes that occur near cities can cause property damage injuries and loss of life.

Checkup V.   Writing Sentences Correctly

Write these sentences correctly.

1. Jim is going to the concert but Jo will stay home.
2. Rebecca will sing a folk song or her sister will play the harmonica.
3. Ted will play the banjo and Donna will yodel.

Checkup VI.   Subject and Verb Agreement

Read the sentences below. Decide whether the subject is singular or plural. Write each sentence, using the correct form of the verb.

1. The poems and stories (is, are) original.
2. Sam or Dennis (has, have) other copies.
3. The twins and their sister (has, have) enjoyed reading them.
4. The first poem or the last one (is, are) my choice.
5. It's too bad that my sister or the twins (doesn't, don't) have more poems.

In this chapter you will study different kinds of stories. Here is your chance to find out how much you already know.

Tryout I.   Stories of the Past and Present

Number your paper from 1 to 3. Write the letter of the phrase that best completes each sentence.

1. The purpose of a fable is (a) to tell an exciting story, (b) to point out a human weakness, (c) to explain the forces of nature.
2. Many legends are (a) biographies, (b) stories about heroes and heroines, (c) nonfiction.
3. Most characters in modern fiction resemble the heroes and heroines in (a) myths, (b) legends, (c) real life.

Tryout II.   Forms of *be*

Write each sentence below. Choose the correct word in parentheses.

1. There (is, are) apple trees in this yard.
2. (Wasn't, Weren't) there many apples here?
3. Now there (is, are) only one apple.

Tryout III.   Writing Book Opinions

Read the following book opinion for a class file. Decide on a good subject heading for it. Then write the opinion correctly, supplying the heading and your own signature.

Dragon prows westward was written by william h bunce. It is a story of how eric crossed the atlantic ocean in a viking ship. He landed on the shores of north america, which the vikings called vineland. Then, eric was captured by the indians.

I enjoy reading about the adventures of the early explorers. and this is one of the most exciting ones.

14

Tryout
Time

14

Sharing Stories

Myths

Long before most people knew how to read, people told stories to one another. Sometimes they acted them out or made up songs about them. They painted pictures of favorite scenes and characters. Stories told by one generation to the next for hundreds of years are known as folk literature. Common forms include fables, legends, fairy tales, ballads, and one of the oldest forms of all, myths.

Among the most popular myths are those made up by the ancient Greeks and Romans. These myths tell stories of gods and goddesses. They had powers humans could never possess. They also had human weaknesses that often led them to trouble.

Several myths concern Mercury, son of the god Jupiter. Mercury was a fun-loving, quick-witted youth, a great story-teller and athlete. Because of Mercury's grace and speed, Jupiter chose him to be messenger to the gods. (You are probably already familiar with Mercury. He is the god who is shown with wings on his sandals and on his cap. He carries a magic wand that is decorated with two golden snakes inter-twined and a pair of tiny wings at the top. Where have you seen his picture? Next time you pass a flower shop, see if there's one in the window.)

On pages 298 and 299 is a myth about Mercury.

How Mercury Played a Trick on Apollo

On the very day of his birth, Mercury began to develop godlike powers. Growing swiftly in strength and cleverness, he soon left his crib and walked into the hills to see the world. In a meadow he saw a herd of beautiful cattle that belonged to Apollo, his brother.

Apollo was nowhere near, for as the sun god he was busy driving the chariot of the sun across the sky. Mercury thought it would be fun to lead the cattle away and hide them. The difficulty was that, in the soft earth, his own footprints and the cattle's would give him away. As he pondered this problem, a solution came to him. Under his feet he tied small bundles of twigs. As for the cattle, he made them back away to their hiding place so that the direction of the footprints would lead toward their home meadow rather than away from it.

At the end of the day, when Apollo found his cattle gone, he was angry and puzzled. He saw only the strange marks of the sticks and the tracks of the herd leading to their own pasture. Then a stranger, in chatting, told him about seeing a mere baby making the cattle back down the hill and into a hidden valley.

This clue was enough for Apollo. Soon he found the herd grazing in the secret meadow and realized that his new brother Mercury was the thief. He felt that punishment for such a crime must surely follow and that Jupiter, their father, should be the judge.

Jupiter agreed. Then Apollo set down two requirements. Mercury had to promise never again to play such a trick on his brother. Mercury also had to give him the lyre which he had that morning cut out from a tortoise shell. Mercury found the promise of better behavior easy to make, but the loss of his lyre was difficult to bear. Realizing that the punishment was severe for one so young, and pleased that Mercury complied willingly, Apollo gave him the magic wand.

To Discuss

1. What parts of the story show that Mercury was super-human? What parts show that he had human traits?
2. Mercury has been used in modern advertising. Why would advertisers want to link their product with him?
3. How would you define a *myth*?

Telling a Mythical Story

Two kinds of people are needed for a story to be told successfully, good storytellers and good listeners.

Plan to read some myths about gods and goddesses or heroes and heroines in books your teacher or the librarian will recommend. Select an interesting one to tell the class. Good stories can be found about these subjects.

Narcissus	The Wooden Horse	Pandora's Box
Hercules	Pegasus	Prometheus
Ceres	Daedalus	Pygmalion

Follow these steps in preparing to tell a story:

1. Read the selection until you know it well. Notice how the story opens. Think of the steps of the plot.
2. Learn to pronounce the words correctly by using a dictionary.
3. Notice interesting words and expressions and plan to use some of them when you tell the story.
4. Practice telling the story aloud to a member of your family or a friend.
5. Be a courteous, intelligent listener as others tell their stories.

Now you are ready to tell your story. Here are some guides to follow. Add others to the list as you think of them.

How to Tell a Story

Wait until you have the attention of your listeners. Give the title and the name of the author (when known). Speak distinctly and loud enough to be understood. Speak with expression.

Present the incidents in the correct order. Keep the final outcome until the end.

Use vivid verbs, adjectives, and adverbs.

Begin your sentences in different ways.

● Practice

Tell the story you selected to your class. Follow the guides above.

Using Words Correctly: *is* and *are*

You have learned when to use singular and plural forms of action verbs. The subject and verb in a sentence must agree in number. Read the sentences below. Name the subject and tell whether it is singular or plural. Notice the form of the verb *be* that is used.

Bill *is* on the roof. I *was* on the ladder.
The tools *are* in the box. They *were* inside the house.

In sentences that begin with *There is* or *Once there was*, the subject follows the predicate or part of the predicate. Study each sentence below. Name the subject and tell whether it is singular or plural.

Once there *was* a beautiful goddess named Venus.
There *were* many stories about her.
Once there *were* two goddesses who competed with her
for a golden apple.

In any sentence that you write or speak, make sure that the subject and the verb agree in number.

● **Practice**

Write each sentence below. Choose the correct word in parentheses.

1. (Are, Is) there really monsters called Gorgons?
2. There (is, are) Gorgons in myths.
3. There (was, were) one named Medusa.
4. (Wasn't, Weren't) there something unusual about her hair?
5. Once there (was, were) lovely curls on her head.
6. There (wasn't, weren't) anything she prized more than her wonderful hair.
7. One day Medusa touched her head and found that there (was, were) serpents where her hair had been.

Fables

Fables are very short stories that point out human faults or weaknesses. Usually a fable suggests a way to improve human conduct. It teaches a moral lesson and often ends with a proverb, or wise saying.

Some of the most famous fables were first told 2,600 years ago by a Greek slave named Aesop. These fables were passed from one generation to another by word of mouth. Then about 200 years after Aesop's death, they were written down. Today you can read many versions of Aesop's fables.

In Aesop's fables, animal characters show the same weaknesses and faults that human beings have. The fable below is from *Aesop's Fables*, retold by Anne Terry White. What human qualities does the animal in this fable have?

The Fox and the Grapes

One fine fall day a Fox was running lightly through the woods when the cry of a bird made him look up. What did he see right over his head but a big bunch of grapes! They were wild but quite large and perfectly ripe.

The Fox licked his lips. "Grapes are just the thing for my thirst," he thought.

Now the grapevine had trailed itself over a high tree branch, and the bunch of grapes hung out of reach. "They are worth leaping for," the Fox told himself.

So he leaped high with open mouth. Not quite high enough, though, for his jaws snapped on empty air.

"Well, next time I shan't miss," he said. He leaped again. Once more he came down with nothing to show for it.

"I'll try from the other side," he thought. He took a run, leaped, and—missed. Then he tried again—and again. A hundred times he jumped in vain.

At last the Fox gave up, turned his back on the grapes, and went crossly on his way. "I am sure they are sour anyway," he said.

It is easy to say something is no good if you cannot get it.

To Discuss

1. What human traits does the Fox in the fable have?
2. How would you define a fable?

● **Practice**

Find a fable in a book of fables your teacher or the librarian will recommend. Prepare to read it to the class, following the guides to reading aloud that you have learned.

COMPOSITION: WRITING A FABLE

A. Choose a proverb that points out a human weakness. Some proverbs from which you may choose are listed below. Write a paragraph telling about something that might have occurred to which your chosen proverb applies.

> Actions speak louder than words.
> Look before you leap.
> Don't cry over spilled milk.
> A bird in the hand is worth two in the bush.
> A stitch in time saves nine.
> Too many cooks spoil the broth.

B. Choose an incident that illustrates a human weakness to which a proverb might apply. Substitute animals for people and use conversation to bring out the attitudes and traits of the characters. Write the conversation correctly. Keep your fable brief.

At the end of the fable, write the proverb you chose. Read your fable to the class without identifying the proverb. See whether your classmates can tell what proverb your fable illustrates.

Review Practice

Punctuation

1. Write these sentences correctly, using commas as needed.

    1. One of Aesop's fables is about a wolf a fox and an ape.
    2. Fables tell about animals but they point out human faults.
    3. No Aesop did not write down his fables.
    4. Can you imagine Harry how exciting that myth was?

2. Write the following fable correctly. Remember the rules for writing conversation.

    One day the mice held a council to decide how to guard against their enemy, the cat. A young mouse solemnly offered his advice. Someone he said should fasten a bell to the cat's collar. Then every step he takes will cause a tinkling. In this way we will all be warned when the cat is near. Almost everyone cheered upon hearing such a new and excellent idea. Then up rose an old gray mouse, whose age and wisdom everyone respected. My young friend he said has an admirable idea. One difficulty must be overcome, however, before it can be put to work. We must find someone among us who is willing to place the bell on the cat. Not I said one and then another and then another. No mouse has yet volunteered to bell the cat.

3. The sentences below contain interjections. Write them, using capital letters and punctuation marks as needed.

    1. Whew this is a hot day.
    2. Help the fish is getting away.
    3. Oh Paul tells such funny stories about big ones that got away.

Legends

When you tell someone about an adventure, you may exaggerate some of the events to make a more exciting story. If your friend then repeats the story, the events may become further exaggerated.

Legends are the stories that people have told about their favorite heroes. Some of them are based on events that really happened, but in the retelling they have gone beyond truth.

The complete story of one legendary figure may include many separate adventures, or episodes. For example, here are some famous episodes in the story of King Arthur.

How Arthur became King
How Arthur wins the sword Excalibur
How Sir Galahad searches for the Holy Grail

To Discuss

1. Look back at page 225. What legendary hero is described there? What makes him legendary? What other legendary heros or heroines do you know?
2. How would you define a legend?

Reading an Episode Aloud

As you read legendary tales, look for episodes that others may enjoy. If a story is short enough, the class might like to hear you read it.

In oral reading, the first step is to understand the meaning yourself. Then use your voice to convey the meaning to others.

How to Use Your Voice in Reading Aloud

Separate your words from one another just enough for listeners to hear each word distinctly.

Pause after reading the title or at the end of a paragraph to show that you are beginning a new part.

End a statement with a drop in voice tone; end a question requiring a "yes" or "no" response with a rising tone.

Stress words and phrases to show emphasis.

Use natural ups and downs of intonation to excite interest and relieve vocal monotony.

● **Practice**

1. Select an incident from a legend to read to the class. Follow the guides above in preparing to read it aloud. You might also tell it in your own words, using the guides on page 300.
2. Listen carefully to the stories. You may hear several versions of the same tale. Decide which you like best and why.
3. After you have heard a number of legends, discuss the characteristics of the legendary heroes and heroines. What traits do they all have? How do they differ?

Going Ahead

If you like to draw, sketch scenes from episodes or descriptions in books. Here are two possible projects to carry out.

1. Plan a mural with several pupils who have read the same stories. You might draw different episodes or incidents on the chalkboard or on colored paper.
2. If you draw easily and rapidly, give a chalk talk, sketching the scenes and events as you tell a story.

Dramatizing a Story

After you have read and heard a number of myths, fables, and legends, choose several of them to act out, or *dramatize*. Choose stories with plenty of action and opportunities for good speaking parts, or *dialogue*.

Planning the Acts or Scenes

Divide the story into acts or scenes, according to the parts or main events of the story. Then write a description of what is going to happen in each act.

Read the following descriptions of scenes and acts.

Aladdin and His Wonderful Lamp

Act I

The Discovery of the Magic Lamp

SCENE 1. Tricked by an evil magician, Aladdin becomes the amazed owner of a magic lamp and ring. He discovers that his pockets are full of priceless jewels.

SCENE 2. By chance Aladdin discovers the Genie, who keeps Aladdin and his mother from starving to death.

Act II

The Rise of Aladdin

SCENE 1. Aladdin asks to marry the Sultan's daughter. The Sultan grants his request.

SCENE 2. Aladdin uses the magic lamp and the Genie to build a lovely palace for the Princess.

Act III

Aladdin's Encounter with the Wicked Magician

SCENE 1. During Aladdin's absence, the evil magician tricks the Princess and gains the lamp.

SCENE 2. Aladdin saves the Princess and himself.

Read a version of Aladdin's adventures. Would you plan different acts?

Planning the Characters

Choose a literary or historical episode and plan the dramatization. List the characters you will need for each act. Plan to have as many speaking parts as possible. For example, for the second act described on page 307, you might have the members of the court speaking to one another. You may wish to review the story to see how the author showed the nature of each character through action and talk.

The examples below may refer to some part of history you have recently studied, or to a book you have read. You could use either of these sources as a basis for a dramatization, or you may think of other sources.

Historic source: A dramatic event preceding the American Revolution. A well-known event concerning a great discovery.

Literary source: Robin Hood and his adventures in the forest. A Hans Christian Andersen fairy tale.

When you have decided upon the episode for each scene, list the characters and their traits on the chalkboard. Make sure they have contrasting traits which show in both actions and words. Show how you would dramatize the traits you have listed by different ways of walking and talking.

Planning the Action and Dialogue

When the action for each scene has been carefully plotted, let volunteers show how they would act out a small part of one scene. Part of the fun in acting out a story in class is in seeing different groups of actors put on the same play. The class should be divided into groups so that everyone will have a chance to participate. After one group has presented part of a scene, another group may try.

Preparing a Formal Play

Most of your plays will be put on without scenery, costumes, or much rehearsal. You will not need to write out the dialogue or memorize the lines.

Sometimes, however, you may wish to put on a favorite play before an audience other than your own class. When you do this, plan as you would for an informal classroom dramatization. After several groups of actors have presented the same scenes, choose the best dialogue.

When you put on a formal play, be sure to have each member of the class contribute. Some of you may participate as actors. Others may serve on committees to prepare scenery, collect the props for the stage, or make the costumes.

● **Practice**

Agree on several stories that would be suitable for classroom dramatization. Then participate in planning and acting out plays. Follow the suggestions you have just read.

309

How Our Language Grows

And Grows and Grows!

You have read about many ways in which our language grows. Look at the summary below:

Technological advances	windshield
Combinations	smog
Prefixes, root words, suffixes	prejudicial
Ups or downs in meaning	sly
Words from myths	titanic
Words from other languages	succotash
Shortened words	cab
People	Braille
Places	Dutch treat
Onomatopoetic words	splash

Now it's your turn to help our language grow. The shorter your words are and the more they sound like English, the easier it will be to use them. Write your own word for each description below.

1. *verb*—the act of turning off all unnecessary lights
2. *adjective*—how the roof of your mouth feels when you have eaten pizza that was too hot
3. *verb*—the act of blowing noisily on your soup
4. *noun*—briefcases with many zippered compartments, first carried by Ms. Kartoffel
5. *adjective*—describing the bottom of your gym shoes when all the tread has worn off
6. *noun*—a basketball-sized potato that has recently been developed in laboratories in Arthursknee, MO
7. *adverb*—describing how your stomach churns before you make a speech
8. *noun*—a dog that wags its tail and growls at the same time

Fiction

In most present-day short stories and fiction, the characters resemble real people. Yet, like legendary heroes and heroines, they may set out to do great deeds and prove to be courageous in the face of danger or hardship.

Examine some books of fiction in your library. Choose one to read. After you finish it, plan to tell your friends about it. Point out the story's outstanding features. The following questions may help you think of some.

1. Who are the main characters?
2. Where and when did they live?
3. What is the story about? What dangers, hardships, or problems do the characters face?
4. What traits do the characters reveal? Which characters do you admire most? Why?
5. Is there some interesting detail or incident which you might describe without giving away the whole story?

Holding a Book Chat

Here are some suggestions to follow when you participate in a book chat with four or five classmates.

1. *Show the book to your audience.* You may also wish to show an interesting illustration. Pass the book around the class.
2. *Give the name of the book and the author.* Write the names on the board. Present any interesting facts you know about the author, and name other books he or she has written.

3. *Describe the outstanding features of the book.* Tell who the main characters are and give the time and place of the story. Describe the heroes. Explain what danger, hardship, or difficulty they tried to face. You may tell some incident that brings out the nature of the adventure. However, do not spoil the story by telling too much.
4. *After the book chat, display the book* in an interesting way.

Plan with several classmates to hold a book chat.

Writing a Book Opinion

Write book opinions on cards which can be filed. At the top of the card, write a heading that tells the subject of the book. Cards on books of the same subject can be arranged together in the file.

Read this opinion. Notice the information given and the form.

Pioneer Adventures

Courageous Comrades was written by Fredrika Shumway Smith. The setting is Milwaukee, Wisconsin, in the year 1836. The story tells how two pioneer children and the son of an Indian chief became good friends and how they did a remarkable thing together.

The pictures help to make the story interesting. The map inside the front cover shows the Indian village, the trading post, the sawmills, and a cluster of stores. I like pioneer stories, and this is one of my favorites.

Ben Meyer

To Discuss

1. Tell what Ben included in writing his opinion of the book. What does the title of his paper tell us?
2. What information did Ben give in his opinion?

How to Write a Book Opinion

Write a heading that tells the subject of the book.
Give the name of the book and its author.
Tell when and where the story takes place.
Tell what or whom the book is about.
Mention an interesting detail about the book.
Give your reason for enjoying it.

COMPOSITION: WRITING A BOOK OPINION

A. Write your opinion of a book you have read.
B. Write a brief description of a book character. Do this from memory without using the book.

Woman with Flower

I wouldn't coax the plant if I were you.
Such watchful nurturing may do it
    harm.
Let the soil rest from so much digging
And wait until it's dry before you
    water it.
The leaf's inclined to find its own
    direction;
Give it a chance to seek the sunlight
    for itself.

Much growth is stunted by too careful
    prodding,
Too eager tenderness.
The things we love we have to learn
    to leave alone.

NAOMI LONG MADGETT

What else do you think this poem could be about besides caring for a plant? How would the final line sound if you read it by itself? Is it appropriate in the context of the poem?

Review Practice

is and **are**

**Capitalization and
Punctuation**

1. Write each sentence below. Choose the correct word in parentheses.

    1. (Is, Are) you going into that cave?
    2. Don't you know that bats and spiders (is, are) in it?
    3. Tina and Joe (was, were) in there earlier.
    4. They (isn't, aren't) going back.
    5. Neither (is, am) I.

2. Write these sentences, using capital letters correctly.

    1. The city of chicago is in cook county, illinois.
    2. Many americans were born in europe.
    3. Are you writing a composition for fire prevention week?
    4. We will visit grandmother and grandfather.
    5. The metropolitan museum of art is located on fifth avenue in new york.

3. Write these greetings for friendly letters.

    dear aunt maria   my dear richard   dear ms. weiss

4. Write this greeting for a business letter correctly.

    dear dr. belski

5. Write the following outline, using capital letters and punctuation marks correctly.

    uses of copper

    I electrical appliances
    II utensils

Checkup I. Stories of the Past and Present

Number your paper from 1 to 4. After each numeral, write the letter of the phrase which best completes the sentence.

1. Aesop was (a) a character in Greek folk tales, (b) a writer of modern fiction, (c) a creator of fables.
2. An example of a legendary figure is (a) Robin Hood, (b) Aesop, (c) the Tortoise or the Hare.
3. An example of an episode is (a) the story about Sir Galahad's quest for the Holy Grail, (b) the complete legend of Robin Hood, (c) any fable.
4. A major part of a play is called an (a) episode, (b) act, (c) chapter.

Checkup

Checkup II. Forms of *be*

Write the sentences below. Choose the correct word in parentheses.

1. Now there (is, are) several planes waiting to take off.
2. Ten minutes ago there (wasn't, weren't) a single plane on the runway.
3. (Was, Were) there a big delay yesterday?
4. There (wasn't, weren't) many flights scheduled then.

Checkup III. Writing Book Opinions

1. When you write a book opinion for your class file, why should you supply a subject heading for your opinion?
2. Write a book opinion for the class file.

Review Handbook

Contents

THE SENTENCE

A **sentence** has a subject and a verb, begins with a capital letter, and ends with a mark of punctuation. It makes sense by itself. There are four kinds of sentences.

1. A **statement** is a sentence that tells something.

    Statement: We are flying to Chicago.

    A statement is also called a **declarative sentence.**

2. A **question** is a sentence that asks something.

    Question: May we board Flight 607?

    A question is also called an **interrogative sentence.**

3. A **command** or **request** is a sentence that gives an order or tells someone what do do.

    Command: Hurry through Gate 22.

    A command or request is also called an **imperative sentence.**

4. An **exclamation** expresses a strong feeling.

    Exclamation: Your plane is about to take off!

    An exclamation is also called an **exclamatory sentence.**

● **Practice**

1. Write the numerals 1 to 5 down the side of your paper. Write *S* after the numeral of each group of words that is a complete sentence.

    1. The tunnel has been closed for two weeks.
    2. For repairs.
    3. Cars on the bridge.
    4. Were in a traffic jam.
    5. Leave now.

2. Write a statement, a question, a command or request, and an exclamation.

Subject and Predicate

The **subject** of a sentence names what the sentence is about. The **predicate** tells something about the subject.

In the sentence below, a vertical line separates the complete subject from the complete predicate.

The woman in the plaid jacket | walked rapidly.

The main word in the complete subject is called the **simple subject.** In the sentence above, it is the noun *woman.* The other words in the complete subject are **modifiers** of the simple subject.

The key word in the complete predicate is called the **simple predicate.** It is always a **verb.** In the sentence above the verb is *walked.* The other word in the complete predicate, *rapidly,* is a modifier of the verb.

● Practice

1. Write each sentence below. Draw a vertical line between the complete subject and the complete predicate.

1. The woman with the yellow umbrella is my mother.
2. The thirsty boys gulped the water.
3. Actors must speak with expression.
4. The tired children slept soundly.

2. Draw a single line under the simple subject and a double line under the verb in the sentences above.

THE PARAGRAPH

A **paragraph** is a group of sentences about a single idea or topic. The first line of a paragraph is indented.

To write a good paragraph, follow these suggestions.

1. Decide on the main topic.
2. Make your first sentence state or hint at the topic.
3. Write other sentences that develop the topic.
4. Follow the correct paragraph form.

Read this paragraph. Answer the questions below.

Maria Callas, the soprano, had an international reputation as an opera star. She was born in New York City; her parents were Greek. She studied opera in Athens. Her world debut was made in Athens. Her American debut came in 1954, when she sang the leading role in *Norma*.

1. What is the topic sentence?
2. Which sentence does not keep to the topic?

THE LETTER

Both friendly letters and business letters have these five parts: a *heading*, a *greeting*, a *body*, a *closing*, and a *signature*. In addition, a business letter has an *inside address*.

Read the business letter below. Name its six parts.

> 126 Oak Drive
> Sperry, Colorado 80610
> April 11, 19___

Ms. R. A. Wallace, Editor
Silver Creek News
122 Main Street
Silver Creek, Colorado 80607

Dear Ms. Wallace:

I am looking forward to the interview next Friday at 3:30 P.M. It is very kind of you to let me see the presses. Thank you for everything.

> Yours truly,
> Dan Riley

● **Practice**

Study the letter above carefully. Then, close your book and write the letter as your teacher dictates it.

THE NOUN

The words below are all nouns.

president	Clara Barton	freedom	honesty
leader	Mulberry Street	Ohio	Nigeria
ocean	path	health	lizard

A noun that names a particular person, place, or thing is a **proper noun.** In the list of nouns above, *James Monroe, Mulberry Street, Ohio,* and *Nigeria* are proper nouns. The other nouns in the list are **common nouns.**

Proper nouns begin with capital letters. If a proper noun consists of more than one word, each important word begins with a capital letter—for example, *Museum of Fine Arts.*

● Practice

1. Write a proper noun for each of these common nouns.

mountain	street
leader	ocean
continent	historic event
country	building

2. Write common nouns for ten things you see around you.

Singular and Plural Nouns

A noun that names one is called **singular.** A noun that names more than one is called **plural.**

Nouns form their plurals in the following ways:

1. Most nouns form their plurals by adding *s.*

table tables   chair chair*s*

2. Nouns that end in *s, sh, ch, x,* and *z* form their plurals by adding *es.*

bus bus*es*	wish wish*es*	fox fox*es*
guess guess*es*	torch torch*es*	waltz waltz*es*

3. Nouns ending in *y* following a consonant change *y* to *i* and add *es*.

    baby bab*ies*   fly fl*ies*

Nouns ending in *y* following a vowel add *s*.

    convoy convoy*s*   journey journey*s*   day day*s*

4. Some nouns ending in *o* add *s*.

    piano piano*s*   dynamo dynamo*s*   banjo banjo*s*

Other nouns ending in *o* add *es*.

    echo echo*es*   cargo cargo*es*   tomato tomato*es*

5. Most nouns ending in *f* or *fe* change *f* to *v* and add *es*.

    wharf whar*ves*   half hal*ves*   knife kni*ves*

A few nouns do not follow the above rule but add *s*.

    chief chief*s*   roof roof*s*

6. Some nouns form their plurals irregularly.

    child child*ren*   ox ox*en*

7. Some nouns form their plurals by changing vowels within the word.

    goose g*ee*se

8. Some nouns have the same form for both the singular and the plural.

    Portuguese   deer   sheep

● **Practice**

Write the plural form of each noun listed below. Use your dictionary if necessary.

sister	tax	mosquito	life
play	hero	solo	mouse
candy	potato	leaf	tooth
dwarf	march	country	torpedo
turkey	radio	moose	family

Possessive Forms of Nouns

A noun changes its form to show possession. Here are some rules to follow in forming possessive nouns.

1. Form the possessive of a singular noun by adding an apostrophe and *s* (**'s**).

      dog's ears   baby's toy

2. Add only an apostrophe to plural nouns ending in *s*.

      dogs' ears   babies' toys

3. Form the possessive of a plural noun that does not end in *s* by adding an apostrophe and *s*.

      oxen's yoke   children's voices

● Practice

1. Write the possessive form of each of these singular nouns: *man, Jane, calf,* and *country.*

2. Write the possessive form of each of these plural nouns: *women, boys, animals,* and *foxes.*

THE VERB

Every sentence contains a verb. Some verbs express action that can be seen or heard.

      The cowhand *branded* the calf.
      The bacon *sizzled* in the pan.

Other verbs express action of the mind, which cannot be seen or heard.

      Jack *thought* about the problem on his way home.

Some verbs do not express action. They are usually found in predicates that tell what or where the subject *is* or what the subject *is like.* They are called *verbs of being.*

      The rose *is* bright yellow   *Are* you ready?

Find the verb in each sentence below. Tell whether it is an action verb or a verb of being.

1. Harry toasted the marshmallows.
2. The bacon was crisp.
3. The dry twigs crackled in the fire.
4. The lemonade is in the cooler.

Helping Verbs

A verb may include more than one word, as in *may have been chosen*. In that example, *chosen* is the main verb; the verbs *may have been* are **helping verbs.**

Practice

Copy each sentence below. Draw one line under the main verb and two lines under the helping verb.

1. Elena may go to the library tomorrow.
2. Have these books been read?
3. Someone else may be waiting for them.

How Verbs Express Time

A verb may express present, past, or future time by changing its form or by using a helping verb. The time which a verb expresses is called **tense.** Study these tenses.

I often *hike* through the woods. (present tense)
Nino *hikes* every Saturday. (present tense)
We *hiked* to the lake last week. (past tense)
Will you *hike* with us next Saturday? (future tense)

Practice

Write six sentences. Use the present, past, and future tenses of the verbs *work* and *climb*.

THE PRONOUN

A **pronoun** is a word that is used in place of a noun. Like nouns, pronouns may be singular, plural, or possessive in form.

Subject Pronouns

SINGULAR	PLURAL
I	we
you	you
he, she, it	they

Object Pronouns

SINGULAR	PLURAL
me	us
you	you
him, her, it	them

Possessive Pronouns

SINGULAR	PLURAL
my, mine	our, ours
your, yours	yours
his, hers, its	their, theirs

Subject pronouns are used in place of noun subjects or in place of nouns after verbs of being.

Object pronouns are used after a verb of action or after a preposition.

Possessive pronouns are used in place of possessive nouns.

● **Practice**

1. Write each sentence, using any correct pronoun.

1. This baby crocodile is for Jim and _____.
2. You and _____ are in for some surprises.
3. Did you see Roberta and _____?
4. Roberta had to give _____ baby alligator to the zoo when it grew too big.

2. Write sentences using these possessive pronouns correctly: *its, yours, theirs.*

THE ADJECTIVE

An **adjective** is a word that modifies a noun.

red flannel   *short* column
those horses   *seven* cards

● Practice

Copy each sentence below. Draw an arrow from each adjective to the word it modifies.

1. The lucky team just won its seventh game.
2. Those students were overjoyed with the result.
3. Excited fans waved their crimson pennants.
4. The cheerleading squad led the victory parade.

THE ADVERB

An **adverb** is a word that modifies a verb, adjective, or another adverb. It usually answers the questions *How?*, *When?*, *Where?*, *How much?*, or *To what degree?* Notice the use of the adverbs in the sentences below.

The schooner drifted *slowly* from its course.
A *perfectly* reasonable explanation was given.
The boat docks *very soon*.
It is *almost here*.

● Practice

Find the verb in each sentence below. Then write the sentence, using an adverb that modifies the verb.

1. The campers _____ made a fire in the clearing.
2. They watched as a deer leaped _____ over the log.
3. In the stream, the water bubbled _____.
4. The stars shone _____.

ADJECTIVES AND ADVERBS IN COMPARISONS

Adjectives and adverbs may compare persons or objects.

Adjective Forms

POSITIVE	COMPARATIVE	SUPERLATIVE
slow	slower	slowest
useful	more (less) useful	most (least) useful
good	better	best

Adverb Forms

soon	sooner	soonest
distinctly	more (less) distinctly	most (least) distinctly
well	better	best

The **positive degree** is the simple form of the adjective or adverb. The **comparative degree** is used to compare two persons, objects, or actions. The **superlative degree** is used to compare three or more.

The Comparative and Superlative Degrees

1. Most adjectives and adverbs of one syllable add *-er* to form the comparative degree and *-est* to form the superlative degree.

   adjective: tall — taller — tallest
   adverb: near — nearer — nearest

2. A few adjectives and adverbs of two syllables add *-er* and *-est.*

   adjective: pleasant — pleasanter — pleasantest
   adverb: early — earlier — earliest

3. Most two-syllable adjectives and adverbs use *more* or *less* and *most* or *least.*

   adjective: active — more (less) active — most (least) active
   adverb: slowly — more (less) slowly — most (least) slowly

4. Adjectives and adverbs of more than two syllables use *more* or *less* and *most* or *least.*

> *adjective:* popular — more (less) popular — most (least) popular
>
> *adverb:* quietly — more (less) quietly — most (least) quietly

5. Some adjectives and adverbs form the degree of comparison in irregular ways.

> good (well) — better — best
> bad (badly) — worse — worst

● **Practice**

1. Write each sentence below. Use the correct form of the adjective in parentheses.

    1. (old)   Which is the _____ of the two houses?
    2. (small)   This apple is _____ than that one.
    3. (active) Tom is _____ than Lisa in the club.

2. Write each sentence below. Use the correct form of the adverb in parentheses.

    1. (fast)   Fred runs _____ than Al.
    2. (clearly) Carol speaks _____ than Patricia.
    3. (well)   Of all the performers, who dances _____?

THE PREPOSITION

A **preposition** is followed by a noun or pronoun which is called the **object of the preposition.**

> for Juana   over the steep hill

Each of the word groups above is a **prepositional phrase.** A prepositional phrase consists of a preposition, its object, and any modifier of the object.

● **Practice**

Make up sentences, using six different prepositions.

THE CONJUNCTION

The **conjunction** is a word that is used to join words, phrases, or sentences. The words *and, but,* and *or* are common conjunctions.

Practice

1. In each sentence, name the conjunction and tell what words, phrases, or sentences it connects.

  1. The horses pranced, trotted, and galloped.
  2. Then one dashed into the bushes and out of sight.
  3. Nina or Carlos will help me find him.
  4. Divide the other volunteers between Nina and me.
  5. I called for Dennis, but he had left.
  6. Helen must hurry, or we will never catch him.

2. Write three sentences, using the conjunctions *and, or,* and *but* to connect words or phrases. Use a different conjunction in each sentence.

THE INTERJECTION

An **interjection** is a word that is used to express a feeling. A strong interjection at the beginning of a sentence is followed by an exclamation point. Notice the strong interjection at the beginning of this sentence.

        Ouch! The water is hot.

A mild interjection at the beginning of a sentence is followed by a comma, as in this example:

        Oh, I left my pen home.

Practice

Write five sentences, using these words as interjections: *hurrah, ha, help, oh dear, bah.*

CAPITALIZATION

Capital Letters for Beginnings

1. Capitalize the first word in a sentence.
2. Capitalize the first word in the second part of a divided quotation if it begins a sentence.

    "Those are dark clouds," Tony observed. "Dad believes it's going to rain."

3. Capitalize the first word in the greeting and closing of a letter.

    My dear Aunt Emily,
    Very truly yours,

4. Capitalize the first word of each topic of an outline.

    I. Educational programs
       A. News broadcasts
       B. Science shows

Capital Letters for Proper Nouns

5. Capitalize the names of particular persons, including their titles and initials.

    Cynthia A. Edwards   Uncle Walter

6. Capitalize the names of cities, counties, states, and countries.

    Denver, Colorado   Los Angeles County

7. Capitalize the names of geographical areas.

    Mount Everest   Gulf of Mexico
           the Southeast

8. Capitalize the names of streets, bridges, monuments, natural wonders, and buildings.

    Statue of Liberty   Museum of Modern Art

9. Capitalize the names of particular documents and historical events.

Bill of Rights   War of 1812

10. Capitalize the names of peoples of a country.

Spanish   Israeli   American

11. Capitalize the names of institutions, businesses, organizations, and departments of government.

Jones Pharmacy   Department of Labor

12. Capitalize the names of days, months, holidays, and special events.

Library Week   Fourth of July

13. Capitalize the names of ships, aircraft, and trains.

Queen Mary   Spirit of St. Louis   Zephyr

14. Capitalize the names of races and religions.

Oriental   Buddhism

15. Capitalize abbreviations for proper nouns.

St. Paul   Wed.   U.S.A.

16. Capitalize proper adjectives.

American flag

17. Capitalize the pronoun *I*.
18. Capitalize the first and all important words in titles.

The House of Dies Drear

● **Practice**

Write the sentences, using capital letters correctly.

1. alice giggled. "whatever is a unicorn?"
2. "a unicorn is a mythical beast," i replied. "here is a picture of one in the *new york times*.
3. "what a fine looking animal!" exclaimed alice. "was there an american myth about it?"

PUNCTUATION

The Apostrophe

1. Use an apostrophe in a contraction.   hadn't

2. Use an apostrophe in nouns that show possession.

   horse's bridle   cowhands' saddles   children's toys

The Colon

3. Place a colon after the greeting of a business letter.

   Gentlemen: Dear Macy's: Dear Mrs. Green:

4. Place a colon between the numerals that represent the hour and the minutes.

   4:16 P.M.   9:30 A.M.

The Comma

5. Use a comma in dates to separate the day from the year and the weekday from the month.

   November 11, 1918   Thursday, January 1, 1970

6. Use a comma to separate city and state or country.

   Dallas, Texas   London, England

7. Use a comma after a greeting in a friendly letter.

   Dear Sandy,   My dear Mrs. Hill,

8. Use a comma after the closing of a letter.

   Yours truly,   Your friend,

9. Use a comma between last and first names when listing last names first:

   Smith, Mary   White, Edward

10. Use a comma, or commas, in a sentence to set off the name of the person addressed.

    I saw you, Tom, at the grocery store.

11. Use a comma after mild interjections and words such as *yes* and *no* at the beginning of a sentence.

> Yes, this is a surprise.

12. Use commas to separate words and phrases in a series.

> The children raced, jumped, and tumbled.

13. Use a comma to set off a quoted sentence.

> They shouted, "Over the fence is out!"

14. Use commas to separate any words that interrupt a quoted sentence.

> "I hope," said the spider, "that you will come into my parlor."

15. Use a comma before a conjunction that joins two sentences.

> Martha bought the stationery, but she left it in her locker.

16. Use a comma to make the meaning of a sentence clear.

> After painting, Sam cleaned the brushes.

● **Practice**

1. Write the contractions for each expression below.

will not	they are
are not	we are
I have	it is

2. Write each sentence below. Use commas correctly.

1. "I believe" Fred said "that we are late."
2. We hurried to the station but the train had left.
3. Fred checked the schedule Julie watched for the train and I waited with the luggage.
4. "There's another train" he said "in less than ten minutes."

The Exclamation Point

17. Place an exclamation point at the end of a sentence that is an exclamation.

That house is on fire!

18. Place an exclamation point after a strong interjection at the beginning of a sentence.

Hurrah! We won the game.

The Hyphen

19. Use a hyphen to divide a word between syllables at the end of a line.   Help us recon-
struct the plot.

20. Use a hyphen in writing some compound words and two-digit number words.

make-believe   thirty-three

The Period

21. Place a period after statements and requests or commands.

Terry has baked an apple pie.
Open the window, Tom.

22. Place a period after numerals and letters of an outline.

I. The many uses of steel
A. In the automobile industry
B. In construction

23. Place a period after an initial and most abbreviations.

Dr. L. S. Patterson   Ariz.   8:00 P.M.

The Question Mark

24. Place a question mark at the end of a question.

Where are you going?

Quotation Marks

25. Place quotation marks around direct quotations.

"You've done a good job," said Uncle Bill, "but don't forget to clean the paintbrushes."

26. Place quotation marks around the title of a story, poem, article, or chapter in a book.

Have you read "The Runaway" by Robert Frost?

Underlining

27. When writing or typing, underline the titles of books, magazines, and newspapers.

Across Five Aprils

● Practice

1. The sentences below require some punctuation marks. Write each sentence correctly.

1. Have you read M. C. Higgins the Great? asked Kay.
2. Yes said Leon it's one of my favorite books.
3. The House of Dies Drear is a good one too said Elizabeth Ann.
4. Where can I find more of Virginia Hamilton's books? she asked.

2. Write the following divided quotation correctly.

If you listen carefully Ruth whispered you'll hear it.

3. In the following sentences there are errors in capitalization and punctuation. Write the sentences correctly.

1. We traveled six hours. Along the Blue Ridge Parkway.
2. We will have baked beans, they are easy to prepare.
3. Then we will pitch our tent. Under the stars.

USAGE

a or an

Use *a* before a word that begins with a consonant sound. Use *an* before a word that begins with a vowel sound.

● Practice

Write each sentence, choosing the correct word or words in parentheses.

1. We waited (a, an) hour for (a, an) taxi.
2. Bring (a, an) raincoat and (a, an) umbrella.

Adjective or Adverb

Use an adjective to modify a noun and an adverb to modify a verb.

> John's room is *neat*. (adjective)
> John paints *neatly*. (adverb)

● Practice

Write sentences using these words correctly: *easy, easily; quiet, quietly;* and *patient, patiently.*

any or no

Use *any* with words that have a "no" meaning, such as *not, none, never,* or contractions that end in *n't.*

> We have *no* paper.   We haven't *any* paper.

● Practice

Write each sentence, choosing the correct word from those in parentheses.

1. There were (any, no) signs of life on the street.
2. We didn't see (any, no) people or animals.
3. There weren't even (any, no) street lights.

at and to

Use *at* when you mean "already there." Use *to* when you mean "going toward."

The girls are *at* camp.   They went *to* the park.

● **Practice**

Write four sentences using *at* and *to* correctly.

begin, eat, give, and write

Turn to page 341 and study the correct forms of these verbs: *begin, eat, give,* and *write.*

● **Practice**

Write each sentence, using the correct form of the verb in parentheses.

1. The hot dogs have been (ate, eaten).
2. Has the game (began, begun)?
3. The announcer (began, begun) to speak.
4. They have (given, gave) free tickets away.
5. Have you (wrote, written) to get yours?
6. I (gave, given) some thought to writing after the last game.

between and among

Use *between* when you refer to only two. Use *among* when you refer to more than two.

● **Practice**

Write these sentences, using the correct word in parentheses.

1. Let's divide the workers (between, among) the other supervisor and me.
2. Distribute the trowels (between, among) the workers.
3. We will dig (between, among) the two rows of trees.
4. (Between, Among) the six of us, we can finish this job in just a few hours.

Turn to page 341 and study the correct forms of these verbs: *blow, come,* and *draw.*

Turn to page 341 and study the correct forms of these verbs: *blow, come,* and *draw.*

● Practice

Write sentences, using each of the following verbs correctly: *blew, came, drew, had blown, have come, has drawn.*

The word *of* is a preposition and may not be used as a helping verb. Do not use *of* when you should use *have.*

● Practice

1. Read aloud each sentence below. Supply the correct helping verb.

   1. Wouldn't Mary _____ called before this hour?
   2. Frank could _____ won the race.
   3. I should _____ told them to come earlier.

2. Write or give six sentences of your own, using *could have, couldn't have, should have, shouldn't have, would have, wouldn't have.*

Use *doesn't* when the subject of a sentence is a singular noun or when it is the pronoun *she, he,* or *it.*

Use *don't* with any plural subject and when the subject is *I* or *you.*

● Practice

Write each sentence below. Choose the correct word in parentheses.

1. Jane (don't, doesn't) shop here often.
2. Carol and she (doesn't, don't) know the price.
3. Why (doesn't, don't) she ask one of the salespersons to help her?
4. The prices (doesn't, don't) appear on the merchandise here.
5. It (doesn't, don't) take long to ask someone, though.

Turn to page 341 and study the correct forms of these verbs: *fly, grow, know, take,* and *throw.*

● **Practice**

1. Write each sentence below. Choose the correct word in parentheses.

1. Look how your elm tree has (grew, grown)!
2. An oriole (flew, flown) to that big branch.
3. She (knew, known) it was time to make a nest.
4. Have you (took, taken) the bird seed?
5. I hope it wasn't (thrown, threw) out.

2. Write five sentences, using these verbs correctly: *flew, knew, grew, took,* and *has thrown.*

good and well

The word *good* is an adjective. It may be used to modify a noun, as in each of these sentences.

This is a *good* sketch of your grandfather.
That still-life painting is *good.*

Never use *good* as an adverb. You may use *well* either as an adjective or adverb.

Mother is *well.* (adjective)
Ed swims *well.* (adverb)

● **Practice**

1. Write or read these sentences. Use *good* or *well* correctly.

1. This is a _____ match.
2. Do you play tennis _____?
3. No, but Larry is very _____.
4. He has a _____ coach.

2. Write two sentences using *well* correctly. Use it as an adjective in one sentence and as an adverb in the other.

The words *hear* and *here* sound alike but differ in meaning and spelling.

The word *hear* is a verb which means "to gather sounds." The word *here* is an adverb which means "this place."

● Practice

Write two sentences, using *hear* and *here* correctly.

Think of the sounds which the italicized letters in these words should be given: hi*m*self and the*m*selves.

● Practice

Read these sentences aloud, saying *himself* and *themselves* correctly.

> Donald hurt himself.
> The girls are enjoying themselves.

Use *in* when you mean "within" or "already inside." Use *into* when you mean "movement from the outside to the inside."

> The salt is *in* the cupboard.
> We drove *into* the parking lot.

● Practice

1. Write each sentence below. Choose the correct word in parentheses.

1. The horses went (in, into) the barn.
2. The cowhands drove the steers (in, into) the corral.
3. Tex dashed (in, into) his room.
4. Were his spurs put (in, into) a drawer?
5. He was deep (in, into) concentration when he noticed them on the bunk.

2. Write two sentences, using *in* and *into* correctly.

Irregular Verbs

Some verbs in our language do not form their past tense in the regular way, that is, by adding *d* or *ed* to the present tense. They are called **irregular verbs.**

In the list of verbs on the next page, you will find the three principal parts of common irregular verbs.

● Practice

1. Write each sentence below. Choose the correct word in parentheses.

    1. Have you (went, gone) to the circus?
    2. The acrobats (did, done) the stunt again.
    3. They have (rode, ridden) bicycles on the high wire.
    4. Last summer we (saw, seen) them in a performance at Niagara Falls.
    5. The sword swallower (ate, eaten) his lunch.
    6. He (began, begun) with a sturdy dagger.
    7. Then he (chose, chosen) a tasty stiletto.
    8. He has just (lay, lain) down for a snooze.
    9. His dog likes to (lie, lay) beside him.
    10. Where have the trapeze artists (went, gone)?
    11. A helicopter has (flew, flown) them over the city.
    12. They have (began, begun) their daring act.
    13. They have never (broke, broken) any bones.
    14. Have the clowns (rang, rung) the bell?
    15. Yes, then they (rode, ridden) into the big top.
    16. Has the trainer (lain, laid) his head in the tiger's mouth?
    17. He even (set, sat) on the largest one's back.
    18. I have never (saw, seen) such a show!

2. Write eight sentences, using the past and the past participle of these verbs: *freeze, drink, speak,* and *steal.*
3. Be prepared to read your sentences aloud to the class.

Irregular Verbs

PRESENT	PAST	PAST PARTICIPLE
begin	began	*(has, have, had)* begun
blow	blew	*(has, have, had)* blown
break	broke	*(has, have, had)* broken
bring	brought	*(has, have, had)* brought
choose	chose	*(has, have, had)* chosen
come	came	*(has, have, had)* come
do, does	did	*(has, have, had)* done
draw	drew	*(has, have, had)* drawn
drink	drank	*(has, have, had)* drunk
eat	ate	*(has, have, had)* eaten
fly, flies	flew	*(has, have, had)* flown
freeze	froze	*(has, have, had)* frozen
give	gave	*(has, have, had)* given
go, goes	went	*(has, have, had)* gone
grow	grew	*(has, have, had)* grown
know	knew	*(has, have, had)* known
lay	laid	*(has, have, had)* laid
leave	left	*(has, have, had)* left
let	let	*(has, have, had)* let
lie	lay	*(has, have, had)* lain
ride	rode	*(has, have, had)* ridden
ring	rang	*(has, have, had)* rung
run	ran	*(has, have, had)* run
say	said	*(has, have, had)* said
see	saw	*(has, have, had)* seen
set	set	*(has, have, had)* set
sing	sang	*(has, have, had)* sung
sit	sat	*(has, have, had)* sat
speak	spoke	*(has, have, had)* spoken
steal	stole	*(has, have, had)* stolen
take	took	*(has, have, had)* taken
teach	taught	*(has, have, had)* taught
throw	threw	*(has, have, had)* thrown
write	wrote	*(has, have, had)* written

is and are

Use *is*, *isn't*, *am not*, *was*, and *wasn't* with subjects that name only one.

Use *are*, *aren't*, *were*, and *weren't* with plural subjects.

● **Practice**

Write each sentence below. Choose the correct word in parentheses.

1. Both teams (was, were) late today.
2. (Is, Are) the uniforms new?
3. (Isn't, Aren't) Tom and Amy playing?
4. The coach and I (was, were) pleased with the way the team performed.

its and it's

Notice the differences between *its* and *it's*.

The ring had lost *its* luster.   (a possessive pronoun)
Yes, *it's* a beautiful moon.   (a contraction for *it is*)

● **Practice**

Write two sentences using *its* and *it's* correctly.

lay and lie

Use a form of the verb *lay* when you mean "to put or place something."

Use a form of the verb *lie* when you mean "to rest or recline."

Refer to the table on page 341 to review the principal parts.

● **Practice**

Write each sentence below. Choose the correct word in parentheses.

1. A long road (lies, lays) ahead of us.
2. The swimmers (lay, laid) on the beach.
3. Have you (lain, laid) the extra blanket on the bed?
4. Lonny had (lain, laid) in the hammock.
5. He (lay, laid) his book in the grass beside him.

Use a form of the verb *learn* when you mean "to gain knowledge or skill."

Use the verb *teach* when you mean "to give instruction."

This year Karen *learned* to play the recorder.
Her neighbor, Mr. Jones, *taught* her.

● **Practice**

Write four sentences, using these verbs correctly: *learned, taught, have learned,* and *has taught.*

Use a form of the verb *leave* when you mean "to go away from" or "to go away." *Left* is the past form of *leave.* Use *let* to mean "allow."

Please *leave* us by ourselves.
The bus for St. Louis *left* a few minutes ago.
My brother *let* us borrow his camera.

● **Practice**

Write or read aloud these sentences. Use forms of the verbs *let* or *leave* correctly.

1. Did Emily _____ you know where she went?
2. She _____ without saying a word.
3. Did she _____ a message?
4. She _____ me keep her valuables for her.

Regular Verbs

Verbs that form their past tense by adding the ending *ed* or *d* are called regular verbs.

PRESENT	PAST	PAST PARTICIPLE
hear	heard	*(has, have, had)* heard
learn	learned	*(has, have, had)* learned
carry	carried	*(has, have, had)* carried

343

say or said

Use *say* or *says* when you speak of present time. Use *said* when you speak of the past.

The sign ahead *says,* "Fresh Raspberries for Sale."
Yesterday, Mrs. Roberts *said,* "Good work, Paula."

● **Practice**

Write four sentences, using these verbs correctly: *says, said, have said,* and *say.*

sit and set

Use a form of the verb *sit* when you mean "to rest." Use *set* when you mean "to place" or "to put in order."

● **Practice**

Write or read aloud each sentence below. Choose the correct word in parentheses.

1. The sun has just (set, sat).
2. We (set, sat) on the lawn.
3. (Set, Sit) the boxes on the porch.
4. Have you (set, sat) in the new chair yet?

their, there, and they're

Study the different meanings of the italicized homonyms.

The twins have *their* new bicycles. (possessive pronoun)
They live *there.* (adverb, telling *where*)
Look, *they're* coming. (contraction for *they are*)

● **Practice**

Write each sentence below. Choose the correct word in parentheses.

1. In a moment, (their, there, they're) leaving.
2. My friends are already (their, there, they're).
3. The Clarks have left (their, there, they're) house.
4. (Their, There, They're) going to the surprise party.
5. They will take (their, there, they're) camera along.

In sentences that begin with *There is, There are, Once there was,* or *Once there were,* the subject and the verb are in inverted order. If the subject is singular, use *is* or *was;* if plural, use *are* or *were.*

there with forms of <u>is</u>

● Practice

Write each sentence below. Choose the correct word in parentheses.

1. Once there (was, were) two mules and a fox.
2. There (was, were) a disagreement between the mules.
3. (Was, Were) there nothing the fox could do?
4. There (is, are) the beginning of a fable.
5. There (is, are) more fables like that in this book.

The words *this* and *that* modify singular nouns.

<u>this</u>, <u>that</u>, <u>these</u>, <u>those</u>

> *this* tie   *that* shirt

The words *these* and *those* modify plural nouns.

> *these* raspberries   *those* bushes

● Practice

Write four sentences, using the following adjectives correctly: *this, that, these, those.*

Them is an object pronoun. It may be used after an action verb or as an object of a preposition, but not as an adjective to modify a noun. Use *those,* not *them,* to modify things or persons.

<u>those</u> and <u>them</u>

● Practice

Write the sentences below. Use *those* or *them* correctly.

1. _____ daisies are mine.
2. I put the flowers in water after I had picked _____.
3. Are _____ my flowers, too?

Unnecessary Words

Do not use an unnecessary pronoun after the noun subject of a sentence.

WRONG: The girls they wore masks.
RIGHT: The girls wore masks.

● Practice

1. Read each sentence below. Notice that the meaning of each one is clear without the crossed-out word.

1. Where is he staying ~~at~~?
2. Jack dived off ~~of~~ the boat.

2. Write each sentence below. Choose the correct word or words in parentheses.

1. Our cat jumped (off, off of) the roof.
2. Do you know where he (landed, landed at)?
3. (The dog, The dog it) was sleeping under the window!
4. (Rosa, Rosa she) saw the whole thing.

we or us with nouns

Use the expressions *we girls* and *we boys* when they are subjects or when they follow a verb of being. Use the expressions *us girls* or *us boys* when they follow a verb of action or a preposition.

● Practice

Write each sentence below. Choose the correct word in parentheses.

1. The writers of the play are (we, us) girls.
2. Mr. Daniels and (we, us) boys are going to see it.
3. Dr. Andrews directed (we, us) students.
4. Mother helped (we, us) actors with our costumes.

Making Sure

Contents

More Practice on Chapter 1

I. Listening Skills

Read the quotes below. Tell whether the person who said each one was a good listener by writing *Yes* or *No*.

1. "The directions were short, so I tried to remember key words."
2. "I know it was a long speech, but I don't need notes to remember it."
3. "As I listened, I tried to form mental pictures of what I was hearing."
4. "The directions were long. I couldn't bother to listen to all that."

II. *let* and *leave*

Write each sentence below. Fill in the blanks with *let* or *leave*.

1. Jean had to _____ school in the middle of a class on Wednesday.
2. Will the doctor _____ her come back on Monday?
3. Yes, because he _____ her get up today.
4. Perhaps she can _____ early if she feels ill again.
5. Should one of us _____ with her?

III. Good Usage

Rewrite these sentences, choosing the correct word or words from those in parentheses.

1. Please take this caterpillar (off of, off) my arm.
2. You can brush it (off of, off) my sleeve with a leaf from that tree.
3. Where did he say the birds (are at, are)?
4. I know where they (are, are at).
5. One just flew (off, off of) that branch.

More Practice on Chapter 2

I. Sentences

Read the word groups below. Then copy them. Add words to those groups of words which are not sentences in order to make them sentences. Punctuate all the sentences correctly.

1. My mule Sal
2. She can pull a canal boat
3. One day, she pulled very hard the boat went sailing on dry land
4. When she puts her mind to it and really chooses to do her job well
5. DeWitt Clinton would have admired Sal
6. From the Erie Canal
7. Do you know the song about Sal
8. What a marvelous mule she is
9. If you had heard of her

II. Subject and Predicate

Copy each sentence below. Draw a vertical line between the complete subject and the complete predicate.

1. A moonwinder is a whittled wooden toy.
2. The mountain people of North Carolina know how to make it.
3. It has a string on it.
4. The string "winds the moon."
5. Moonwinders cost very little.
6. They are quite easy to make.
7. Young people enjoy them so much.
8. Many adults like them, too.
9. Some people prefer flipper-dingers.
10. These are more difficult to use.
11. A little wooden ball has to hook onto a circle.

III. Finding Simple Subjects and Verbs

Copy each sentence below. Underline the simple subject with one line and the verb with two lines.

1. The scent of water refreshed me.
2. Across the water I saw berry trees.
3. Through the branches flew tiny birds.
4. The birds were brown with bright eyes.
5. Their gay chirping sounded cheerful.
6. The spray from the water soaked into the grass.
7. A few berries lay among the blades.
8. Who ate the fallen berries?

IV. Writing Sentences Correctly

1. Rewrite these groups of words so that they form complete sentences.

    1. My coat needs to be cleaned, will you take it to the cleaner?
    2. That's the one around the corner. With Dorkin's Dry Cleaning on the front.
    3. Sy Goldberg has been the owner. For ten years.

2. Add words to each of these fragments to make it a complete sentence.

    1. on the darkest night
    2. by the light of the moon
    3. with garlic and tomatoes

V. Writing Paragraphs

Write a paragraph about one of these topics:

> The Street Where I Live
> My Favorite Game
> Monday
> My Favorite Place

More Practice on Chapter 3

I. Prefixes and Suffixes

Match the words below with the prefixes and suffixes to make new words. You should make at least eight words.

WORDS		PREFIXES	SUFFIXES
light	cap	re-	-ness
kind	do	un-	-ful
play			

II. Finding Entries in a Dictionary

Alphabetize each row of words.

1. hairy, handsome, hasten, haste, hank
2. sunder, Sunday, sundry, sundial, sundown
3. gorge, Gorgon, gorgeous, gory, gorse
4. trust, talk, tumble, teach, thimble
5. peasant, peace, peck, pearl, pear

III. Discovering Word Meanings

Read each sentence below. Then write the meaning of each italicized word. Do not use a dictionary.

1. Amy joined the *Feline* Friends' Club after she bought her fourth cat.
2. Marion's *culinary* ability was praised by everyone who tasted her good meals.
3. *Pedestrians* must be careful when they cross streets full of fast cars.
4. This *pugilist* was the heavyweight boxing champion for three years in a row.
5. John's *epidermis* felt hot and painful after a long day at the sunny beach.
6. The *belligerents* reached an agreement with the help of a United Nations advisor.

More Practice on Chapter 5

I. Common and Proper Nouns

Write each sentence below. Begin each proper noun with a capital letter.

1. joan is flying to paris.
2. She will visit the louvre museum.
3. Perhaps she will ride up the eiffel tower.
4. How fortunate that she speaks french as well as she does english!
5. Many americans stay at the ritz hotel.

II. Singular and Plural Nouns

Write the plurals for these nouns.

1. country
2. sheep
3. watch
4. handkerchief
5. man
6. pear
7. tree
8. tomato
9. wife
10. foot
11. cow
12. typewriter

III. How Nouns Show Possession

Write the singular and plural possessive of each of the nouns below.

1. establishment
2. planter
3. teacher
4. ribbon
5. dog
6. mystery
7. church
8. racer

More Practice on Chapter 6

I. Writing a Bibliography

List the books below in alphabetical order by the authors' last names. Use the correct form for a bibliography.

1. golden cities, golden ships, by glen dines
2. the blind colt, by glen rounds
3. hans brinker, by mary dodge
4. the buffalo soldiers in the indian wars, by fairfax downey
5. yvette, by leon harris
6. secret of the emerald star, by phyllis whitney

II. Outlining

Write the following items in correct outline form.

> pea soup
> sandwich
> turkey salad
> soup
> cookies
> dessert
> lunch
> tuna
> chicken soup
> fruit

III. Using *teach* and *learn*

Write each sentence below. Write the correct form of *teach* or *learn* in each blank.

1. Who _____ you to crochet?
2. I _____ it from my mother.
3. Would you _____ me how to do it?
4. Yes, you'll _____ it quickly.

More Practice on Chapter 7

I. Recognizing Verbs

Read the words below. Write those which are verbs.

door	eat
write	staircase
enjoy	frighten
three	choose
listen	sometimes

II. Verbs of Action or Being

Write these two headings on your paper: *Action Verbs* and *Verbs of Being*. Write the verb in each of the following sentences under the proper heading.

1. The air seemed unusually clear.
2. We saw the rising sun.
3. It glowed like a fresh orange.
4. Then it became a bright, pale yellow.
5. It was the color of a lemon drop.

III. Verbs in Contractions

1. Find the verb in each of these sentences.

1. Couldn't Sancha come to the movie?
2. I've been here since nine o'clock.
3. She'll never catch the first showing.
4. That's too bad.
5. Didn't she hear about the coming attractions?

2. Make contractions from these words.

you have	it is
should not	you are
they will	were not
I am	could have

IV. Principal Parts of Verbs

Write each sentence below. Use the form of the verb called for in parentheses.

1. (start, *past*)   The rain _____ early this morning.
2. (expect, *past part.*)   We _____ _____ it last night.
3. (pour, *past part.*)   It _____ _____ for three hours.
4. (stop, *past*)   In Portland, it _____ before noon.
5. (drop, *past part.*)   The temperature _____ _____ quickly.
6. (predict, *past part.*)   The announcer _____ _____ snow.
7. (rake, *past*)   Yesterday Emilio _____ the leaves.
8. (want, *past part.*)   He _____ _____ to make a bonfire.
9. (burn, *past*)   Last year's fire _____ out quickly.

V. Irregular Verbs

Write each sentence below to express past action. Write the correct form of the verb in parentheses.

1. (speak)   Have you _____ to Mr. Gutierrez about that?
2. (write)   Sheila _____ about Scotland.
3. (drink)   Have you _____ the whole bottle?
4. (lay)   They have _____ the foundation for the new apartment house.
5. (lie)   The reports have _____ on her desk for a week.
6. (take)   Miss Benkovitz, you _____ my umbrella by mistake.
7. (sing)   My parents _____ "Happy Birthday" to me.
8. (eat)   The worms have _____ into the apples.

More Practice on Chapter 8

I. Using Negatives Correctly

Read each sentence. Use the correct word in parentheses.

1. I don't get (any, no) respect.
2. You never worked to earn (any, none).
3. That doesn't have (anything, nothing) to do with the problem.
4. You won't (ever, never) know whether something will work until you try.

II. Expressing Yourself Well

Correct these groups of sentences to form good paragraphs.

1. Greta comes from Delft in Holland and she has been in America for only six weeks and she speaks English quite well. She began to learn it in Holland. She still has an accent. She will soon lose it.
2. I have always wanted to go to Holland. I have heard so much about the tulips there. I love tulips. I like lilies too. I prefer tulips.

III. Capitalizing and Punctuating Correctly

Rewrite these paragraphs correctly.

1. Trolls and elves are described in some detail by j. r. r. tolkien in his book the hobbit. The story tells of Bilbo Baggins' adventures in the east.
2. The old guide book said, ride five kilometers north and three kilometers west. You'll be at the highest point in nevada, the best state in the west.
3. Many animals are in danger of extinction. One such animal is discussed in an article in the latest issue of natural history magazine. The article is entitled the search for the tasmanian tiger.

More Practice on Chapter 9

I.   Singular and Plural Pronouns

List the pronouns used in the conversation below under the headings *Singular* and *Plural*. Beside each pronoun, write the noun or nouns for which it stands.

Tina turned her head so she could look at the hen. "Have you laid any eggs for John and me?" she laughed. "Mama wants them for our breakfast. We are so hungry."

II.   Possessive Pronouns

Write a different possessive pronoun for each blank.

1. Is that _____?
2. No, it's _____.
3. Joe said it was _____.
4. Well, it's certainly not _____.

III.   Writing Pronouns Correctly

1. Write a sentence for each of these words: *there's, theirs, their*. Which two words are possessive pronouns? Which one is a contraction?
2. Write a sentence using *its* correctly. Write a sentence using *it's* correctly.

IV.   Pronoun Forms

Write each sentence below. Choose the correct pronoun in parentheses.

1. (She, Her) and Carol want to go to the movie.
2. The picture features (he, him) and Wayne Marvel.
3. Buy some popcorn for Jody and (I, me).

More Practice on Chapter 10

I. Writing a Friendly Letter

Write the following parts of friendly letters correctly.

1. 399 hermosa street
tempe arizona 85283
december 4 19___
2. syracuse new york 13210
may 15, 19___
425 shaker road
3. your friend
linda

II. Using *sit* and *set*

Write each sentence below. Choose the correct word in parentheses.

1. He had (sat, set) in the dentist's chair for an hour.
2. If I have to (sit, set) here much longer, I'll scream.
3. Doctor, you (sat, set) my appointment for six o'clock.
4. If you'll (sit, set) still for ten minutes, I'll be finished.

III. Interjections

Complete the following sentences, using interjections and correct punctuation.

1. _____ A giant turtle has grabbed my leg.
2. _____ perhaps I can help you later.
3. _____ that would be nice.
4. _____ It's going to bite me.

IV. Writing Business Letters

List these parts of a business letter in order.

signature body heading
greeting closing inside address

More Practice on Chapter 11

I. Adjectives

1. Write two adjectives to describe each of these.

   1. The color of a streak of lightning
   2. The sound of a baby's cry
   3. The way your hair feels

2. Write the paragraph below. Choose adjectives to fill the blanks.

> An octopus lived in a _____, _____ cave. The octopus was very _____ and _____. He was so _____ that he could eat _____ fish at a time. He ate _____ fish. His favorite meal was _____ fish with _____ clams.

II. Making Comparisons with Adjectives

Write each sentence below. Use the comparative or superlative form of the adjective in parentheses.

1. Her mother cooks (well) than she does.
2. They're (greasy) than any of the others.
3. Is this the (effective) of all the ways to do it?
4. No, but it's probably the (easy).
5. She is the (intelligent) of the two sisters.

III. Proper Adjectives

1. Write four sentences of your own using proper adjectives correctly.
2. Change each of the proper nouns in parentheses into a proper adjective. Write the completed phrases.

   1. (Argentina) peso
   2. (Jamaica) beaches
   3. (Alaska) oil
   4. (China) pandas

IV. The Adverb

Read the sentences below. Write all the adverbs on your paper.

1. The gray cat ran quickly.
2. Suddenly she saw a little toy.
3. Soon she had snatched it.
4. Then she batted it and bounced it.
5. She had never had a catnip mouse.
6. She pushed the toy up and down and around.
7. Sometimes it would slip from her.
8. She would soon recover it.

V. Making Comparisons with Adverbs

Write each sentence below. Choose an adverb for each blank.

1. Cicely has always played _____ than I.
2. Gloria plays more _____ than she.
3. Of the three girls, Anita plays most _____.

VI. Using Words Correctly

Write each sentence below. Choose the correct word in parentheses.

1. How (good, well) do you know him?
2. He works in one of (them, those) factories.
3. Doesn't he know (anything, nothing) about cars?
4. He's not familiar with (any, none) of the latest models.

More Practice on Chapter 12

I. Improving Your Word Choice

1. Match each adjective in column 1 with its synonym from column 2. Then use each word from column 2 in a sentence.

1	2
nice	blunt
unhappy	miserable
fast	sluggish
slow	pleasant
dull	swift

2. Match each verb from column 1 with its synonym from column 2. Then use each word from column 2 in a sentence.

1	2
cry	modernize
joke	weep
renew	liberate
smell	jest
free	sniff

II. Using the Correct Expression

Read each sentence below. Rewrite each one that is incorrect.

1. Miriam should have come by now.
2. Could she of missed the bus?
3. I think she would've called in that case.
4. Wouldn't she have gotten a lift from Mr. Akers?
5. She couldn't of taken the wrong bus.
6. Shouldn't Jack of offered to bring her?
7. I would have brought her myself.

III. Writing Conversation

Rewrite this conversation correctly.

This horse said the tall cowhand must be the fastest animal in the world Do you really think so asked the greenhorn or are you just fooling This horse is so fast retorted the cowhand that it makes a hurricane seem slow

IV. Using the Comma

Rewrite these sentences, using commas correctly.

1. "See here young man that's my coat you have."
2. "I'm sorry sir. I didn't realize it."
3. "Well we all make mistakes."

V. Using *say, says,* and *said*

Write each sentence below. Use the correct form of the verb in place of each blank.

1. Last night June _____ she was going to Rita's.
2. Did she _____ what time she'd be home?
3. This note _____ she'll be back at midnight.

VI. Writing Stories

On your paper, write the word or words that make each sentence below correct.

1. When one incident in a story leads to another, they form the story's _____.
2. After the _____ of a story, there is nothing left.
3. The _____ of the story is usually the most interesting part.
4. An unexpected problem can be the _____ of the story.

More Practice on Chapter 13

I. Recognizing Prepositions

On your paper, write all the prepositions from the following sentences.

1. Run around the reservoir three times.
2. Turn a somersault under the tree in the wheat field.
3. Go over Pine Hill, through Bridal Vale, across the brook, and up to the dale.
4. Do all this with your hands behind your back.

II. Prepositional Phrases

Read each sentence below. Copy each prepositional phrase. Write the word or words it modifies next to it.

1. This card has been left inside the book.
2. Was the book on the counter?
3. No, it lay in the bin.
4. That bin beside the door is always full.
5. No one reads the sign above it.
6. The sign directs students to the circulation desk at the front of the library.

III. Using Words Correctly

Write the sentences below. Choose the correct word in parentheses.

1. Is Elena (at, to) home now?
2. No, she's (in, into) school.
3. She's coming to our clubhouse (among, between) the two oaks.
4. Don't get (in, into) the boat.
5. We'll just go (at, to) the old barn and back.
6. Here are some cookies to share (among, between) all of you.

IV. Words in a Series

Rewrite each sentence below. Use commas where they are needed.

1. Brian Dick and Meg went to the stadium.
2. Amati Stradivarius and Guarneri were violin makers.
3. Irene may eat spinach potatoes and meat and then have dessert.

V. Writing Sentences with Conjunctions Correctly

Write these sentences using commas correctly.

1. Jaime plays the guitar and the oboe and his brother plays the drums.
2. Cats are smart but pigs are said to be smarter.
3. My friend likes *Captains Courageous* but I prefer *Kim*.

VI. Subject and Verb Agreement

Rewrite each sentence below. Choose the correct word in parentheses.

1. (Haven't, Hasn't) Bob and Linda gone to Hawaii?
2. Yes, they (was, were) going to see their son.
3. I'm sure he (are, is) awaiting them eagerly.
4. Snapshots, slides, and a movie of their trip (make, makes) good memories.
5. A Nikon or two Kodaks (were, was) left on the plane.
6. Three rolls of film or one flash attachment (cost, costs) the same.

More Practice on Chapter 14

I. Stories of the Past and Present

Number your paper from 1 to 3. Choose the word or words in parentheses that best complete the sentence.

1. An (animal, exaggeration) is part of a legend.
2. A fable is often based upon a (human weakness, real-life person).
3. Do you prefer factual books or works of (biography, fiction)?

II. *is* and *are*

Write the sentences below. Fill each blank with *is* or *are*.

1. That truck _____ making a lot of noise.
2. _____ there a police officer nearby?
3. There _____ ordinances against making loud noises in a residential area.
4. Who _____ the driver of the truck?
5. _____ you the owner of the truck?
6. Yes, but who _____ you?
7. We _____ members of the Noise Pollution Committee.

III. Writing Book Opinions

Read the book opinion below. Write down what information was left out.

A Brave Rescue

The Rescuers is a very exciting story. It tells about three mice who helped a poor young poet escape from a guarded castle.

I like the story because the mice have such different backgrounds and characters. Each one makes a different contribution to the rescue.

Index

Verbs (*continued*)
  object of, 190
  past participles, 131, 141, 208, 340
  predicates, simple, 28, 32–34, 46
  principal parts of, 131, 144, 152, 355
  recognizing, 130, 133, 151, 354
  regular, 343
  sentence patterns, in, 99, 136, 142, 196
  tense, 143, 323
  testing for, 133, 134
  usage, correct, 57, 67, 94, 113, 131, 152, 192,
    236, 268
    See also Usage, correct
Vocabulary, improving, 56
Voice. *See* Oral expression *and* Speech
Vowels, 64–65

was, were, wasn't, weren't, 301
we or *us* with nouns, 177, 195, 198, 286, 346
Word order:
  inverted, 32
  natural, 32
  questions, in, 34, 187
    See also Sentence Patterns
Words:
  choosing correct, 23, 246
  context, in, 68–69
  dividing correctly, 63
  forming new, 56–57
  improving choice of, 246, 270, 294, 361
  listing, 54, 59
  meaning of, 47, 54–58, 62, 66, 68–69, 73, 351
    See also How Our Language Grows
  origin of. *See* How Our Language Grows
  root, 56–58, 68–69, 203, 279
  series, in a, 273, 289, 294, 364
  studying parts of, 56
  unnecessary, 1, 16, 348
  vivid and specific, 135, 149, 223, 225, 230, 249,
    251, 253, 254–257
would have, wouldn't have, 258, 270, 337
write, 94, 336
Writers and poets:
  Aesop, 302
  Alden, Carella, 269
  Anonymous, 83, 88, 116, 262
  Babbitt, Natalie, 218
  Behn, Harry, 80
  Billings, Josh, 71

Bodecker, N. M., 90
Bothwell, Jean, 223
Burgess, Gelett, 88
Burnford, Sheila, 163
Carroll, Lewis, 262
Chute, Marchette Gaylord, 76–77
Coatsworth, Elizabeth, 37
Conkling, Hilda, 83
DeJong, Meindert, 149
Dickinson, Emily, 87
Driscoll, Louise, 283
Emerson, Caroline D., 89
Enright, Elizabeth, 251
Fall, Thomas, 38
Franklin, Benjamin, 161
Frost, Robert, 86
George, Jean Craighead, 197
Giovanni, Nikki, 75, 79
Glenn, John H., Jr., 189
Gray, Elizabeth Janet, 249
Greene, Bette, 175
Hamilton, Virginia, 128
Hunt, Irene, 72
Johnson, Georgia Douglas, 141
Koriyama, Naoshi, 82
Lawson, Robert, 105
L'Engle, Madeleine, 292
Lewis, C. S., 150
Madgett, Naomi Long, 313
Manry, Robert, 163
Michelangelo, 209
Minor, Carlton, 85
Nervo, Amado, 81
Newsome, Effie Lee, 78
O'Brien, Robert C., 44
Poor Richard, 161
Sandburg, Carl, 11
Teasdale, Sara, 81
Terhune, Albert Payson, 236
Twain, Mark, 227
Wadsworth, Wallace, 225
White, E. B., 252
Wojciechowska, Maia, 243
Writing systems, 9–10
Written expression:
  theme for writing original sentences, 15, 27, 35,
    38, 42, 45, 59, 99, 131, 139, 144, 196, 198, 210,
    219, 233, 237, 239, 240, 262, 271, 276, 289, 317,
    324, 328, 335–340

C
D
E
F
G
H
I
J